Gender and Diversity in the Middle East and North Africa

The images of women in chadors or burqas as contrasted with images of belly dancers which circulate today as representations of Muslim/Middle Eastern women do not fluctuate from the images propagated by Orientalist paintings and colonial photographs which also offer contrasting representations of the veiled thus secluded and the naked or semi-naked thus eroticised Muslim/Oriental woman.

As well as challenging the prevailing stereotypes of Middle Eastern and North African women, the book aims to highlight the element of diversity which characterises the lives of these women and the regions to which they belong. The sense that most of the Middle Eastern and North African countries are Muslim does confer a common identity, a distinction from others that may serve to bridge wide social, cultural, and economic differences among them. However, it is also important to stress that significant elements other than Islam contribute to the making of MENA societies and women's cultural identities.

This book was published as a special issue of the *British Journal of Middle Eastern Studies*.

Zahia Smail Salhi is Senior Lecturer in Arabic Literature and Gender, at the Department of Arabic and Middle Eastern Studies, University of Leeds. She is an executive member of the Centre for Gender Studies at Leeds, and the Executive Director of the British Society for Middle Eastern Studies (BRISMES).

Gender and Diversity in the Middle East and North Africa

Edited by Zahia Smail Salhi

Routledge
Taylor & Francis Group

LONDON AND NEW YORK

First published 2010 by Routledge
2 Park Square, Milton Park, Abingdon, Oxfordshire OX14 4RN

Simultaneously published in the USA and Canada
by Routledge
711 Third Avenue, New York, NY 10017

First issued in paperback 2014

Routledge is an imprint of the Taylor & Francis Group, an informa business

Typeset in Times by Value Chain, India

British Library Cataloguing in Publication Data
A catalogue record for this book is available from the British Library

ISBN 978-0-415-54975-2 (hbk)
ISBN 978-0-415-81606-9 (pbk)

Contents

Notes on Contributors

Nadje Al-Ali is a Reader in Gender Studies, SOAS, University of London, UK.

Ayşe Gunes Ayata is based at the Middle East Technical University, Department of Political Science and Public Administration.

Anila Daulatzai is currently conducting anthropological research with widows in Kabul, Afghanistan. She is completing her PhD in Social Anthropology at the Johns Hopkins University.

Moha Ennaji is Professor of Gender and Linguistics, Rutgers University, USA and Université Sidi Mohamed Ben Abdellah, Fès, Morocco.

Amel Grami is based at the Department of Arabic Studies, Faculty of Literatures, Arts and Humanities, Manouba, Tunisia.

Lina Khatib is a senior lecturer at the Department of Media Arts at Royal Holloway, University of London, UK.

Amalia Sa'ar is a cultural anthropologist at the University of Haifa.

Fatima Sadiqi is Professor of Linguistics and Gender Studies, University of Fes, Morocco.

Naomi Sakr is based at the Communication and Media Research Institute, University of Westminster, London, UK.

Zahia Smail Salhi is Senior Lecturer in Arabic Literature and Gender, at the Department of Arabic and Middle Eastern Studies, University of Leeds.

Fatma Tütüncü is a visiting scholar at Harvard University, Women, Gender and Sexuality. And has also worked at Abant Izzet Baysal University in the Department of Public Administration.

Taghreed Yahia-Younis is a Political Sociologist. She is a post-doctorate fellow at the University of Haifa.

Introduction

ZAHIA SMAIL SALHI

The theme of Gender and Diversity in the Middle East and North Africa (MENA) is, in my opinion, a very topical theme in view of the often disconcerting stereotypes of the women of this specific region that continue to circulate within both learned and less learned circles, sometimes in the same way as they were generated by the Orientalist media in the last two centuries.

The images of women in chadors or burqas, contrasted with images of belly dancers, that circulate today as representations of Muslim/Middle Eastern women do not fluctuate from the images in Orientalist paintings and colonial photographs, which also offer contrasting representations of the veiled, thus secluded, and the naked or semi-naked, thus eroticized, Muslim/Oriental woman.

The chapters in this volume are written against these stereotypes and in an interventional way in the representations of the women in question. Wherever possible the authors are either native of the country of study or have based their field research on the countries in question, and worked directly with their subject matter, which has ultimately resulted in first-hand experiences being analysed and presented.

As well as challenging the prevailing stereotypes of Middle Eastern and North African women, the chapters in this volume aim to highlight the element of diversity that characterizes the lives of these women and the regions they belong to; it is a known fact that Western audiences are informed by images of Middle Eastern women as a single entity; they are the suppressed, secluded, veiled, and passive victims of a hostile religion. The sense that most Middle Eastern countries are Muslim does confer a common identity, a distinction from others that may serve to bridge wide cultural, social, and economic differences among them.[1] However, it is also important to stress that significant elements other than Islam contribute to the making of MENA societies and women's cultural identities.

Tunisian women, for instance, do not essentially suffer from the same dilemmas as those from Iraq, Afghanistan, or Saudi Arabia, nor do they share similar pre-Islamic ethnic origin, language, socio-economic status, colonial experience, modern national identity, and so on.

Likewise, while it is often believed in the West that all MENA women are or should be veiled, that they are all subject to honour killings, female genital mutilation, physical violence, marital rape, social discrimination in the work place, and so forth, it is of paramount importance to stress that these forms of oppression are not experienced in the same manner nor with the same intensity by women across the region. Therefore the notion of 'Muslim women' proves to be more reductive because it diminishes the composite identity of millions of nationally, ethnically, economically,

---

[1] Herbert L. Bodman and Nayereh Tohidi, *Women in Muslim Societies: Diversity within Unity* (Boulder, CO and London: Lynne Rienner, 1998), pp. 2–3.

and geographically diverse women to a single element, the religion of Islam. What usually underlies such a one-dimensional identification is an essentialist perception of Islam, which sees Islam as a reified entity that has been the primary, if not the only factor in determining the conditions of women's lives.[2]

It is the aim of this volume to demonstrate that while Middle Eastern and North African women are unified by their adherence to Islam as the religion of the vast majority, and often live under the dictates of Islamic family laws, a large amount of diversity is to be found not only from one region to another and from one country to another but also within each country.

Such diversity within the overall unity of MENA must always be emphasized in any discussion, but especially of its women, for gender identity is informed to a great extent by local cultural and historical elements, which distinguish each country from another across a region where millions of women lead diverse patterns of day-to-day lives.

In MENA as in other regions of the world, culture is often gendered and violently masculinized so that particular countries or nation-states are marked by their crimes against women. As such Egypt and Sudan are characterized by female genital mutilation; Lebanon and other Levantine countries are known for honour killings. And while Afghanistan is known for the burqa worn by its women, Iran is often associated with the chador.

As such, culture becomes highly gendered to the point that countries in the region are marked by their patterns of gender oppression. It is almost global knowledge that women in MENA are restricted by religion and patriarchy to the point where the US invasion of Afghanistan in 2001 was said to have the rescue of Afghan women from the Taliban and their burqas as part of its agenda.

This connects in a very interesting manner with French colonialism at the turn of the last century and its declared agenda to liberate and thereafter civilize native North African women as a swift and efficient way to civilize the whole region. Frantz Fanon warns about the French campaign directed towards native Algerian women in his book *L'An V de la révolution algérienne*, where he declares: 'To convert the woman, to win her to foreign values, to rescue her from her status, is both a means to have full control on the man and to have the practical and efficient means to demolish Algerian culture'.[3] Fanon explains how the French colonists tried to culturally dominate the Algerian society through targeting its women: 'The colonial administration could then define a precise political doctrine: "if we want to hit the Algerian society in its deep contexture, in its resistance strategies, we must start to conquer the women; we must go and find them behind the veils under which they conceal themselves and in the houses where the men hide them".'[4]

As part of the colonial French acculturation programme the authorities in colonial Algeria launched a fierce campaign against the community's cultural and religious identity through targeting women and the veil. While in the first years of colonization

---

[2] Ibid., p. 278.

[3] Frantz Fanon, *L'An V de la révolution algérienne* (Paris: La Découverte, 2001), p. 20. My translation.

[4] Ibid., p. 19.

the veil was purely viewed as an exotic item, it later became the shield which protected native women from the invaders' gaze.

Having failed to assimilate Algerian society through the closure of Arabic schools and religious establishments together with the enforcing of laws of discrimination against Muslim communities, the colonial French administration quickly became aware that Algerian women played a pivotal role in preserving Algerian cultural identity both through keeping themselves impenetrable to French culture and colonialists' gaze and by keeping their homes as heavens of authenticity, impenetrable to foreign culture and influence. In brief, they were the main axis around which the whole society revolved.

Fanon demonstrates that the more the French tried to assimilate the Algerians, the more the latter resorted to the veil and seclusion of women. In their campaign to assimilate Algerian society through targeting its women, men's honour and the values of masculinity were directly targeted. Not only did the French colonize the nation, which is often symbolically portrayed in national literature as a woman, but they reached far deeper to sully the men's honour and diminish their masculinity on a personal level. As a natural reaction to the French 'civilizing mission', native men adopted more restrictive measures against women and therefore the drastic efforts of the French to unveil Algerian women resulted in a deeper fixation on the veil as a token of national identity and authenticity.

As such within the domestic realm, women maintained an identity strongly resistant to colonial influences and became the guardians of tradition and cultural values. On the other hand, the home became a place of safety, a refuge where the man, constantly undermined by colonialism, could regain his pride and identity.

While I have frequently claimed that colonization 'increased veiling, seclusion and unequal treatment of women often as a reaction against colonial rule and Western ways',[5] I would now add that colonization targets native men's masculinity on both the symbolic and factual levels. The colonized man is humiliated by being defeated in the defence of his mother land, and threatened in his honour by losing control over his women folk who eventually become symbols of identity and authenticity. Therefore while I have always claimed that in colonized countries women are irrefutably the colonized of the colonized, I would add that this condition is a direct result of injured masculinities.

The consequences of injured masculinities are further developed and discussed by Amalia Sa'ar and Taghreed Yahia-Younis, in their chapter 'Masculinities in Crisis: The Case of Palestinians in Israel'. They argue that the Palestinians in Israel are undergoing a deep crisis of masculinity that is at once a reaction to, and a reflection of, their collective situation. They demonstrate how blocked paths to masculine performance often result in the seemingly inward-turned wave of violence experienced by Palestinian men.

While a vast amount of research on gender has studied the predicament of Palestinian women, very little is written on Palestinian men and how their experiences of daily patterns of oppression result in them replicating the same patterns on their

---

[5] Zahia Smail Salhi, 'Algerian Women as Actors of Change and Social Cohesion', in Fatima Sadiqi, *Women as Agents of Change in the Middle East and North Africa* (London: Routledge: forthcoming).

women folk. This chapter offers a view of the vulnerable side of what is usually considered the hub of power and control, through the study of masculinity as a site for a critical reading of the situation of Israeli Palestinians.

Based on the analysis of a discourse on crisis as it appears in the printed Arabic press in Israel, which Amalia Sa'ar and Taghreed Yahia-Younis have read using gender theory, this chapter argues that the sense of predicament among Palestinian citizens is implicitly articulated in terms of a crisis in masculinity.

The political-economic location does not allow the realization of militaristic masculinities, which hold gross hegemony in the area, while alternative scripts of less violent masculinities are also hardly viable for Palestinian men. Growing numbers of men are incapable of supporting their families, men generally are barred from positions of effective political leadership, and more generally still, because of their interstitial position in the region, Palestinian Israelis are marginalized in terms of cultural production.

The authors conclude that while their research has demonstrated destructive behaviours, and the anger and frustration that they evoke, their material also points to the potential of redirecting norms and behaviours towards more productive, and conceivably to a certain extent less militaristic, masculinities.

The second chapter in this collection sheds light on 'The Central Role of the Family Law in the Moroccan Feminist Movement'. Fatima Sadiqi provides a critical review of the Moroccan feminist movement and scrutinizes the early beginnings of the movement during both the colonial and post-colonial eras.

One question I would like to ask here is whether the liberated male whose masculinity is no longer under threat from the colonial hegemony would act differently towards his female counterparts.

Siddiqi demonstrates that the men's feminist views were different from the women's in that while the women aimed at improving their lives, the men's views were more abstract as they saw the emancipation of women as part of the emancipation of the country. They firmly believed that Morocco could not progress without educating and training its women. While these views could be, to some extent, justified during colonial times when the nation is often seen as a woman to be liberated from colonial rule, one is surprised to see such symbolism perpetuated during the post-colonial era.[6]

Siddiqi reveals that the newly independent state espoused these male feminist views for more or less the same reasons. As an example, she cites the event in 1957 during which King Mohamed V unveiled his eldest daughter in public and proclaimed the necessity to emancipate women in order to develop society. Following this event thousands of women in cities unveiled, and religious preachers in mosques associated unveiling and working outside the home with nation-building.

Things were only to become even more complicated when the Moroccan family law, known as the Moudawana, was introduced in the same year.

Fatima Mernissi and other female academics and activists were deeply disillusioned with the promises of the newly liberated nation and denounced the undemocratic practices of the former national male leaders who had suffered torture

---

[6] Morocco obtained its independence from France in 1956.

at the hands of the French colonizers in order to achieve democracy and equity but who then treated half of their society unfairly by institutionalizing a Code of Personal Status that denied them their rights. They underlined the inconsistency between the conservative nature of the Code and the promotion of a liberal economic system. While the Moroccan Constitution granted women equal political rights with those of men, the Mudawana inscribed them as essentially domestic beings with limited rights. Accordingly, post-colonial Morocco designated male supremacy and female subordination as symbols of cultural specificity and political legitimacy.

Women, however, never ceased their battle against the social injustice legally inflicted on them by the dictates of the Mudawana. The emergence of Islamism as a movement for cultural authenticity stood as an obstacle in the way of feminist struggle which it saw as a pro-western movement, an endeavour against which Islamist ideology positioned itself.

The long struggle of the Morrocan feminists resulted in the Mudawana being altered and in the demystification of the 'sacredness' of Shari'a law. Male feminism, which once constituted the necessary background for the birth of the Moroccan feminist movement, is now joining this movement without jeopardizing the latter's independence from other actors. The major issue today is to seek efficient ways to implement the new Family Law through the sensitization of women, men, and families to the important changes that have been introduced in the Personal Status Code and to incite judges to apply the new law without any reservation.

In 'Steps to the Integration of Moroccan Women in Development', Moha Ennaji casts a gender perspective on developments in Morocco. He affirms that the reform of the Mudawana in 2004 has led to more democratization, and the emergence of numerous women's associations with a great national and regional impact. He observes, however, that while Moroccan women contribute to development, their socio-economic situation has hardly improved over the years as a result of their participation. Despite the increasing aid afforded to the country and despite the numerous programmes of development financed by world organizations, all the indications suggest that there exists an increase in poverty, particularly among women. The evaluation of projects specific to women's promotion has shown the limits of the economic approach.

Ennaji insists that the role of women in development and growth is crucial and that education and training are important for women to enable them to meet the new challenges, and to help them safeguard their rights and interests. While he reiterates the male feminist view that the development of society cannot be achieved without the integration of women in the process of growth, Ennaji calls for the promotion of women's emancipation by the state, which ought to provide opportunities for women to become adequately trained to use the new information technology. Ennaji's chapter demonstrates that by gaining new skills, Moroccan women can develop their productivity and improve their standards of living and those of their families.

This chapter provides a valuable set of data to help understand the possibilities at hand and the achievements as well as the shortcomings of various governmental and international programmes for the promotion of women's welfare. One thing is certain; it is no longer a matter of choice whether women should work or not, their contribution to development is a necessity both for the development of the nation and for their own welfare.

In 'Gender Equality in Tunisia', Amel Grami provides an interesting insight into the condition of women in Tunisia. Grami states from the outset that the Middle East shows a great degree of diversity in the formulation of legal codes and their relevance to women's everyday lives. She remarks that while Tunisia, Algeria, and Morocco share many cultural characteristics, the extent of the legal reforms redefining gender relations has varied greatly from one country to another. The elaboration of family laws differed in harmony with the differences in the political leverage of kin groupings and the form of central authority in the pre-colonial society. In these three *Maghribi* countries, post-independence family laws were formulated in accordance with the political leadership's choice of either maintaining Islamic law or oscillating between alternatives.

Grami explains that in Tunisia, where the power base of the post-colonial state was independent of tribes and lineages, a liberal policy on family law greatly expanded women's rights, while in Morocco the post-colonial state, which had strong alliances with tribes, promptly promulgated a conservative family law favourable to lineages and unfavourable to women. In Algeria, the post-independence government was in partial alliance with forces anchored in kin-based formations and unable to resolve internal divisions. Algerian law was trapped in prolonged gridlock until a conservative legal code was eventually adopted in 1984. The type of family law enacted in each country was in fact an expression of the model of kinship favoured by the political actors in the newly formed nation-state.

It is common knowledge that Tunisian women are the most favoured in the MENA region in terms of citizenship rights. Grami explains that the reason for this is the colossal work of its first president Bourguiba who, for the development of Tunisia, promulgated a family law reform which redefined the rights and responsibilities of citizens by presenting a new concept of gender relations that not only departed from the model associated with kin groupings, but steered individuals away from the extended kin group.

Despite this state of affairs Grami shares the belief of many Tunisian feminists that Tunisia is not a wholly egalitarian state as its women still face discrimination. She argues that the gap between the legal framework and the lived reality on the one hand, and between law and mentalities on the other remains quite large. She highlights the dualism between the 'public' social, economic, and political rights women are guaranteed under family law and the restrictions placed on their 'private' home lives by cultural norms. Recently, cultural heritage has become for some Tunisians the symbol of their Islamic identity and most men refuse to support women's rights movement in family law and even the application of rules. Some men are worried about the emancipation of women with no clear landmarks ahead. They don't have the family and work place privileges by right of their gender that they see in other Arab countries. Grami poses the question as to whether we can speak about a masculinity crisis in Tunisia, a view that I totally support, as many neighbouring Arab countries publicize that Tunisian men are being deprived of their masculinity by a set of rules that render them vulnerable before the law.

Recently, many moves towards conservatism have been observed in the Tunisian landscape, a fact that questions the secular aspect of the state and the emancipation of women. Grami demonstrates how the example of Tunisia shows that a legislation empowering women is necessary but insufficient to guarantee them a real promotion.

In 'Party Politics of the AKP and the Predicaments of Women at the Intersection of the Westernist, Islamist and Feminist Discourses in Turkey', Fatma Tütüncü and Ayse Gunes Ayata discuss the case of women politicians in the AKP[7] as well as its policies on gender equality and relations. Their chapter aims to analyse the party on three angles: women's representations and visibility, changes in political ideology and rhetoric, and the adaptation of party organization to the demands of women.

Like the women in Tunisia, Turkish women had enjoyed only public and legal equality since the foundation of modern Turkey. The inequalities in the private realm were widely disregarded. In this connection, the feminist women in the 1980s, whose emergence coincided with that of the Islamist party as two anti-establishment movements, focused primarily on the private sphere issues, including domestic violence, sexual harassment, control over women's bodies, and the like. Tütüncü and Ayata ponder on the issue of the headscarf which dominated the political scene in Turkey. Is it an individual right, or an expression of freedom of religion and conscience? Is it an assault on public neutrality, or a symbol of the Islamist agenda which aims at abolishing the secular and modern establishment in Turkey?

The rise to power of the AKP, a party rooted in political Islam, on the eve of Turkey's integration into the EU gave the situation a new twist. On the one hand, the AKP launched several legal amendments for harmonization with the EU, including significant legal transformation for equality between women and men as a way of expressing loyalty to the long-lasting desire for European integration of the country, and, on the other hand, it established women's auxiliaries on a national scale. The AKP promised to integrate women into politics and increase their political literacy.

The chapter concludes that while it is true that the AKP increased the visibility of conservative and Islamist women in politics, this was more or less an introduction to politics through the headscarf debate and as an auxiliary for vote mobilization. The women in the AKP have had very little impact on increasing representation, or changing the rhetoric and programme, as well as not being close to power positions in the organizational structure.

Naomi Sakr, in 'Women and Media in Saudi Arabia: Rhetoric, Reductionism and Realities', uncovers the uneven picture in Saudi Arabia whereby heightened visibility for women in the press and on television was not matched by large-scale promotion of female media professionals to decision-making positions.

She asserts that contradictions inherent in restrictions on women in Saudi Arabia have been shown to create space for renegotiation of women's personal and political status in the kingdom. The Saudi media offer a window onto this renegotiation process, not because there is any automatic correlation between women's visibility in the media and their status in other areas of public life, but because analysis of media institutions can shed light on the contingent and historically specific nature of legal and social constraints on women. It can thus reveal whether these constraints are undergoing change.

---

[7] The Justice and Development Party (Adalet ve Kalkinma Partisi, AKP).

Sakr remarks that Saudi Arabian public discourse about women's status is puzzling. While official statements are replete with rigid essentialist rhetoric about 'women's nature' and limitations on what women may do and where they may go, government policies have produced considerable change in women's education, employment, and legal standing in recent years. The chapter questions whether these measures signify that established constructions of womanhood in Saudi Arabian society are being revised in response to the exigencies of an economy in which women's material assets, purchasing power, and earning potential carry increased weight. Do they mean that interpretations of Islam promulgated by the kingdom's unbending religious establishment are being gradually modified or set aside?

Sakr concludes that restructuring and diversification of the Saudi media has helped to open up a wider range of media portrayals of women and channels of participation. Just as the range of portrayals had been closed by powerful interest groups after the Grand Mosque siege in 1979, its opening up in 2004–6 was due in part to initiatives driven by the domestic and foreign policy interests of influential elements in the Saudi ruling establishment. Behind these high profile initiatives, however, was a parallel process of renegotiation for the status of all citizens, male and female, vis-à-vis government and the state.

In 'Iraqi Women and Gender Relations: Redefining Difference', Nadje Al-Ali explores the changing roles of women and gender in Iraq from the 1950s pre-revolutionary period through 35 years of the Ba'th regime and economic sanctions to the current post-2003 period. She claims that against the historic background of both state repression and state feminism, gender relations changed rapidly during the period of economic sanctions (1990–2003) which was marked by a drastic turn towards greater social conservatism. It is, however, in the current context of occupation and the rising influence of Islamist political parties and militias that gender ideologies and relations are at the centre of political contestations, increasing violence and the instrumentalization of human rights issues.

This chapter challenges the notion of diversity in the context of Iraqi women as represented in the prevailing political and media discourses which focus on ethnic and religious differences. Historically, as Al-Ali argues, social class, place of origin, and political orientation cut across ethnic and religious boundaries and presented the main markers of difference.

Al-Ali views diversity as a marker of difference not only between women's experiences from one country to another but also between the women of the same country. In this instance Iraq is a good example; the period after the first Ba'th coup in 1963 is generally associated with increased political violence, greater sectarianism, and a reversal of progressive laws and reforms. The experiences of this period differ most significantly in terms of class and political orientation. While many secular and apolitical middle-class women concurred in their appreciation of the achievements of the early Ba'th in education, modernization of infrastructures, and welfare provisions, those who were politically active in opposition to the regime testify about political repression, mass arrests, torture, and executions, though they too appreciate the developmental policies of the regime.

From the late 1970s, differences on the lines of secular and Islamist political positions started to assume greater significance and influence on women's experiences of the regime. Members of the Islamist Shi'i Da'wa party, for example, were targeted not so much because of their religious affiliation but because of their separatist agenda. Without wanting to diminish the suffering and hardship that members of the Shi'i Islamist opposition parties endured, the narrative about being the main recipients of state repression not only belittles the suffering of Kurds, but also other segments of the population, including those Sunni Arabs who actively resisted the regime.

The chapter highlights the media portrayals of the violence against Iraqi women in the aftermath of the 2003 invasion as being an unfortunate part of Arab or Muslim 'culture'. This reflects a commonly held assumption that gender-based violence in the Middle East derives from Islam. Pinning violence against women on Islam, remarks Al-Ali, is politically useful: it helps to dehumanize Muslims and justify foreign intervention in their countries.

In 'The Discursive Occupation of Afghanistan', Anila Daulatzai writes against the same concept of justifying the invasion of a country for the sake of saving its women. She refers to a radio address by Laura Bush on 17 November 2001,[8] as well as the so-called 'Campaign to Stop Gender Violence in Afghanistan'. She describes these two interventions as being both emblematic and rather problematic in the ways in which they capitalized on the schematic idea of the suffering, veiled, and oppressed Afghan woman, as well as in the manner in which they distorted the recent history of Afghanistan for reasons of political expediency. The latter was accomplished by privileging the damage caused by the Taliban over a cumulative aetiology of sufferings that would account for the decades of crisis. While the Laura Bush address is criticized for hijacking the feminist agenda in order to justify the occupation of Afghanistan, the Feminist Majority campaign exploited feminism's reputation as a liberating ideology in order to advance an agenda of cultural imperialism.

Daulatzai's critical assessment of contemporary writings on and representations of Afghanistan grows out of the realization that the conceptual tools used to understand Afghanistan and its predicaments urgently need to be reassessed. In her view, discussions of contemporary Afghanistan have reached an impasse and consequently seem to spin in circles. Explanatory frameworks privileging mechanistic descriptions of the workings of gender, culture, or religion in Afghanistan need to be recognized as tropes, and these tropes can no longer serve as the underlying epistemological axes along which our understandings unfold, but need to be incorporated into the analyses as objects of investigation. The tropes themselves, and not just the social forces they were supposed to describe, have become contingencies inflecting the details of everyday life in Afghanistan.

The chapter pleads that the lives of Afghans, men and women alike, need to be situated within the larger social, historical, political, and economic webs of significance, and not only within the narrow grid of tropes (lest understandings be gridlocked); it would not be fair to privilege certain vulnerabilities over others. But as we zoom out to incorporate these larger-scale contingencies, we simultaneously need to zoom in and carefully focus on the social worlds and the experiences of

[8] See http://www.whitehouse.gov/news/releases/2001/11/20011117.html (accessed 22 December 2005).

Afghans; the ways in which the decades of violence and deprivation are mapped onto the lives of Afghans need to be studied in detail, as must the subjectivities rendered dependent on international and institutional interventions.

It is a fact, however, that war reinforces the patriarchal subjugation of women and, in the case of women from rural communities, war deepens their economic deprivation. This is a concept developed by Lina Khatib in 'Gender, Citizenship and Political Agency in Lebanon'.

Khatib argues that while the wartime preoccupation with maintaining basic standards of living diverted attention from women's rights, the war also had a positive effect on women as it opened up new avenues for them to participate in public life. The post-war period saw a surge in the number of women's rights groups, campaigns for women's rights, and on-the-ground challenges to patriarchy through women's changing lifestyles. While this chapter analyses gender relations in Lebanon through the frameworks of social change and the rise of civil society, it also emphasizes the challenges facing women in post-war Lebanon, where many aspects of their lives, from personal status laws to sexual rights, are still governed by taboos.

Khatib demonstrates that behind the glossy façade of published figures about women's participation in civil society lurks the bleak reality of a patriarchal system which prevents women from enjoying their legal rights.

Another aspect analysed in this chapter is women's political participation. Khatib affirms that politics in Lebanon is conceived of from within a patriarchal framework, which hinders women's participation as electoral candidates. One result of the framework is the lack of recognition of the ability of women to be politicians. The three women elected to the Lebanese parliament in 1992 only achieved this through their family connections to male politicians, in other words all three are extensions of the politics of their male relatives rather than politicians in their own right. The same pattern repeats itself in the parliamentary elections of 2005.

While it can be understood that men hold negative views of women's political participation it is rather disconcerting that such views are shared by women and are passed from one generation to another as a social phenomenon. Furthermore, the few women elected to parliament show little concern with pushing for a change in Personal Status Laws or for implementing legislation against gender discrimination.

Khatib concludes that there is a need to focus on changing the systems and perceptions that trap women in a culture of passivity and self-denial. Women in Lebanon suffer from what may be called a 'fear of power', where women are afraid to engage in politics.

The final chapter in this volume, 'Gender and Violence in Algeria: Women's Resistance against the Islamist Femicide', demonstrates how as a reaction to the institution of the Family Code by the Algerian government in 1984, Algerian women were forced out of the trap of political passivity and self-denial.

The institution of the Family Code was a strong wake-up call for Algerian women and a re-launch of the Algerian feminist movement which started in the 1940s as the Algerian Women's Union (UFA: Union des Femmes Algérienne). The Women's Union, which was mainly affiliated to the Nationalist political parties, joined the National Liberation Front (FLN) and the armed struggle (ALN) from 1954 to 1962.

In the post-independence period the Women's Union was made into a state controlled organization, namely the UNFA (Union Nationale des Femmes Algériennes: National Union of Algerian Women), an organization which was stripped of its militant platform and turned into a conformist organization, and was ultimately deserted by feminist women.

Women war veterans and a new generation of women who opposed the UNFA in their struggle to stop and eventually repeal the Family Code merged together and solidified their ranks in a new feminist movement whose political platform is the abolishing of the Family Code. They view the Code as a major act of state violence against them because it codifies their subjugation and renders them more vulnerable in the face of gender segregation in both the private and public spheres.

Women found themselves stranded between a patriarchal society generally hostile to women and a set of laws that institutionalize discrimination against them. Their condition was exacerbated by the rise of Islamic terrorism in Algeria, which had women as one of its principal targets.

This chapter argues that the discriminatory provisions of the Family Code are symptomatic of the growing misogyny in Algerian society and have facilitated violence against women, legitimized discrimination in practice, and made it particularly difficult for women to deal with the consequences of widespread human rights abuses brought about by Islamic terrorism, which have amounted to femicide, the most extreme form of sexist terrorism.

Throughout the 1990s, Algerian women led a dual struggle: while the urgency of the situation engaged them to resist the Islamist femicide whose main aim was to preserve male supremacy under cover of Islamic legitimacy, this did not detract the women's groups from their primary battle to have the Family Code repealed. This violent decade was a formative period for women who intensified their actions to raise awareness and build strong solidarity networks among women both nationally and internationally.

While this chapter strives to investigate and analyse the causes and effects of the Islamist femicide and the reasons why women were at the centre of the Algerian Islamist venture, it also looks at the ways in which organized and spontaneous resistance by women worked together for a mutual cause, and adopted various strategies in the face of terrorist violence.

The coming of age of the Algerian feminist movement benefited from the political reforms that followed the 1988 riots, which allowed women to organize themselves in associations, three of which were created and were granted permission to operate as of summer 1989. These are the Association for the Emancipation of Women, the Association for Equality before the Law between Women and Men, and the Association for the Defence and Promotion of Women's Rights. Nevertheless, despite the genuine will and determination of the women's groups to exercise full political citizenship, the disjuncture between political and civil citizenship has hampered them from enjoying full participation in public life and from achieving autonomy in the conduct of their private lives.

The new political climate in Algeria positioned women's organizations and the Islamists as clear opponents in a game in which the first group fought for their civil rights while the second fought to suppress them, by resorting to violence which often reached the level of femicide.

This chapter argues that targeting women's bodies and using them as battlefields makes it obvious that gender is at the core of the issue of Islamic terrorism, and inflicting violence on their bodies is a means of controlling women and terrorizing their community. The forms and persistence of violence against women's bodies in Algeria is not seen with the same intensity nor did it reach the same levels across the MENA region. This leads me to conclude this section with Dorothy F. Beck's statement: 'the Middle East is a fascinating land of great contrasts'.[9]

It is very much hoped that this collection of articles, though in different ways, has done justice to the convolution of the lives of the many millions of women who across the diverse cultural, historical, and ethnic landscape that comprises the region lead equally diverse patterns of daily life.

---

[9] Dorothy F. Beck, 'The Changing Modern Moslem Family of the Middle East', *Marriage and Family Living* 19 (1957), p. 340.

Masculinity in Crisis: The Case of Palestinians in Israel

AMALIA SA'AR and TAGHREED YAHIA-YOUNIS

ABSTRACT *This paper argues that the Palestinians in Israel are undergoing a deep crisis of masculinity that is at once a reaction to, and a reflection of, their collective situation. Notwithstanding some important benefits that accrue to them as citizens, they are subjected to structural violence, which includes policing, racism, and discrimination. Their socio-economic conditions are poor, and their sense of identity and cultural vitality are on the defense. The paper describes several coexisting scripts of hegemonic masculinity and their inbuilt tensions and reads the seemingly inward-turned wave of violence as emanating from blocked paths to masculine performance.*

Despite the abundant literature on Palestinian women, the discussion of Palestinians as a national collective tends to be blind to the double role of gender, and particularly of masculinity, as a model of and model for the production of cultural meaning. Masculinity therefore is an apt site for a critical reading of the situation of Israeli Palestinians, whence to view the vulnerable side of what is usually considered the hub of power and control.

I. Introduction

Over the past decade, and increasingly since the outbreak of the second Palestinian uprising (*intifada*) in October 2000, the Palestinian Arab citizens of Israel seem anxious about growing violence inside their localities.[1] Violence erupts over boundaries of plots of land, due to shared ownership, or over municipal politics. But increasingly it just breaks out during quarrels between youngsters, sometimes even children, which then create a factional dynamic that quickly draws entire extended families or even clans into circles of ongoing attacks and counter attacks. In this paper we document a cumulative sense of moral predicament that is created by numerous stories of aggression in the local press. We examine what seems to be a discourse on crisis and interpret it, paying close attention to language and symbolism, as a discourse on *masculinity* in crisis. Although we could find some

---

[1] A note on terminology: as critical scholars writing on issues pertaining to identity, we acknowledge the impossibility of a neutral term for this national group, whose location is fraught with contradictions. In order not to reify any specific title and to draw attention to the shifting and contextual character of identity, we have chosen to alternate between several local and external titles (Palestinian-Arabs, Israeli-Palestinians, the Arabs Inside, the Arabs of '48, and Arabs).

statistical support to the local impression of increasing violence,[2] we do not attempt to engage in 'objective' assessments of whether violence in the Palestinian-Arab communities in Israel has actually been on the rise. Internal aggressions are quite common among communities all over the world that suffer poverty, marginalization, and exposure to state and racial violence. The members of such communities are frequently convinced that the scope of the violence is *objectively* enormous – certainly greater than in the past or in comparison with other places, although they cannot know this 'for a fact'. As Jean and John Comaroff show for the case of South Africa, the application of statistical measurements to crime rates does not necessarily produce neutral evaluations, since the very procedures of counting and defining facts tend to be embedded in the discourse that imagines the phenomenon to be grave.[3] Our focus, instead, is on the discursive construction of crisis and relapse.

In the most basic sense the discourse on violence that seems to be getting out of hand is a discourse on collective identity. Not surprisingly it is fraught with gender undertones, which only rarely are articulated explicitly. For one thing, the fact that the perpetrators tend almost invariably to be males is never remarked upon as such, yet the discourse is rich in symbols of masculinity and occasionally even includes explicit discussions of proper manhood. Emphatically, the discourse is about collective morality, not men per se. By analyzing it in terms of masculinity we use an etic[4] term in order to bring to the surface an unmarked component that we consider to be one of the organizing schemes of collective identity. We therefore hope to contribute to ongoing scholarly efforts to unearth the underlying gender aspect of the political economy of Israeli Palestinians.

A Constructionist Approach to Masculinity

Our approach to masculinity is guided by the constructionist theory of gender. Treating masculinity as a social construction has several implications, which are by now well-established in feminist literature. We review them here stenographically, borrowing from Robert Connell's presentation merely to position our analysis.[5] In any given cultural context masculinity is never singular. Instead, various models of masculinity coexist and inform one another.[6] These models are hierarchical and compete for hegemony. Yet despite their self-imagined differences, in the Israeli–Palestinian context, as in many other places,

[2] A quantitative study conducted in fall 2005 by the Center for the Study of Crime, Law and Society at the University of Haifa found that the Arab citizens of Israel are concerned about violent crimes in their residential communities, including car accidents, drug-related offenses, and the use of arms, at much higher rates than Jewish citizens. The majority of the violent cases, this survey revealed, occurred among neighbors, family members, or residents of the same community (Personal communication from Dr. Badi Hassissi who conducted this survey, 4.1.2006). For more on violence inside Arab communities, see www.arabs48.com

[3] Jean Comaroff and John Comaroff. 2006. 'Criminal ac/counting: Quantifacts and the production of the unreal', Talk presented at the University of Haifa, May 2006.

[4] The terms 'etic' and 'emic' are widely employed in a variety of social science disciplines to denote a distinction between an outsider and insider perspective on knowledge, respectively. They were originally coined by Kenneth Lee Pike, *Language in Relation to a Unified Theory of Structure of Human Behavior* (The Hague: Mouton Rawl, 1967).

[5] Robert W. Connell 'Arms and the Man', in Ingeborg Breines, Robert Connell and Ingrid Eid (eds.) *Male Roles, Masculinities and Violence: A Culture of Peace Perspective* (UNESCO, 2000).

[6] See also Andrea Cornwall and Nancy Lindisfarne (eds.), *Dislocating Masculinity: Comparative Ethnographies* (London: Routledge, 1994); Maurice Berger, Brian Wallis and Simon Watson (eds.) *Constructing Masculinity* (New York and London: Routledge, 1995).

they share a formidable interest in maintaining patriarchal and heterosexist principles.[7] Thirdly, alongside the competition between various options masculinities are also divided, in the sense that masculine identities embody tensions between contradictory desires or practices. A fourth important aspect of masculinities is that they are collective. Masculinities are sustained and enacted by individuals, but also by groups, institutions, and cultural forms such as the mass media. Fifth, there is no necessary or automatic link between masculinities and men. Notwithstanding their strong exclusionary nature,[8] masculine identities, images and ideologies may be enacted by men *and* women, although at the level of individual experience they are likely to affect men more acutely. Next, like gender more generally, masculinity is embodied, which opens a space for performativity. People do not 'have' gender. Rather, masculinities and femininities are things that people 'do'.[9] In this respect, Esmail Nashif argues that Palestinian men tend to *overdo* their gender, and he marks 'overmanning' as a ritualistic response to the crisis of male productivity in the Arab world.[10] Another important corollary of the performative aspect is that in practical reality, any heuristic models of masculinity are translated into nuanced and located scripts of action. The notion of scripts here is borrowed from the work of Carol Stack and Linda Burton on the ways in which kinships are realized 'on the ground'.[11] Masculine scripts, as opposed to models, by their very nature create ongoing tangles of subjugation and subject-making. All too often such scripts involve different forms of aggression/victimization. As Connell notes,[12] the source of violence is probably the ongoing active construction of masculinity rather than the end state. Last but not least, masculinity is created in specific historical circumstances. Along with the emphasis on performativity and scripts, this last point highlights the possibility of change, which is embedded in the very tensions and contradictions of masculinity.

Methodology

This paper is the product of an ongoing exchange between two ethnographers of Palestinian society inside the Green Line, one of whom (Taghreed Yahya Younis) is also a member of this society, while the other (Amalia Sa'ar) is a member of the dominant Jewish-Israeli society.[13]

Through our ongoing research, which actually focuses primarily on Palestinian women, we have observed a certain process that is happening to masculinity. To test what we thought was going on, we set out on a systematic reading of the most widely selling Arab newspapers over a set period of time. During September–October 2005 we sampled eight weekend editions of three newspapers: *Al-Sinnārah*

---

[7] Edna Lomsky-Feder and Tamar Rapoport, 'Juggling Models of Masculinity: Russian-Jewish Immigrants in the Israeli Army', *Sociological Inquiry* 73(1) (2003), 114–137.

[8] See Michael Taussig, 'Schopenhauer's beard' in Berger, Wallis and Watson (eds.), *Constructing Masculinity* (1995), pp. 107–114 on the role of secret knowledge in masculinities.

[9] Judith Butler, *Gender Trouble: Feminism and the Subversion of Identity* (New York and London: Routledge, 1990).

[10] Invited talk, MADA center, Haifa, November 2005.

[11] Carol B. Stack and Linda M. Burton, 'Kinscripts', *Journal of Comparative Family Studies* 24(2) (1993), pp. 157–170.

[12] Connell, 'Arms and the Man'.

[13] Taghreed Yahya-Younis has been carrying out participant observation in her own native village at the center of the country. Amalia Sa'ar did anthropological fieldwork in two urban Palestinian communities inside Israel, in 1992–93 and in 1997–99.

and *Kull-al-'Arab*, which are independent, and *Fasl-al-Maqāl*, which belongs to the secular-nationalistic Tajammu' party.

To gain some sense of time-depth, and to make sure that what we found was not bound to the particular late summer season, we then sampled four winter weekend editions of the earliest year for which each of these newspapers could supply us with copies. The early issues all date back to the 1990s, which is when the Arabic printed press in Israel started flourishing. Until the mid-1980s locally printed Arabic newspapers were very limited. One prominent exception is *Al-Ittihād*, a daily that belongs to the Israeli Communist Party (and the subsequent DFPP coalition that came to include it). A strictly party-line newspaper, *Al-Ittihād* has a somewhat different character from the independent papers, and even from *Fasl-al-Maqāl*, which was first issued when the landscape of Arabic newspapers had changed and became more diverse, less politicized, and more 'yellow'. We did not sample *Al-Ittihād* because we looked for items with a community focus and even a gossipy character. We likewise did not sample the two Islamic-party newspapers *Al-Mīthāq* and *Sawt-al-Haq wa al-Huriyah*, whose distribution is relatively smaller.

When scanning the newspapers, we left out the sections on national and international politics, sports, and economics, where masculinity is omnipresent to the point that it is largely transparent. Instead, we focused on the sections on family and community affairs, as well as on the culture section, and looked for direct and indirect comments on masculinity and on crisis. Note that at the stage of data collection we already had quite a clear idea, because of our ongoing reading of the local press, that there is a discourse on crisis, and that this discourse is imbued with images and underlying motifs of masculinity. To reiterate, we came to this idea through our ongoing involvement with Palestinian society. Our reading, accordingly, was target oriented, rather than completely open-ended. We explicitly looked for direct and indirect expressions of masculinity. In the analysis, we used the notion of *interpretive package*[14] to identify an underlying frame and the set of condensing symbols used to invoke it.

The paper unfolds as follows. After a brief background section on the Palestinian citizens of Israel, we use ethnographic literature as well as our own research to sketch scripts of Palestinian masculinities and point out some of the tensions that they produce. We then review the local discourse on crisis, and highlight the masculine elements that inform it throughout. This section is based almost exclusively on our sampling of newspapers articles. Through the material presented in these two sections we argue that the state of masculinity among the Palestinians in Israel poignantly embodies their collective predicament. In masculine terms, the intense violence that seems to be hitting the Arab communities inside Israel is a response to blocked options. On the one hand, militaristic-heroic masculinity, which surrounds them through the practices of Palestinians in the PA and of Israeli Jews, is a path not available to them. On the other hand non-violent forms of productive patriarchal masculinity, notably the possibilities to accrue political and economic power, are also largely limited, because of class and national discrimination against them.

[14] William A. Gamson, and Hanna Herzog, 'Living with Contradictions: The Taken-for-Granted in Israeli Political Discourse', *Political Psychology* 20(2) (1999), pp. 247–266.

Background on Palestinians in Israel

The Palestinian citizens of Israel number roughly 1.3 million people, or 20% of the citizens of the state, with a majority of Muslims (82%) and two smaller groups of Christians and Druzes (9% each).[15] Although their Israeli citizenship grants them certain rights and opportunities, notably through education, welfare, and the right to vote and appeal to the courts, they are nevertheless structurally discriminated against.[16] Palestinian Israelis are over-represented in poverty and are concentrated in the lowest socio-economic echelons,[17] with soaring rates of unemployment among men over 45 years of age.[18] Their residential areas suffer from stalled urbanization,[19] which entails among other things, under-developed infrastructure, unemployment, and housing shortages. Strikingly, patriarchal clans have largely retained their powerful position in municipal politics[20] despite far-reaching changes, such as nuclearization of households, a changing power-balance between genders and generations within families, a rise in women's education and earning power, relative entitlement to individual civil protections, and an overall shift to cash economy.

As to gender relations, the situation of Israeli-Palestinian women is complex and even contradictory. They navigate between multiple patriarchies, notably the family, the state, their ethnic or religious communities, work places and different community institutions. This potentially intensifies their oppression.[21] However, the different power regimes often compete and conflict with each other, which drives wedges and produces tensions in the broader gender order, in turn creating constant, if fleeting opportunities for women to expand the scope of their entitlement.[22] Over the past half century or so, Arab women in Israel have registered dramatic achievements. Their level of schooling has risen spectacularly, and the average number of children per woman has dropped significantly. Their freedom of movement has increased and their presence in the public sphere has become ever more salient. At the same time, their participation in paid employment remains grossly low, compared with both Jewish-Israeli women and women in neighboring Arab countries, and their participation in formal politics is negligible.[23]

[15] Israel Central Bureau of Statistics, 2002.

[16] As'ad Ghanem, 'State and Minority in Israel: The Case of Ethnic State and the Predicament of its Minority', *Ethnic and Racial Studies*, 21 (1998), pp. 428–448; Sammy Smooha 'The Model of Ethnic Democracy: Israel as a Jewish and Democratic State', *Nations and Nationalism* 8(4) (2002), pp. 475–503; Gershon Shafir, and Yoav Peled, *Being Israeli: The Dynamics of Multiple Citizenship* (Cambridge: Cambridge University Press, 2002).

[17] Fifty-four percent of Palestinian children in Israel are poor (www.arabs48.com); see also Alisa Lewin, Haya Stier and Dafna Caspi-Dror, 'The Place of Opportunity: Community and Individual Determinants of Poverty among Jews and Arabs in Israel', *Research in Social Stratification and Mobility* 24 (2006), pp. 177–191.

[18] Ahmad Sa'di and Noah Lewin-Epstein, 'Minority Labour Force Participation in the Post-Fordist era: The Case of the Arabs in Israel?', *Work, Employment and Society* 15(4) (2001), pp. 781–802.

[19] Rasem Khamaisi, 'Urbanization and Urbanism in the Arab Settlements in Israel', *Ofakim Be-Geographia*, 64–65 (2005), pp. 293–310 (in Hebrew).

[20] Majid Al-Haj, 'Social research on family lifestyles among Arabs in Israel', *Journal of Comparative Family Studies*, 20 (1989), pp. 175–195; Majid Al-Haj and Henry Rosenfeld *Arab Local Government in Israel* (Boulder, CO: Westview Press, 1990); Taghreed Yahia-Younis and Hanna Herzog, 'Gender and kinship-based discourse during primary elections held by hamael to select candidates for local authorities in Palestinian-Arab localities', *State and Society* 5(1) (2005), pp. 1077–1104 (in Hebrew).

[21] See also Suad Joseph, and Susan Slymovics (eds.), *Women and Power in the Middle East* (Philadelphia, PA: University of Pennsylvania Press, 2001).

[22] Amalia Sa'ar, 'Contradictory location: assessing the position of Palestinian women citizens of Israel', *Journal of Middle East Women's Studies,* 3(3) (2007), pp. 45–74.

[23] Taghreed Yahia-Younis and Hanna Herzog, 'Gender and kinship-based discourse'.

Since this paper focuses on a crisis of masculinity and the various forms of violence that this crisis entails, it is pertinent to note that women are frequently exposed to severe measures of domestic and sexual oppression.[24] By and large the state acts as a passive or active preserver of patriarchal control and male domestic violence.[25] However, over the years women's organizations have challenged the state to provide protection for women threatened with death and suffering domestic abuse, as well as to promote women's rights generally, mostly through the court system and legislation.

Lastly, the Israeli-Palestinian social field is informed by several meta-narratives, including modernity, national identity, cultural authenticity, Islamic morality, and liberal entitlement. All these are distinctly modern, and despite the various epistemological contradictions among them, in their institutional forms they all reinforce male domination. These narratives yield several models of masculinity, all of which claim hegemony, and which are then translated into scripts of conduct.

II. Scripts of Palestinian Masculinities

Several authors to date have presented grounded analyses of Palestinian masculinities. Julie Peteet and Esmail Nashif,[26] writing a decade apart, present ethnographic material on Palestinians living under occupation who are exposed to extreme measures of physical and mental oppression. Focusing on men who had been imprisoned, beaten and tortured, they both describe practices and rituals that are intensely centered on male bodies. In both their analyses, masculinity is gained through endurance of severe physical and mental pain. Individual bodies comprise arenas of personal agency; subjects evince great courage and creativity, but at the same time reenact – hence merge into – the collective national body. The most significant finding in both studies is that practices of masculinity serve to transform humiliation into empowerment. Peteet interprets the public relating of confrontations with Israeli soldiers as rites of resistance, which transform not only the individuals who tell them, but also the larger social structure. Nashif shows how prisoners use their bodies as means of communication and for building communal relations within and without the prison. In these depictions, the condition of violent occupation is critical to the construction of masculinities that enshrine militaristic notions of active and bloody combat.

Establishing a new model of anti-colonial masculinity, Joseph Massad observes,[27] is a much more complicated endeavor than its colonial counterpart.

[24] Nabila Espanioly, 'Violence against women: a Palestinian woman's Perspective; Personal is political', *Women's Studies International Forum* 20 (1997), pp. 587–592; Nadera Shalhoub-Kevorkian, 'Law, Politics, and Violence against Women: A Case Study of Palestinians in Israel', *Law & Society* 21(2) (1999), pp. 189–221; Ilza Glazer and Wahiba Abu-Ras, 'On Aggression, Human Rights, and Hegemonic Discourse: The Case of a Murder for Family Honor in Israel', *Sex Roles* 30 (1994), pp. 269–282; Muhammad M. Haj-Yahia, 'Beliefs about Wife Beating among Arab Men from Israel: The Influence of Their Patriarchal Ideology', *Journal of Family Violence* 18(4, August) (2003), pp. 193–206.
[25] Manar Hasan, 'The Politics of Honor: Patriarchy, the State, and the Murder of Women in the Name of Family Honor', *The Journal of Israeli History* 21 (2002), pp. 1–37.
[26] Julie M. Peteet, 'Male Gender and Rituals of Resistance in the Palestinian Intifada: A Cultural Politics of Violence', *American Ethnologist* 21 (1994), pp. 31–49; Esmail Nashif, 'Attempts at Liberation: Body Materialization and Community Building among Palestinian Political Captives', *Arab Studies Journal* XII(2)/XIII(1) (2004/2005), pp. 46–79.
[27] Joseph Massad, 'Conceiving the Masculine: Gender and Palestinian Nationalism', *Middle East Journal* 49(3) (1995), p. 477.

Differently from Peteet and Nashif, Massad's project is not to portray Palestinian masculinities as such but to explore the hegemonic position of masculinity in the generic Palestinian national agent. Using political speeches and legal and political documents, rather than ethnographic observations, the agent that Massad depicts is still quite similar to what his colleagues recorded. Ideally, and notwithstanding important attempts to construct a gender-inclusive category, this agent is healthy, young, and male, and is measured by his willingness and ability to fight and sacrifice. However, the glorious fighter is not the only image active on the scene. Responding to the fact that many Palestinian men have not been involved in military clashes, particularly if they live in exile or have become work-migrants, the national agent is also a provider and a nurturer. 'He *pays* for his brother's and sister's education... *takes care* of his parents... *raises* his children... and *dreams* of returning to Palestine'.[28] In other words, 'he' is also a bourgeoisie in the making.

In another publication, still on Palestinians living under occupation (in the Palestinian Authority), Penny Johnson and Eileen Kuttab note that Peteet's interpretation that 'the beatings (and detentions) are framed as rites of passage... with critical consequences for political consciousness and agency' does not seem to apply in the second *intifada*.[29] The much greater presence of death and injury during the latest eruption of fire, they write, has produced an emphasis on martyrdom. Against the guerilla-type images of courageous protestors, who nevertheless stay alive (!), which were popular in the first *intifada*, the second uprising is much more brutal, and accordingly masculinities endorse ever higher levels of violence. The leadership at once uses and is hostage to the power of insurgent young men, but without changing the relations between them. Consequently, Johnson and Kuttab argue,

> [t]he crisis in masculinity is not resolved through popular resistance, and indeed increased militarism is perhaps the only 'solution' that is offered. As the intifada continues... the crisis becomes more militarized and even more restricted in its participation, except as recipients of increased Israeli violence.... Power is fragmented and disassociated with the community...[30]

In striking contrast to the bleak context in which masculinities are constructed under occupation, Daniel Monterescu frames his ethnographic account of Palestinian masculinities *inside* Israel as part of an attempt to understand the world of leisure. Poverty and unemployment notwithstanding, life in Jaffa, where he did his research, emerges as the extreme antithesis to the ordeals of the former group. According to Monterescu, the dominant cultural categories in the lives of Arab men in Jaffa are constituted within a framework of strangeness, in 'a mixture of dense daily coexistence interwoven with deep cultural distance'.[31] Too familiar with the Jews/occupiers yet too disempowered to attempt violent resistance against them, the men that Monterescu describes seem to spend their days toying with stereotypical images (woman, homo, loser, Westerner/Jew), against which they attempt to construct themselves as proper men. Arab men in Jaffa are helpless

---

[28] Ibid., 478 emphases original.
[29] Penny Johnson and Eileen Kuttab, 'Where Have all the Women (and Men) Gone?', *Feminist Review* 69 (2001) p. 35.
[30] Ibid., pp. 35–6.
[31] Daniel Monterescu, 'A city of Strangers': The Socio-Cultural Construction of Manhood in Jaffa', *Journal of Mediterranean Studies* 1(1) (2001), p. 163.

because the old patriarchal order has lost its power yet in the new, ethnic state-patriarchy their gendered advantages are useless. Compared with the descriptions of masculinities among Palestinians in the PA, the complete absence of militaristic components is remarkable. Instead, Monterescu tells us, strategies of masculinity in Jaffa are patterned after two mutually exclusive ideological poles: Islamic and secular. The first dreams of returning to the old patriarchal norms while the second offers the concept of relative gender equality.

In another ethnographic exploration of masculinity among Palestinian Arabs inside Israel, Rhoda Kanaaneh looks at the quite exceptional category of men who volunteer for the Israeli security forces, which include the police, the military, and border patrol. These men, who number several thousands, are usually seen as traitors in the Palestinian community, especially if they serve in the military. The discourse on their denigration, which is heavily gendered, reveals much about local understandings of masculinity. Besides being cursed as sons of prostitutes, these volunteers 'are attributed a superficial, individualistic, immature, pubescent masculinity... [and seen] as needing the military to bolster their weak masculinities'.[32] Because the Israeli military apparatus is geared, first and foremost, *against* Arabs, the Palestinian citizens are by definition excluded from its masculine culture. They cannot cash in on the invaluable symbolic capital that accrues to army veterans – tangible material benefits, important connections, and above all, entry into the inner circle of Israeli citizenship – because they are not invited to participate in the first place. They do not receive a draft order. However, even those who do serve, whether because they volunteer or if they happen to be Druze (the only ones who do get drafted), they still remain marginalized. To counter their stigmatization, Arab soldiers emphasize particular components of masculinity, the economic benefits that will allow them to fulfill the role of provider. 'The response of many of the criticized men is that theirs is a pragmatic masculinity, not formed by outdated notions of national taboos but, rather, aimed at advancing their families or themselves as current or future family providers'.[33]

Of course, neither the café-goers in Jaffa nor the men who join the Israeli security forces are 'representative' of what Massad refers to as the Palestinian national agent.[34] Rather, they are particular cases that signify stopping points on a continuum of options and ideals. Intriguingly, both constitute radical opposites to the hyper-militaristic scripts portrayed for Palestinians in the PA. Not that the components of the latter, particularly bodily strength, fighting fitness and sexual prowess, are absent from Arabs in Israel. Their presence is evident, for example, in the constructions of masculine sexuality among homosexuals in Jerusalem, where racialized attributes such as 'black' (i.e., Arab origin), muscular, working-class, and young are considered extremely erotic and sensual.[35] The gap between the portraits drawn by Monterescu and Kanaaneh and those presented earlier possibly indicates the absence of an institutionalized cultural path to militaristic masculinities among the Palestinians who are Israeli citizens. In our interpretation, the appearance of growing internal violence is a response to this void.

[32] Rhoda Ann Kanaaneh 'Boys or Men? Duped or 'Made'? Palestinian Soldiers in the Israeli Military' *American Ethnologist*, 32 (2005, 2), p. 263.
[33] Ibid., 270.
[34] Joseph Massad, 'Conceiving the Masculine'.
[35] Jehuda Sofer, 'Testimonies from the Holy Land: Israeli and Palestinian Men Talk about Their Sexual Encounters', in Arno Schmitt and Jehuda Sofer (eds.), *Sexuality and Eroticism among Males in Moslem Societies* (Binghamton, NY: Harrington Park Press, 1992), pp. 105–112.

To be sure, there are other scripts of hegemonic masculinity too. Devout Islamic masculinity is probably the one most rapidly growing in popularity. This masculinity draws on classical sources, namely verses from the Qur'an and Hadith, which are adapted by contemporary religious leaders who highlight certain verses or stories and give them priority over others. Notwithstanding its own stake in authenticity, Islamic masculinity, like any masculinity, is neither static nor monolithic. The ongoing preoccupation with the desired balance between authentic culture, modernity, and claims for women's advancement and gender equality has yielded new forms of patriarchal masculinity among the Islamists also.

Secular education is another important resource for successful masculine performance. Educational credentials are not necessarily seen as contradictory to virtuous Islamic masculinity, and may well be construed as complementing it. However, among a whole generation of secular, progressive intellectuals they often do represent a counter-model to the former. A column titled 'man of the year', which appeared in several of the newspapers we sampled for this research, featured some pertinent examples. Most of the men who were celebrated as success stories were highly educated professionals, whose achievements were noted as a source of communal pride. For Israeli Palestinians, as for other minorities, education and success as white-collar professionals bear great symbolic value, because they are regarded as keys to social mobility. For some, although not for all, they also entail endorsement of ideas of gender equality.

In a piece emphasizing individual achievement and contribution to the community, an inspector of special education was chosen 'man of the year' for his important contribution to the Arab educational system.[36] Note that this type of successful masculinity is emphatically anti-heroic and in fact controversial. Educational inspectors are tainted because of the stamp of approval that they get from the Israeli security apparatus. Their success, therefore, is somewhat reminiscent of the narratives of those who volunteer to serve in the military or the police. They are responsible, hard working, pragmatic, and most probably socially and politically conservative. They may become quite influential, but they can hardly embody national pride. Success in Israeli academia, which is considered relatively independent, is much rarer and much more lucrative. On 1996, on his promotion to the rank of professor, sociologist Majid Al-Haj was quoted as saying, 'I regard this as an achievement of my people and my society, especially [in light of the fact] that my society has given me more than I ever gave it. Any academic achievement of an Arab is an achievement for his people'.[37] A decade later Al-Haj was appointed Dean of Research and deputy president at the University of Haifa. This appointment to one of the highest offices ever held by an Arab in a national Israeli institution received wide press coverage. One commentator described Al-Haj as 'this self-made man from the East [who] has managed to climb up the academic ladder right to the very top and thereby raised our heads up high'.[38]

A third path to successful masculinity, admittedly reserved for the young and healthy, but very glorious, is that of football players. Football seems to be attractive for two major reasons. It offers some substitute for the absent option of militaristic muscle masculinity, which both Palestinians in the PA and Israeli Jews

---

[36] *Kul al-'Arab*, 5.1.1990.
[37] *Fasl al-Maqāl*, 16.12.1996.
[38] *Al-Sinnārah*, 21.10.2005.

exhibit so vigorously, yet which Palestinians inside Israel are barred from realizing. It also offers potential entrance to a high-earning career in a lucrative branch of mainstream Israeli sport. Thus, one 'man of the year' was Arab footballer 'Abas Suan, who was chosen to play in the Israeli national team and won individual fame when he scored some critical goals.[39] Notwithstanding the ecstatic joy and pride that enveloped Suan and other Arab players, and which reached another peak when the Arab team Abna' il-Sakhneen won the State Cup in 2004, the participation of Arabs in Israeli football continues to invoke blatant expressions of racism, which are hurled even at the most celebrated players.

III. Masculinity in Crisis? Reading Gender Undertones in the Discourse on Crisis

As we explained in the introduction, in our reading of the printed press and our listening to people's daily talk, Israeli Palestinian Arabs are engaged in a discourse on crisis. In particular, people are preoccupied with what seem to be unprecedented levels of violence. In this section we review the central themes that recurred in the newspaper sample, concentrating on the various forms of violence. All the clusters of narratives that convey crisis allude directly or indirectly to gender morality, and more specifically to masculinity. We therefore suggest that they be read as a commentary on masculinity.

Outlining the Major Themes of the Discourse on Crisis

The major narrative packages are as follows. One is a narrative on loss of morals/transgression of cultural boundaries. This cluster, which positions the West and 'Western culture' as the primary source of pollution, includes topics such as the unduly sensual appearance of pop singers. Somewhat countering the first cluster, a second narrative package adopts a rational-secular approach to social problems. This package includes the appeal to experts, such as psychologists or educators, who prescribe methods of anger management or dialogical child upbringing. A third cluster encompasses the issue of violence against women. Here opinions are commonly pitted against one another that condemn such violence as barbarian and those that support it on grounds of cultural propriety. Significantly in this cluster, the concept of domestic abuse has expanded to include spousal abuse alongside 'honor' killings, as well as aggression among males of different generations. Communal violence is yet another narrative package. It includes a range of topics, from road rage that leads to death and injuries, through ethnic/religious riots and clashes, to criminal violence and severe vandalism. Fifth, juvenile violence emerges as yet another growing source of preoccupation. This cluster includes not only what has normatively been termed juvenile delinquency, but also school children carrying knives and using abusive language, and what appears to be a growing license to offend teachers. Because of space limitation, we will not elaborate on each of the five clusters. Instead, we dwell on domestic male violence and on communal violence. We will then integrate the other topics into a presentation of some of the prominent masculine

[39] *Al-Sinnārah*, 7.10.2005.

symbolism that informs the discourse, as well as into an extended case study presented in the discussion.

Domestic Male Violence

A central aspect of violence and masculinity is violence against women, which ranges from physical, mental, and sexual abuse to murder. The cultural option of taking women's lives has undergone some challenges and changes, yet all in all, women and girls in different sectors of the population remain at risk, in some places higher than in others. Although no official figures can be had from official state authorities, documentation from feminist organizations indicates that women and girls continue to be killed. Importantly, over the past fifteen years or so, Arab feminist organizations have made significant progress in challenging state authorities regarding their incompetence in defending women at risk, and in winning growing segments of Arab public opinion against the practice. Yet ironically, while 'honor' killings may have gone down *in some sectors*, the risk to women's lives has not diminished. In fact, it has magnified, since in addition to the cultural license to murder by blood relatives, husbands too, who in the past would have been at risk of retaliation from the same blood relatives, have now joined the circle of potential killers. The traditional killing of women to preserve the 'honor' of their kin group is now joined by killing in a so-called 'romantic' setting.

Still on the scene of gendered and sexual violence, public discourse is increasingly concerned with spousal abuse, which is portrayed in the press in graphic detail. Physical and sexual violence is particularly likely to get coverage, probably because of its sensational aspect and because it activates professional intervention more than mental or spiritual abuse does. Reported cases of husbands' aggression during the months we surveyed include the use of fists, knives, poison, or a rope (in one case). Sexual assault within marriages, previously impossible to spot because of the norm of men's unconditional entitlement to their wives' sexual services, is now increasingly reported. One newspaper article, for example, described a case of a man who raped his wife in front of their children.[40]

Alongside the diversifying implications for women, domestic violence operates in other directions as well. Parental abuse, which until recently was also largely unmarked, because it was seen as a legitimate extension of parental authority, now receives headlines. The state law for Defense of the Underage and the Helpless is likewise gaining in popularity, although people still worry about its potential encroachment on parental authority. Newspapers report severe injuries of children at their fathers' hands, in some cases through the use of firearms. One article gave the story of a father who, during an argument with his son over the latter's alleged descent to crime, pulled a gun and started shooting in the house.[41] The opposite case, of sons attacking their parents, is seemingly still quite rare, but violent nevertheless. One article reports a youngster who, following an argument with his father brought his friends, one of whom had a licensed gun. They fired into the house and set the father's two vehicles alight. Domestic violence of that kind, it should be noted, happens within nuclear families, but also among extended relatives.

---

[40] *Al-Sinnārah*, 7.10.2005.
[41] *Al-Sinnārah*, 7.10.2005.

Communal/Religious-based Violence

Fights that erupt in the communities often assume an added religious tone. However, because religious factionalism is a highly sensitive issue (it is often regarded as an Israeli divide-and-rule ploy to weaken its Palestinian citizens), such tones are not always expressed explicitly. Religious motives tend to reverberate in criminal or other framings, and vice versa. Hence, religious-based vandalism may serve as a pretext to unleash violence of any of the kinds enumerated above. In one case a man entered his next-door neighbor's garden and shot five family members who were standing there, seriously injuring them. Although the shooter was Christian and his neighbors Muslim, the explanations given by the wounded family to the many who came to express their shock and dismay insistently avoided the option of religious motives. Instead, they said, it was a case of a minor neighbors' dispute, which took a tragic turn for no logical reason whatsoever. Besides dismissing the shooter as a low-life, the arguments persistently focused on the outrageous ease with which people get to own firearms.

Masculine Symbolism

Three objects that recur in the discourse on a violence got out of hand, and which are particularly laden with masculine symbolism, are arms, cars, and dogs.

Arms. Private ownership of arms by Palestinian citizens has visibly been on the rise. Men own personal pistols, rifles, and even missiles and bombs. Some of these arms are held legally, mostly through employment in the security forces or as civilian guards (an underpaid occupational branch that has grown exponentially with the latest wave of suicide bombings). Others are obtained illegally, through involvement in criminal activity, including the smuggling of arms and drugs across the borders. A growing number of news items report chance fights in which the participants are quick to draw arms. Quite often these fights end up in injury, or even death. Yet as some of the commentaries emphasize, such unfortunate developments are not necessarily premeditated. It is simply that people are unaware of the severe consequences of carrying and pulling guns. More often than not, such violent incidents entail similarly violent retaliation attempts.

Cars. Although driving and even car ownership has long been an activity open for women, it continues to be regarded as a male sphere. Women's attitude to driving is constructed as functional. Considering the distances between communities and the bad public transportation, women's driving is often seen as the safest and most efficient path to their participation in the public domain. Men's driving, on the other hand, is invested with value and gender identity. Among young adults, ostentatious driving with music blaring from the car radio is a common ritual of display. Speeding, especially in narrow alleyways, represents virtuoso control of the vehicle and of space. Older men too tend to invest a disproportionate part of their income in their cars. Lastly, the maintenance, fixing, buying and selling of cars, including of cars owned by women, are nearly exclusively male activities.

Driving-related violence has several aspects. The most common, which results in fatal accidents, is a tendency to drive too fast, irrespective of road conditions, and not obeying traffic laws. Another particularly tragic aspect is the high incidence of small children run over by cars being driven in reverse inside villages. A third type of driving-related violence is road rage. Drivers may consider overtaking as an offense to their honor and attempt 'retaliation' by driving faster, running the other driver off the road, etc. Some traffic laws, such as yielding the right of way, are considered a particular affront to manliness. In fact, among young adult males unruly driving is a common masculine performance. Another corollary of road rage is the apparently expanding phenomenon of 'taking the fight outside the car'. Fiction writer Sayed Kashua relates the following exchange between an intellectual who lived in Jerusalem for many years and his brother, who is initiating him upon his return to the village,

> You are driving in a narrow road, a car is coming toward you and there is no room for both of you, you immediately back up. Even if he only needs to back up one meter and you need to back up a hundred, *you* will be the one who backs up. Because it can end up in shootings, depending on who is sitting in the car. You are driving in the street and two cars are blocking the road because the drivers are talking to one another through the window? Wait silently. Don't dare honking! Wait until they finish their conversation. Even if it takes them an hour, you just wait silently and when they let you pass, smile and say thank you.' Ashraf is laughing as he recites to me the lexicon of survival.[42]

Dogs.   Last but not least, training attack dogs and walking them in public seems to be one of the latest male fashions. One newspaper article that was dedicated to this trend was among the few that explicitly named men and masculinity. The fascination with these dangerous dogs, according to the explanation given in this piece, lies in the sense of control and power that they provide for their owners.

> We raise these dogs in order to satisfy machismo (*al-matshoism*) ... People say that they want the dogs for defense purposes, but the real goal is different. The dogs make for a display of masculinity (*al-rujula*) [and youngsters raise them] to be in line with their friends from the neighborhood or from school. As one dog trainer said: 'We raise these dogs because they make us feel men and powerful. I can walk the street with this dog knowing that no one will challenge me, or the dog will attack him'.[43]

Masculinity, Violence and Nationalism

Notably, the growing public discourse on the alarming rates of violence makes constant links between aggressions that emerge from, and are directed at the community, and what is portrayed as spirally growing national and global levels of aggression. American-British aggression in Afghanistan and Iraq has stirred acute resentment. But mostly, Israeli aggression against Palestinians in the West Bank and Gaza, and lately against Lebanese civilians has been a permanent source of pain and anger. The daily practices of watching these aggressions live on TV, and the mixture of strong antagonism and helplessness that they arouse, surely affect the local atmosphere of license to violence.

But probably more than the violence 'out there', which is present through the media, a necessary aspect of the violence within the Arab communities is the much more direct and personal context of civil discrimination and national exclusion. Indeed, the national defeat of the Palestinians, and the personal and communal

---

[42] Sayed Kashua, *Let it be Morning* (Tel Aviv: Keter 2004), p. 31 (in Hebrew).
[43] *Al-Sinnārah*, 2.9.2005.

losses that it entailed, has been a constitutive element in the collective consciousness of the Palestinians, within and outside Israel. However, compared with the grand narrative of *al-nakba* (the tragic defeat of 1948) the current discourse on crisis bears a distinctly ordinary character. It likewise digresses from the highly political tones that have characterized local debates and increasingly shifts attention from external oppression to internal behaviors and world views.

The highly gendered character of the Palestinian national discourse has been widely documented.[44] Our analysis, therefore, draws on a rich interpretive legacy. Yet whereas for the most part the discussion has focused on dramatic articulations of femininity and masculinity, our focus is on mundane and often anti-heroic versions of the same phenomenon. In the larger discourse on Palestinian destiny and identity, the Arabs of 1948 occupy a precarious position. For better or for worst, they do not live under occupation, even though as an indigenous minority they are not granted full citizenship, nor do they live in exile from their homeland. They likewise have not been able to participate, culturally and economically, in the broader Arab-Middle Eastern region, and their reunion with Palestinians in the West Bank and Gaza has seen interruptions and has been riddled with significant and multiple gaps. Within this context their discourse on crisis, and the images of masculinity that embody this discourse, tend to assume a somewhat ordinary character, compared with the dramatic representations that feature in parallel Palestinian expressions.

In the hyper-nationalistic Israeli-Palestinian scene, violence is a central mode of behavior, yet within this complex, the Arabs inside are left with no defined role. Despite their Israeli citizenship they are not drafted into its armed forces. At the same time, as official citizens of the state they cannot join the organized Palestinian resistance either. They are at once potential traitors to their national group and a potential fifth column within their state. Considering the restricted space allowed for their collective expression, Israeli-Palestinian Arabs do not have legitimate, institutionalized channels for militaristic-violent masculine performances. They can neither identify with Israeli national military heroes nor endorse openly Palestinian heroes, whose very glory is derived from their resistance to Zionism and later to Israel. This blocked path is important for the interpretation of the local concern about growing communal violence that seems to have encroached ever closer to home.

We conclude the description of the phenomenon with a narrative that ties together some of the main themes that have been raised thus far. In July 2005 a 60-year-old man from a large community in the Galilee was murdered in what was presented as a case of utter arbitrariness. According to the account in one of the newspapers, which dedicated a long article to the case, the man had berated a 19-year-old youngster from the same village for driving too fast in his street. Shortly after the incident, when the man was sitting on his porch, the driver returned, accompanied by his father (allegedly to hold a *sulha*, ritualistic peace making),[45] who drew his automatic weapon, shot at close range, and killed the older man in his own home. Having described the facts, the authors of the article comment, 'It is as if after he failed to kill

[44] Sheila H. Katz, 'Adam and Adama, 'Ird and Ard: En-gendering Political Conflict and Identity in Early Jewish and Palestinian Nationalisms', in Deniz Kandiyoti (ed.), *Gendering the Middle East; Alternative Perspectives* (London: I.B. Tauris, 1996), pp. 85–105; Rosemary Sayigh, 'Palestinian Women and Politics in Lebanon', in Juditt Tucker (ed.), *Arab Women: Old Boundaries, New Frontiers* (Bloomington, IN: Indiana University Press, 1993), pp. 175–194; Joseph Massad, 'Conceiving the Masculine'; Julie M. Peteet, 'Male Gender Rituals of Resistance'.
[45] This detail, which we learned from personal communication with the victim's relatives, was not included in the newspaper article.

by running someone over, he decided to do it by pulling a gun. As everyone knows all too well, such guns abound in the village. And they are illegal. Yet the police turn a blind eye for [they say], "At the end of the day, they kill one another".[46] After describing the act and giving some biographical details about the slain man, the article cites excerpts from eulogies that were made on the man's grave and from interviews with some of his acquaintances. The episode forms a dense narrative on masculinity in crisis.

The victim was a scientist who had lived in the US for many years, enjoying a highly successful career. He had married an American woman and had three children with her. After his marriage collapsed he decided to return to his land, where he married a young woman and had another son. Over the previous five years he was employed in his profession with an Israeli firm. The eulogies and personal testimonies abound with positive images of masculinity. '[He had a] wide and big heart, full of love, compassion, and warmth... He was modest... Always smiling... had a noble character... He was a faithful husband, always sacrificing and never complaining that he was tired. Always swift to respond when asked... never liked to boast about his credentials and his knowledge'. The manly traits that were recounted include acquired success, in the form of high educational credentials, ambition, hard work, and standing up to challenges. The allusion to the man's rural background emphasizes his achievements (from *fellah* to a renowned scientist) and celebrates the modernistic ethos of individual upward mobility despite the odds. At the same time, individualism is balanced by a strong commitment to give back to society (his love, his compassion...). And ultimately, he 'came back to his land'. Having left a divorced wife and three children behind is not an issue. Instead, his *fellah* background underscores his love of the soil and autochthonous roots. Lastly, he was a good spouse – always sacrificing and not complaining. Here the theme of a modern man recurs, yet the idea of the egalitarian husband is ambivalently presented as sacrifice, possibly of his traditional patriarchal prerogatives.

The portrait of noble masculinity is made all the more vivid through the denigration of the murderers (quoted from the same article):

> Knifing in the back is not among the attributes of the noble and has nothing to do with masculinity... our response was a cultured response. We have followed our original morality and not allowed the blood to boil. We did not burn down houses; we did not even consider it. We did not seek revenge; we did not even consider it. We did not follow the tradition of blood revenge. We do not hold the one responsible for the deeds of another. Our avoiding revenge is not a sign of cowardice, but of strength. We refuse to sink to the animal level of the murderers and those who assisted them, and do not let our instincts rule us. God made man superior to the rest of beings in wisdom and brains. Any human being whose brain does not lead him cannot be counted among men.

And later in reference to the reactions of the murderer and his son, 'They think of this as a sign of masculinity'.

Importantly, the lack of control that is associated here with 'wrong' masculinity is related to two sources. One is the young age of the driver (the age gap between the murderer and the murdered is noted several times in the article). True masculinity entails maturity, and above all self-control. A second source of failed control is related to the state, which lets illegal weapons flood the village. Also according to this version, 'true' masculinity

---

[46] *Fasl-al-Maqāl*, 2.9.2005.

means rational, pragmatic adherence to the state's law, regardless of national sentiments, instead of following the old laws of group honor and the blood feud, which have ceased to be relevant. Lastly, the argument about maturity notwithstanding, the fact that it was the young driver's *father* who allegedly fired the fatal shot cannot reduce the deed entirely to lack of maturity. Rather, this means that what this narrative presents as 'wrong' masculinity is not unanimously seen as such. Greatly to the contrary, the very fact that the authors of the article go out of their way to emphasize that 'this is not true masculinity' implies that the two scripts exercise a hold in the society.

IV. Discussion

Paul Farmer uses the term structural violence for brutality that resides in taken-for-granted arrangements, notably poverty and sharp social inequalities, where oppression results from many conditions that are both 'sinful' and ostensibly 'nobody's fault'.[47] In the case of the Palestinian citizens of Israel, structural violence entails, alongside official and latent measures of constitutional discrimination, also routine violence from state institutions and the Jewish public alike. After the state's decades-long control of its Arab citizens[48] significantly relaxed in the 1990s, the outbreak of the second *intifada* brought the process of Israeli democratization to an abrupt halt. The violent clashes that ensued following the visit of Ariel Sharon in the Temple Mount in late September 2000 sparked protests inside Israel as well, and these were violently suppressed by the Israeli police, an operation that left 13 dead and hundreds kept in detention without trial for months on end. These events, which later received the title *habbat octobar* (October gust), marked a traumatic setback in Arab–Jewish relations inside Israel. Following intense public protest, a state-run commission of inquiry (the Orr Committee) was eventually appointed to investigate the conduct of the police, yet despite its severe conclusions no indictments were ever filed, and the politicians who had been in charge lost no public credibility. For all its shortcomings, the Orr Committee did manage to inscribe on Israeli public opinion the death of 13 citizens as a regretful failing of democratic protection. It also instigated a certain rhetoric of government commitment to undertake a compensatory policy on the Arab sector as a whole (a promise that has never been delivered). Ironically, however, the settling of the October gust did not mark the end of casualties among the Palestinian citizens at the hands of the security forces. A report released by Mossawa Advocacy Center for Arab Citizens of Israel in 2004 surveys 16 more incidents which occurred after the October 2000 events. Only for two incidents were indictments filed against two security officers who had shot and killed Arab citizens.[49]

Racism, or hostility on account of their national background, is another prominent experience of the Palestinian citizens of Israel.[50] A poll conducted for

[47] Paul Farmer, 'An anthropology of structural violence', *Current Anthropology* 45(3, June) (2004), pp. 305–325.
[48] Ian Lustick, *Arabs in the Jewish State: Israel's Control of a National Minority* (Austin, TX: University of Texas Press, 1980).
[49] http://www.mossawacenter.org/en/reports/2004/06/040601.html
[50] In a study of the impact of the armed conflict on women in Israel, 15% of the Palestinian respondents reported having been exposed to either verbal or physical offenses related to their national affiliation, Dalia Sachs, Amalia Sa'ar and Sarai Aharoni, 'How can I feel for others when I myself am beaten? The impact of the armed conflict on women in Israel', *Sex Roles* 57(7) (2007), p. 593.

Mossawa shows that 70% of the Jewish public thinks that the Arab citizens constitute a threat to state security; almost 34% accuse the Arab citizens of taking over their jobs and of exacerbating the poor economic situation; 22% state that they would vote for the extreme right Kach party (which preaches ethnic cleansing) if it were allowed to run for election.[51] Beside routine acts of discrimination and racism, in the past few years several incidents were registered of armed terrorism against Arab citizens. In 2004, the car of an Arab MK was booby-trapped; other bombs were placed in mosques and even in some homes. In the summer of 2005, a Jewish IDF soldier stormed a bus in the city of Shafa-'amer and murdered four passengers. At the level of parliamentary politics, the Arab representatives are subjected to gross de-legitimacy as partners to the coalition. Jewish politicians and religious leaders repeatedly hurl insults at them, not fearing charges of racial agitation, while Arab MKs are routinely subjected to investigation despite their parliamentary immunity. Similarly, the football fields, which as shown in the previous section are often celebrated as neutral and spontaneous sites of democratic participation and coexistence, and which many Arabs cherish as an opportunity for civic inclusion, have at the same time served as sites of blatant racist incitement.

Directions for Future Research: Comparative Analysis and the Question of Subjectivity

Before concluding, we want to point out two pertinent issues that remain outside the scope of the present paper, but which we find important to outline for future research. The first concerns a comparative outlook. One of the immediate reference groups that comes to mind is Palestinians in the PA, who despite having an internationally recognized polity remain subjected to Israeli military and economic rule. There, more extreme forms of structural violence also breed internal violence, which is again enacted through scripts of masculinity. While our paper is empirically restricted to Palestinians inside Israel, the cultural, historical and political affinities between these two groups challenges our decision to stop at the border, as it were, and calls for an initial inclusion of both in the same analytical endeavor. Notably, despite the resemblance of masculine performances, among Palestinians in the PA the scope and degree of brutality, and indeed the sense of predicament, are much graver. Not wishing to engage in ranking and making taxonomies of violence, our noting the closeness among Palestinians on both sides of the Green Line is meant to highlight the point that like in so many other cases, the political borders and their concomitant official identities are themselves part of the violent structure. Note that we do not expect that enlarging the lens to include Palestinians from the PA will in the least take the edge off the admittedly less extreme violence that preoccupies the Palestinians inside Israel. Rather, we endorse Arthur Kleinman's insistence on a broad definition of social violence that includes extremes of political violence as well as everyday forms of suffering through images, institutional practices, and cultural expectations. He writes: 'through violence in social experience, as mediated by cultural

---

[51] http://www.mossawacenter.org/en/reports/2004/06/040601.html. On increased racism against Palestinians among the Jewish citizens of Israel during the years of the second *Intifada*, see also M. Elran, *Israel's National Resilience: The Influence of the Second Intifada on Israeli Society* (Tel Aviv: Tel Aviv Jaffee Center for Strategic Studies, Tel Aviv University, 2005).

representations, social formations are not just replicated, but the ordinary lives of individuals are also shaped, and all too often/ twisted, bent, and broken'.[52]

The second issue is subjectivity. As outlined in the introduction, masculinity is dynamic and contradictory. Concomitantly, the term 'scripts', which we preferred over 'models', better acknowledges agency and subjectivity. Nevertheless, the present paper relied primarily on printed newspaper passages, which leaves relatively little room to consider the active engagement of members of the community with whatever picture such texts produce. Complementing our data with accounts obtained through participant observation would no doubt yield a fuller and more complex picture of the intersection of violence, masculine scripts, and cultural morality. Not that the material that we did collect conveyed a static picture: the last case that was cited, for example, included a clash between masculine scripts. The declaration, 'we have followed our original morality and not allowed the blood to boil', referring to the conduct of the victim who admitted the offender into his home, apparently accepting the latter's offer of a *sulha*, ultimately invested him with moral superiority, hence subjectivity.[53]

In the printed media that circulates among Israeli-Palestinian Arabs, the dominant moral tone creates an atmosphere of lost direction. Yet the contents of the stories also give a sense of vitality. Take, for example, the notion of wife abuse. Stories similar to those above about the brutal rape of a wife or the attempted murders of women by their husbands produce voyeuristic, sensational narratives whose moral is nevertheless complex, as they are given to diverse interpretations. Besides seemingly obvious depictions of women as victims and of men as brutes, such stories at one and the same time rearticulate the terms of legitimate male domestic violence, and re-inscribe the nexus of subjugation and moral laxity traditionally attached to women's sexuality. Then again, the very talk about rape and other forms of violence within marriage lifts the categorical ban on discussing such issues in public, even as the protagonists remain anonymous. These and other competing interpretations, which are already intimated within the printed presentations, suggest that gender morality is not simply falling apart, but may actually be rejuvenating. A future ethnographic study, therefore, may seek to document the ways in which, when translated into kinscripts, seemingly conflicting models of masculinity/femininity in effect mutually inform one another.

V. Conclusion

In this paper we explored a discourse on crisis in the printed Arabic press in Israel, and read it using gender theory. We argued that the sense of predicament among the Palestinian citizens is implicitly articulated in terms of a crisis in masculinity. Their political-economic location does not allow the realization of militaristic masculinities, which hold gross hegemony in the area, while alternative scripts of less violent masculinities are also hardly viable for them. Growing numbers of

---

[52] Arthur Kleinman, 'The Violence of Everyday Life: The Multiple Forms and Dynamics of Social Violence', in Maurice Berger, Brian Wallis and Simon Watson (eds.), *Constructing Masculinity* (New York and London: Routledge, 2000), p. 238.
[53] For the ability to notice the dialectic, if charged, relations between victimization and subjectivity we are indebted to the illuminating work of Veena Das and partners in Veena Das, Arthur Kleinman, Mamphela Ramphele and Pamela Reynolds (eds.), *Violence and Subjectivity* (Berkeley, CA: University of California Press, 2000).

men are incapable of supporting their families, men generally are barred from positions of effective political leadership, and more generally still, because of their interstitial position in the region, Palestinian Israelis are marginalized in terms of cultural production.

The contribution of this paper lies in the application of gender theory to issues of cultural morality and social order that are locally deemed collective, as opposed to being specific to women, hence in marking a layer of power dynamics that conventional studies of the *collective* affairs of this group usually leave unmarked. The notion of masculine scripts, in particular, facilitates dialectical consideration of structural components and transformative capacities, since such scripts operate as models of/model for the production of cultural meaning. While we have demonstrated destructive behaviors, and the anger and frustration that they evoke, our material also points to the potential of redirecting norms and behaviors toward more productive and plausibly somewhat less militaristic masculinities. Conceptualized in this way, masculinity comprises a timely site for critical reading of the situation of Palestinians inside Israel, as it allows a glance at the vulnerable side of what is usually considered as the hub of power and control.

Acknowledgements

This paper was originally presented at the workshop on Cultural Critique and Gender Critique in the Middle East and Mediterranean Region, held by the European University Institute in March 2006. The authors thank the workshop participants and particularly Zahia Salhi for their valuable comments. We likewise thank Murray Rosovsky for his careful editing of the manuscript and Nadeem Karkabi for his assistance in data collection.

The Central Role of the Family Law in the Moroccan Feminist Movement

FATIMA SADIQI

ABSTRACT *Ever since its inception in the mid-forties of the last century, the Moroccan feminist movement has evolved around the family law Code. The post-independence family law denied women basic rights and thus fueled the disappointment and anger of the female intellectual elite (journalists, writers, politicians and activists). Legal rights have always constituted a priority in Moroccan women's struggle for dignity in and outside the home. These rights became central with women's increasing access to education and the job market. Today, women's legal rights are associated with democratization and political openness. This paper addresses these issues and underlines the impact of the family law in generating and accelerating feminist ideas in Morocco.*

I. The Beginnings

The beginning of the Moroccan feminist movement goes back to 1946, the year in which the 'Akhawat Al-Safaa' (Sisters of Purity) Association[1] issued a document which embodied a number of legal demands, among which the abolition of polygamy and more visibility in the public sphere. This document is considered the first 'public' voice of the Moroccan feminist movement.[2] Some of these pioneer women wrote articles in the mainstream newspaper of the 'Istiqlal' (Independence) Party: *Al-Alam*.[3] Their views were generally supported by the male liberal nationalists of the time.

The first voices of women in the public sphere were made possible by the liberal views of key political male actors such as prominent nationalist thinkers, the monarch, and political parties. 'Akhawat Al-Safaa' belonged to the middle and upper classes of the city of Fes, and all of them had influential male relatives in the then sole popular party: the 'Istiqlal' (Independence) party.

At this juncture, it is important to distinguish the pioneer women's feminist views from the then prevailing male 'feminism' which targeted the promotion of

---

[1] This association was part of the 'Istiqlal' (Independence) Party.
[2] Cf. Sadiqi et al. (eds.), *Women Writing Africa: The Northern Region* (New York: The Feminist Press), forthcoming in 2008.
[3] Ibid.

women from larger perspectives in which society as a whole, and not women as individuals, constituted the priority.[4] Thus, although they belonged to the same historical era (the Protectorate and Post-Independence era), Allal Al-Fassi, a Salafist, a religious reformist, and a prominent nationalist, who studied and lived in Egypt, dismissed polygamy, not because it harmed women as individuals, but because it was a practice that 'tarnished' the image of 'modern' Islam,[5] and Mohamed Hassan Ouazzani, a modernist intellectual, who studied and lived in France, called for equitable inheritance laws, not only because these laws were harmful to women as women, but also because equitable inheritance laws were 'tokens' of a modern egalitarian society. The two men had different societal projects and sought the 'emancipation' of women to suit these projects: an 'enlightened' Islamic state in the case of Al-Fassi and a European-style state in the case of Ouazzani.

The newly independent state[6] espoused these male feminist views for more or less the same reasons. For example, in 1957, King Mohamed V unveiled his eldest daughter in public and called for the necessity to emancipate women in order to develop society. After this symbolic gesture, thousands of women in cities unveiled and religious preachers in mosques associated unveiling and working outside the home with nation-building.

As for the political parties (conservative and otherwise), they included 'feminist' ideas in their electoral campaigns, although the more one went into their core priorities, the less 'feminist' these ideas became, as is most attested in the structures and orientations of these parties which bluntly reproduced the same patriarchal visions they claimed to fight against.

Overall, men's feminist views were different from women's: while the latter's aimed at improving women's lives, the former's were more abstract as they formed part of 'remedies' to the 'backwardness' of Morocco. Feminist men of the time endeavored to prove that Morocco could not progress without educating and training its women. The interest in educating women that the intellectuals, the state, and political parties called for was not motivated by a genuine interest in the liberation of women as individuals, but by larger social/national projects. As a result, middle and upper classes sought in educating their girls some kind of social prestige which they used to boost their personal and social status.[7] Likewise, although the state and political parties played a crucial role in inducing women to seek regular remunerated work outside the home, this inducement did not emanate from clear and active policies to integrate women into the job market; rather, women's work was part of unplanned consequences of state policies as well as of development requirements.

Although male feminism did not target the empowerment of women as individuals, the middle and upper class women gained from it in two fields:

[4] This feminism took its roots in the nineteen century 'Nahda' (Renaissance) era in the Middle East and embodied male larger visions of what a targeted society could be. The 'Nahda' scholars, such as Jamal Eddine Al-Afghani and Mohamed Abdou, sought the 'emancipation' of women as part of the overall development of society.

[5] In his *Al-Naqd Al-Dhātī* (Auto-Criticism), Allal Al-Fassi made several criticisms of the Moroccan family law in which he called for the abolition of polygamy, judicial regulation of repudiation, as well as divorce and the equivalent of a set of alimony for repudiated women.

[6] Morocco obtained its independence from France in 1956.

[7] Walters (1999) argues that girl's education in Tunisia was partly geared towards producing more marriageable daughters, thereby, increasing the status of the family.

34

education and job opportunities, that is, the means of entering the public sphere. It was the new post-independence bourgeois class that produced the first women pharmacists, jurists, medical doctors, university professors, etc. The general feminist trend of these women was liberal in the sense that they readily embraced 'modern' ideas and practices without rejecting their local specificities, including being Muslim.[8] This liberal trend was accompanied by changes in dress, as well as other social practices, such as the adoption of the French style and ways of life. However, this style never succeeded in replacing traditional Moroccan practices and ways of life, including dress.

Women's feminist ideas started to be manifested in journalistic and academic writings (mainly sociological and literary). As such, the general feminist trend of these women links with the 'Akhawat Al-Safaa' journalistic practices. Journalistic writings included newspaper reports and magazine articles. These writings circulated widely among the educated population. The Moroccan feminist writer Leila Abouzeid started her carrier as a journalist in the early 1970s and wrote under a man's name, and Zakia Daoud remains a Moroccan professional journalist and a fervent feminist.

II. Journalism

Journalistic discourse, couched in Arabic and French, evolved around two major issues: (i) a cult of domesticity and (ii) feminist ideology. The cult of domesticity included topics that were meant to improve women's health, productivity, education, nurturing skills, household management, childrearing, and 'how to' be a better, more effective wife and mother. As for feminist ideology, it included selected biographies of national and international feminist figures. Indeed, using some sort of feminist hagiography, biographies were used as a means of publicly exposing feminist ideas without directly implicating the writer. It is not just exposing readers to feminist ideas, but also authors' indirectly espousing such a stance. Both types of journalistic writings aimed at stressing the development of women through the development of their gifts, while highlighting their domestic roles. They were also meant to promote the rights of women to remain in the work force. In parallel to journalistic writings, women of the 1960s and 1970s started to write novels and produce sociological analyses. Some of these women, like Khnata Bennouna, belonged to leftist political parties and some readily espoused leftist ideology. Both the journalistic and academic writings challenged patriarchy without displacing or dismantling it.

Along these journalistic and academic writings, women started to organize themselves in political parties. Examples are the 'Union Progressiste des Femmes Marocaines' (Progressive Union of Moroccan Women), which was created in 1962, and the 'Union Nationale des Femmes Marocaines' (National Union of Moroccan Women), which was created in 1969. These were professional, not straightforwardly political, organizations. Likewise, more and more women became skilled politicians in opposition leftist parties such as the 'Parti du Progrès et du Socialisme' (Progress and Socialism Party) and the 'Parti de L'Union Socialiste du Front Populaire' (Socialist Union of the Popular Front).

In the subsequent years, that is in the 1980s, and with the advent of mass education, more outspoken feminist journalistic and academic writings were

---

[8] I will later deal with the dichotomy liberal feminism/Islamism.

produced by women. Magazines such as *8 Mars*[9] (March 8), created in 1983 and *Kalima* (Word), created in 1986 and censured in 1988, addressed feminist issues and aimed to show that gender roles, sexuality, and even the division of labor were neither divinely prescribed nor ordained by nature, but had a historical origin. In parallel, more outspoken women's voices made themselves heard in the academic sphere: Fatema Mernissi[10] argues that Moroccan women's unequal status is attributed to the political and economic systems which exclude them.[11] Leila Abouzeid (1983) wrote *'Ām Al-Fīl* (The Year of the Elephant)[12] where she brilliantly depicts how Moroccan women, who participated in the fight for independence, were fulfilled and had an identity during the nationalist fight, but after independence, felt discarded and useless as the national leaders often re-married younger wives and adopted French-style ways and manners in which indigenous ways of life and illiteracy hardly had any place.

III. The Role of NGOs

Along with the journalistic and academic writings, women's associations (also called local NGOs) started to see the light of the day. The first post-independence women's association, 'L'Association Démocratique des Femmes Marocaines' (The Democratic Association of Moroccan Women) started, like the 'Akawat Al-Safaa' association, as a division of a political party, the Party of Progress and Socialism, this time. Soon after, another strong women's rights association, 'L'Union de L'Action Féminine' (Female Action Union), was created.

These two associations were soon followed by a plethora of similar, but smaller, women's associations which have emerged to combat violence against women, gender-based legal and cultural discrimination, under-representation of women in government and the economic sector, and illiteracy. These associations have given Moroccan women the opportunity to become skilled in the public organization of their demands, the public articulation of their resources, as well as a good opportunity to gain credibility in the public scene. Moroccan feminist associations produced many feminist militants who later became national public figures like Latifa Jbabdi, Nouzha Skalli, Amina Lemrini, and Latifa Smires Bennani.

These associations were greatly helped by international organizations. As liberal feminists and proponents of women's rights across the world have launched worldwide pressures to stop gender-based discrimination and promote women's rights, using powerful organizations like the United Nations, the government of Morocco was constantly being asked to send official delegations and address women's issues in world-wide events like the United Nations Decade for Women (1975–1985) and specific UN meetings (Mexico City 1975; Copenhagen 1980,

---

[9] This magazine ceased to appear for more than a decade before it resumed its activities in 2004.

[10] Fatema Mernissi, 'Etat et Planification Nationale', in A. Alahyane et al. (eds.), *Portraits de Femmes* (Casablanca: Le Fennec, 1987).

[11] It is important to note that the details of feminist struggles and conditionings differ for each Muslim country. For example, Tunisia's political elite positioned Tunisian women very differently by capitalizing on their civil rights. This does not mean that Tunisia is a panacea for women, but its history contrasts in critical ways with Morocco's. Indeed, national differences indicate that the 'Arab Muslim' world is not an undifferentiated whole.

[12] The expression 'Year of the Elephant' is an allusion to a famous period in the history of Islam during which foreign tribes riding elephants marched on the sanctuary at Mecca. Elizabeth Fernea with Robert Fernea (1985) explain the title by stating that the battle was not won by arms and superior numbers of warriors but by 'flocks of birds which miraculously appeared and bombarded the elephants with clay pellets'. The birds were like ordinary men and women who brought about Morocco's independence.

Nairobi 1985, Beijing 1995, etc.).[13] Likewise, Morocco ratified the Convention to End Discrimination Against Women (CEDAW) on August 26, 1993. CEDAW was ratified by Morocco with reservations to articles 2 and 16 which concern marriage and its dissolution and national identity and how it is not passed from mother to child, respectively. These reservations were justified on the grounds that Moroccan officials wanted to reconcile Western views with the Moroccan legal system; they considered that the two articles that were opposed conflicted with the Code of Personal Status known as the 'Mudawana'.

By questioning the sexual division and the ideology on which it was based, the journalistic, academic and associative discourse of liberal feminists questioned patriarchy. In such a discourse, women's condition was not considered a 'natural state', but a state that had historical origins and women's work was seen as production, and not merely reproduction. As such, this discourse tackled issues which, until recently, were taboo, such as female sexuality and the various forms of violence against women. This discourse sought to politicize women's collective consciousness of their oppression and denounced the indifference of political parties, which often used women's issues to enforce their political agendas and demarcate themselves from the fundamentalist rhetoric, to the reality of women's lives.

This overall stance of Moroccan feminists explains their bitter disappointment with the first Code of Personal Status 'Mudawana', which was instituted in 1957, that is, only one year after independence. The Moroccan feminist movement is deeply associated with the 'Mudawana' as the latter constitutes the locus of the legal and civil discrimination against women. The disappointment of liberal feminists with the 'Mudawana' was partly due to the fact that Allal Al-Fassi's liberal ideas were not integrated into the 'Mudawana' although the man was called upon for the drafting of this document.[14] Another aspect of liberal feminists' disappointment is the fact that the 'Mudawana' was based on the religious Maliki law, at a time when other codes were based on civil law such as the Penal Code and the Constitution. For example, many Moroccan laws such as the ones relative to bank interest and the sale of alcohol bypass the precepts of religion even though the Qur'an is very clear on these issues.

The fact that the 'Mudawana' was masterminded by men only and was based on religious law was meant to make it 'sacred' and not open to public debate. The 'Mudawana' also defined women as minors by limiting their rights and allowing polygamy. The Code was seen by liberal feminists as a 'betrayal' and a way of distancing women from the public sphere.[15]

Mernissi denounced the undemocratic practices of the former national male leaders who suffered from torture at the hands of the French colonizers in order to achieve democracy and equity but who then treated half of their society unfairly by institutionalizing a Code of Personal Status that denied them their rights. Mernissi deconstructed the patriarchal biases in gender representation at the official level and postcolonial undemocratic societal projects. She underlined the inconsistency

[13] It is worth noting that participation in international events like these carries an importance and a cachet in Morocco, as well as in North Africa and other countries, that it does not in the US at least, perhaps because though the US government may send delegations, the active and engaged participants are mainly from groups having nothing to do with the government, especially for women's issues.

[14] In 1957, only one year after independence, King Mohamed V created a commission to work with the Minister of Justice to codify Family Law in Morocco; this commission consisted of ten Ulemas (Islamic scholars) and three figureheads of Moroccan Salafism (religious reformism) among whom Allal Al-Fassi.

[15] Zakia Daoud, *Transfiguration of the Maghreb* (Minneapolis: University of Minnesota Press, 1993). Winifred Woodhull, *Féminisme et Politique Au Maghreb* (Casablanca: Eddif, 1993).

between the conservative nature of the Code and the promotion of a liberal economic system. While the Moroccan Constitution granted women equal political rights with those of men, the Code of Personal Status inscribed them as essentially domestic beings with limited rights. According to Mernissi, postcolonial Morocco designated male supremacy and female subordination as symbols of cultural specificity and political legitimacy.

IV. Interesting Developments: The Mudawana as a Pool of Struggle

From the 1980s onward, the Moroccan feminist movement had to deal with a serious challenge: Islamism.[16] In general, Islamists don't have a deep theological or judicial knowledge which leads to require from themselves and from others rigorous religious practices based on the literal reading of the founding texts (Qur'an and Sunnah). In opposing the West, Islamism opposes modernity, and in doing so, it creates confusion between the West and modernity and takes the West, which may be defined as an incomplete historical manifestation of modernity, for modernity itself. Instead of criticizing the West in the name of modernity, Islamism rejects modernity and opposes the 'Self' and the 'Other' in an anti-historic way, using women as the weaker and hence more accessible sex.

Liberal feminists quickly realized that Islamists targeted women, especially the lower classes, through their call for veiling and their carefully packaged discourses that comforted the patriarchal tendencies among men, especially young unemployed males who were easily led to think that women's work outside the home robs them of opportunities. They also realized that by pushing politicized women to demand rights from a religious perspective, they were trying to highjack the discourse, space and fruits of years of efforts by liberal feminists.

The main strategies that liberal feminists used were a gradual downplay of the 'religious' role of the veil in their writings and practices, more and more usage of Arabic, Qur'an and *Hadith*, a call for more flexible readings of the Qur'anic texts, a gradual inclusion of the children's oppression in women's issues, and a reinforcement of Islam as culture and spirituality. These liberal feminists also endeavored to draw the attention of the younger, often veiled, generation to the real problems that women faced: absence of legal protection before the law. These feminists made an excellent use of the media in depicting the social misery of women and child victims of divorce, thus targeting the very social issues that the Islamists capitalized on. By doing this, the liberal feminists maintained their focus on the necessity to reform the Family Law.

Overall, the liberal feminists of the 1980s sought to assert themselves and affirm their own identity and the existence of their own history in spite of the powerful Islamic movement. They did this through journalistic writings, associative work, and anthropological, sociological, and political studies, as well as through narratives and poems. These feminists were conscious that if they rejected Islamic precepts, they would face a double sanction: in Morocco, they would fail to connect with the vast

---

[16] Islamism may be defined as a social movement or organization based on the exploitation of Islam for political aims. More precisely, any such movement or organization that tries to exercise power in the name of religion only. Given its western-most geographical position in the MENA region, Islamism reached Morocco last. Moroccan Islamists do not constitute a homogeneous group: they range from conservative, to moderate, to radical.

majority of Moroccan women who are poor, illiterate and deeply religious and, outside Morocco, they would be accused of not representing their own authentic culture.

This trend in the feminist movement was strengthened in the 1990s at the journalistic, academic and associative levels. In the late 1990s, Moroccan liberal feminism was enhanced at the academic level by the creation of centers for research on women as well as graduate programs on gender/women studies at the university level in Rabat, Fes, and Meknes. These programs have typically been established in state or public Universities, not in private institutions as was the case in the Middle East.[17]

At the level of associations, while the majority of Moroccan women's advocacy NGOs are concentrated in the urban centers of Rabat, Casablanca, and Fes, local NGOs, women's and development organizations have emerged in smaller cities and towns across the country since the late 1990s to address problems unique to women in their regions. In 1992, 'L'Union de L'Action Féminine' launched a huge campaign to establish equality between women and men on Women's International day on March 8 of that year. This association sent a letter to the Parliament calling for changes in the 'Mudawana' and secured a million signatures to support its demands. These demands were strongly opposed by the Islamists, and as a result, King Hassan II, in his capacity as 'Amīr al-Mu'minīn' (Commander of the Faithful), created a Commission of 'Ulemas' (religious scholars) and judges to review the proposed changes and suggest recommendations. None of the members of this Commission was a woman.[18] On May 1, 1993, the king announced changes in articles 5, 12, 30, 32, 48, and 148, such as limiting the marriage tutor control as the woman needed to give her consent and sign the marriage contract; women over 21 who did not have a father were allowed to contract their own marriage without a tutor, before taking a second wife, a husband needed to inform his first wife; a woman could ask for a clause in her marriage contract to the effect that her husband would give her a divorce if he took a second wife, but it was up to the judge to either declare or not the divorce; a man's application to divorce his wife needed to be addressed to two notaries and the wife needed to be summoned to court. The mother was given the right to legally represent her children if their father died (but according to article 142 the mother still could not dispose of the children's property) and in cases of divorce child custody was given first to the mother and secondly to the father. Finally, some type of family counseling institution was to be created to help judges with family disputes. The 1993 reforms were a real disappointment and a step backwards for women's associations because of the child custody issue. Custody was given to the mother and then the father but, in case of the mother's remarriage, custody was given to the father instead of the maternal grandmother.

In spite of their disappointment, liberal feminists considered the 1993 changes big symbolic gains because they made the debate on the 'Mudawana' public for the first time in the history of Morocco, a sign that the Moroccan feminist movement was making significant headway. Indeed, the biggest success of this movement was its ability to bring an almost 'sacred' religious document into the heart of public debate: the 'Mudawana' was not only examined, but criticized and

[17] Margot Badran, Fatima Sadiqi and Linda Rashidi (eds.), 'Language and gender in the Arab world', *Language and Linguistics*, 9 (2002).
[18] Ahmed Taoufik, *The Code of the Personal Law and the Latest Ammendments* (Casablanca: Da Al-Thaqafa, 1993).

even changed. This meant that women's issues were finally open to public discussion and debate. This is a remarkable achievement.

In 1998, the first socialist government took power in Morocco and in March 1999, Mohamed Said Saadi, the then Secretary of State for the Family, the Children and the Disabled, presented the 'Plan d'Intégration des Femmes dans le Développement' (The Plan for Integrating Women in Development), also known as 'The Plan'. Of the 214 points that this Plan contained, eight concerned changes in the Family Law, such as the abolition of polygamy; which immediately infuriated the Islamists who saw in 'The Plan' an outside maneuver to destabilize Moroccan society. During March 2000, two marches were organized: one in Rabat supporting the 'Plan' and one in Casablanca opposing it. The Feminist movement was at the forefront of the supporters of the Plan. Human rights NGOs, democratic NGOs and political parties also supported the 'Plan'. As for the Casablanca march, it was supported by the Islamists. The Casablanca march was characterized by the great number of veiled women who marched in separate rows from men. The latter march was meant to be a show of force on the part of the Islamists who managed, through unprecedented mobilization, to attract greater numbers of people and to launch their first political party. The 'war' between them and liberal feminists took on bigger dimensions. 'The Plan' failed, and Mohamed Said Saadi lost his post. The failure of the Plan was a real blow for the feminist movement which, nevertheless, kept fighting.

In addition to universal laws and global feminism, liberal feminists concentrated more and more on 'maqasid Shar'iya' (Goals of Shari'a) instead of 'Shari'a' per se.[19] Seeing that the state would not favor the rise of Islamism in Morocco, the feminist movement started to rally with the state, thus further politicizing women's issues. This process was greatly enhanced by the enthroning of Mohamed VI, a young new king in July 1999.

With the end of the last century and the beginning of the new one, the Moroccan feminist movement has started to become very visible in the public sphere of power. From its inception to the end of the 1990s, the discourses of the Moroccan feminist movement ranged from a deconstruction of the family and social oppression, through that of the legal oppression, to that of political oppression. As such, this movement evolved through various historical periods and managed to ensure continuity. At the beginning of the twenty first century, and with the coming of the new king, the feminist movement in Morocco has increasingly become a political actor, and an indispensable tool of democratization.

V. Women's Activism and the Democratization of the Public Sphere: The Politicization of Women's Issues and the New Family Law

The impasse that the Moroccan feminist movement reached in 2000 changed dramatically with the coming of the new king, Mohammed VI. One month after he took power, King Mohamed VI said in his August 20, 1999, address: "How can society achieve progress, while women, who represent half the nation, see their rights violated and suffer as a result of injustice, violence, and

[19] Whereas 'Shari'a' rules are more based on a rigid and literal reading of the Qur'an and *Hadith* (the Prophet's Sayings), 'maqasid Shar'iya' target the contextualization of these rules within changing historical eras.

marginalization, notwithstanding the dignity and justice granted them by our glorious religion?"

A series of high-profile female royal appointments followed this statement; in March 2000, for the first time in the country's history, the king appointed a female Royal Counselor, in August 2000, the King appointed a woman to head the National Office of Oil Research and Exploration, in September 2000, he confirmed the first-ever female ministerial appointment, and in October 2000, he appointed the first woman to head the National Office of Tourism. Similar appointments to political and religious posts followed in subsequent years.

In addition to the king's disposition to enhance women's position in the public sphere, the Socialist Party, led by Abderrahmane Youssoufi, set the ground in May 2002 for the democratization of the Parliament by approving a proposal, backed by the King, which sets aside 30 seats for the election of women in the national elections of September 2002.

These top-level political actions greatly boosted the feminist movement in Morocco and confirmed its recognition as a powerful political actor in the public sphere. Although feminist journalists and writers continued to focus their efforts on legal demands, they expanded their domain of action to various related areas. Hence, they endeavored to assert that law is a social construction, that inequality and social relations are socially constructed, and hence subject to historical variability, deconstruction and reconstruction on the basis of equality. They demanded a re-examination of the social, political, economic structures and an analysis of the judicial norms with respect to men–women relations in order to fight the ambivalence in men–women social relations. On other fronts, liberal feminists increased efforts to introduce gender as a powerful tool of analysis in various public institutions.

In parallel, women's associations became more active, proving, thus, more accessible to women than the institutional political parties as they do not require extensive material resources or influential connections. Two main types of women's associations may be discerned at the eve of the twenty-first century: the ones that focus on service provision by filling gaps left by the deficient state structures in terms of social and economic development, such as addressing concrete problems on the ground using available means, and the ones that focus on advocacy and lobbying with the aim of defending a vision of society where women's legal and civil rights are respected. Both types of women's associations kept a dialectical relationship with the broader civil society (Human rights associations, youth organizations that involve women's issues, etc.). This advocacy and lobbying tightened the link between women's associations and other actors of civil society.

Women feminist writers such as Mernissi started to be directly involved in the work of women's associations. Mernissi explains:[20]

> Pour faire fructifier notre capital social, on a besoin de donner confiance aux 13 Millions d'adultes qui existent dans notre pays, hommes et femmes, ruraux et citadins pour qu'ils puissent devenir des 'hallalin al machakil'. Car il faut que nous, les 13 Millions d'enfants deviennent de superbes démocrates, de merveilleux communicateurs, des pionniers de la Méditerranée de la tolérance.

[20] Fatema Mernissi, *ONG Rurales du Haut-Atlas. Les Aït Débrouille* (Rabat: Editions Marsam, 2003), p. 123.

[To fructify our social capital, we need to give confidence to the 13 million adults who live in our country, men and women, rural and urban in order for them to become problem-solvers, because we, the 13 million children, should become superb democrats, marvelous communicators, pioneers in the Mediterranean of tolerance.][21]

Overall, women's associative work started to assume political, social and economic functions, hence strengthening institutional politics. Politically, local activism bridges the gap between women and the institutional political sphere mainly through local activists' networks with more urban/political women's NGOs. Socially, the increasing proliferation of women's associations allowed women to assume more powerful social roles as leaders and managers of public affairs. Economically, NGOs have allowed many women to acquire economic independence through self-generating incomes such as micro-credits.

On a more general level, women's associations started to become carriers of alternative projects of transformative gender roles in Moroccan society, and this protects and guarantees an effective exercise of public freedoms favoring the emergence of pluralist collective identity based on the universal values of the culture of citizenship, for bottom-up development and for empowerment. Indeed, women's associations endeavored to promote participation, social mobilization, and associative lobbying that encourage good governance and a culture of responsible citizens, not passive subjects, thus working towards a dynamic participatory and equitable democracy.[22] They have become real schools of democracy which encourage women to get involved in decision-making in local public affairs and to empower women at all levels of governance. NGOs have enabled women to critically assess their own situation, create and shape a transformation of society.

Because of the social, economic, and political issues they persistently address, women's NGOs, and civil society in general, gradually became the raison d'être of the Moroccan political class not only because of the disposition of the latter as mentioned above, but because of external pressure and pressure from political parties and other human rights NGOs. The government and political parties have realized the need to take account of these new areas of participation and mobilization. The challenge facing the women's NGOs is to elaborate autonomous strategies and to establish themselves as forces for innovation, political pressure and proposals, to push the state to revise its policies. The NGOs autonomy is a basis for genuine partnership with the state and for co-operation with political parties. For the time being, Morocco is perhaps a unique example in the Arab world; a country where the battle led by feminine NGO activists has begun to have a tangible impact on national human rights and development policies. Support for these movements remains essential, not just for Morocco, but for the sake of social development throughout the region. Moroccan women's activism helps to promote awareness and knowledge of legal rights among women, to develop networks between

[21] The translation is the author's.

[22] Valentine Moghadam, *Modernizing Women: Gender and Social Change in the Middle East* (Boulder, CO: Lynne Rienner, 1995).

El-Mostafa Chadli, *La Société Civile ou la Quête de l'Association Citoyenne* (Rabat: Publications Faculté de Lettres et des Sciences Humaines, 2001).

Maria-Angels Roque, *La Société Civile qu Maroc* (Paris: IEMed Publications, 2004).

women's NGOs and community-based groups, and to ensure a broader spectrum of participation in the public sphere.

The impact of the feminist movement was vividly felt after the May 16, 2003, Casablanca bombings. Liberal feminists have been very swift in strongly reacting to the terrorist attacks and they were among the very first who took to the streets. They brilliantly seized the event to take a 'historical revenge' on the Islamists. Their strong public presence was greatly enhanced by the significant diminution in power of the Islamists after the Casablanca attacks.

Overall, the dialectic relationship between the monarch, political parties, the Parliament, and human rights NGOs, on the one hand, and the feminist movement, on the other hand, led to the promulgation of the new Family Law.[23] More than in any period of Morocco's history, the new Family Law is both a subject of its own and a means of studying other topics such as changing notions of state authority, individual decision-making, gender practices, family planning, and family size. It is felt to be an important document that concerns all the components of society, as its impact is attested at the legal, political, religious, socio-cultural, and intellectual levels. At the legal level, the Family law is a central piece in the Moroccan judicial arsenal because it touches on practically all the other aspects of the Moroccan legal system. At the political level, women's judicial status in the family is linked to demands for democracy and full citizenship, and while at the socio-cultural level, the Family Law has been associated with the controversial notion of emancipation,[24] on the intellectual level, the new Family Law has been and still is at the heart of the antagonism between two major tendencies: the conservatives and the modernists.[25]

In spite of the fact that the new Family Law is more 'audacious' than 'The Plan', it succeeded. There are three reasons behind this success: first, unlike the Plan, the new Family Law is first proposed to the Parliament, thus implicating all the representatives of the people; second, it was presented as a 'project of society', and third, it resolves the notorious issue of reference by blending social reality, the 'Shari'a', and the philosophy of human rights. The new Law is designed around

---

[23] The new Family law is presented as a body of rules, practices, and beliefs that govern the home. Its policies govern all aspects of family life from courtship, marriage and child rearing to spousal violence, divorce, and inheritance.

[24] Women's emancipation has always been characterized by passionate debates. The reason is not simply because of the implications on the social and individual lives of Moroccans, but because this emancipation entails a redefinition of the functions and roles of men and women, as well as that of the relations between individuals.

[25] The domain of confrontation is women's rights in the private sphere, the family. The issue at stake is reference (le référential). For conservatives, reference needs to stem from identity 'going back to the source' and 'what singles us out as different: the 'Shari'a'. For modernists, reference needs to stem from universal values. The antagonism is a mirror of the socio-cultural rift within Moroccan society. It is an expression of the ambivalence in the Moroccan judicial and political systems. This ambivalence had local and international causes. It should be pointed out that such antagonisms have always surfaced in the major transitional phases of Morocco's history.

FATIMA SADIQI

three axes: equality between spouses, family equilibrium, and the protection of the children.[26] The inclusion of children was instrumental in passing the law. It circumvented the thorny issue of 'illegal' children in a skilful way: by respecting international laws protecting children's rights, single mothers were given legal visibility.

Although the new Family Law is more audacious than the 1999 'Plan', the latter failed. The reason for the success of the former is the change in overall political context and the weakening of the Islamist ideology after the Casablanca 2003 terrorist bombings. The new Family Law led to many improvements in other laws, such as the criminalization of violence against wives, the law against sexual harassment in the workplace, and the mother's citizenship law. Overall, the new Family Law improves women's status before, during, and after marriage. It strengthens the position of women in the private and the public spheres. However, two issues remain pending: the implementation of the law and the issue of religion.

So far as implementation of the Family Law is concerned, it differs from region to region but in general it is meeting with resistance because of various reasons. First, the Family Law is still very poorly known in rural and sometimes urban areas.[27] Second, many male judges resist the application of the law. On the other hand, even when the Family Law guarantees women's rights, the impact of patriarchy, tradition, illiteracy, and ignorance may prevent women from invoking their rights or reporting crimes against them, such as rape, child abuse, sexual exploitation and domestic violence. For many feminists, the new Family Law can be adequately implemented only in a democratic context. Another problem is that

[26] Equality between spouses

The concept of equality is attested in the following innovations:sexes

- The legal age of marriage is 18 for both sexes
- Equality in family legal responsibility: both spouses are legally heads of the family.
- Equality in rights and duties: abolition of the right of obedience in return to catering.
- No tutorship for 'major' women.
- Severe constraints on polygamy, almost impossible
- Repudiation and divorce in the hands of the judge. The judge also handles consensual divorce, compensation divorce, 'shiqaq' (impossibility of cohabitation).
- Girls and boys choose which parent to live with at the age of 15.
- Grandchildren (from the daughter) inherit in the same way as those from the son.
- The sharing of accumulated property and benefits gathered during marriage

Guarantee of Family Equilibrium

- The public ministry automatically intervenes in any application of the Family Code
- Establishment of Family Courts. Twelve are already operational throughout Morocco (Royal letter addressed to the Ministry of Justice on October 12, 2003).
- Reinforcement of means of reconciliation through family
- Creation of a Fund for family assistance
- Recognition of Moroccan marriages contracted abroad according to the legislations of the host countries

Protection of Children's Rights

- In the interest of children, the right of the mother's tutorship is not lifted if the divorced mother remarries or if her residence is far from that of the father.
- In the interest of children, the judge may alter the order of the family members eligible to tutorship: the mother, the father, the maternal grandmother, etc.
- The social status of the child is taken into consideration at the moment of divorce: decent dwelling, the standard of living should be similar to that he/she was leading before divorce
- Recognition of paternity when the child is conceived during courtship, that is, before marriage is formalized by a contract.

[27] A recent study of 'Leadership Féminin' (a local women's association) reveals that 87% of women in six rural areas in Morocco do not know anything about the new Family Law.

44

the new Family Law is about married women. It leaves out: single women, who are not Moroccan but who are married to Moroccans.

In addition to the problem of implementation, the Family Law has not totally abolished four institutions: polygamy, repudiation, separation by compensation '*talaq al-khol*'', and the sensitive question of inheritance which the Family Law has not touched upon. These institutions were not abolished because, on the one hand, the reforms had already been audacious enough, and on the other hand, polygamy is allowed (albeit in a form that is debatable) in the Qur'an (as the King himself acknowledged, stating he cannot forbid what is allowed) and that inheritance is clearly outlined in the Qur'an.

This raises new questions for the feminist movements. The religious will one day emerge in a different form with secularization being more and more at stake in some feminist NGOs. Some feminist associations raise the question of secularization on the basis that the latter does not exclude religion. Secularization is important for the continuity of the feminist movement. The road is still long for Moroccan women to become full citizens, for equality to leave discourse and enter homes, and for democracy to prevail in both the public and the private space.

VI. Conclusion

The feminist movement has greatly contributed to the feminization of a once male-dominated public space in Morocco. By espousing universal values and adopting local, appropriate and pragmatic strategies, this movement has succeeded to involve the major political actors in the promulgation of the new Family Law reforms. These reforms are by far the most important achievement of the Moroccan feminist movement, for they have succeeded to demystify the 'sacredness' of 'Shari'a' (Islamic law) and have fundamentally contributed to the democratization of the public space and the implementation of human rights on the ground. Male feminism, which once constituted the necessary background for the birth of the Moroccan feminist movement, is now joining this movement without jeopardizing the latter's independence from other actors. The major issue today is to seek efficient ways to implement the new Family Law through the sensitization of women, men and families to the important changes that have been introduced in the Personal Status Code and to incite judges to apply the new law without any reservation.

In the long run, the public debating of once private family issues will force Moroccan society to face the intricate issue of the role of religion in an increasingly secularized public space where women are increasingly visible as actors; this is the next big challenge of the Moroccan feminist movement.

Steps to the Integration of Moroccan Women in Development

MOHA ENNAJI

ABSTRACT *This paper casts a gender perspective on development in Morocco. While Moroccan women contribute to development, their socio-economic situation has hardly improved over the years as a result of their participation. Despite the increasing aid afforded to the country and despite the numerous programs of development financed by world organizations, all the indications show that there exists an increase of poverty, particularly among women. The evaluation of projects specific to women's promotion has shown the limits of the economic approach. The role of women in development and growth is crucial. Education and training are so important for women to enable them to meet the new challenges, and to help them safeguard their rights and interests. The development of society cannot be achieved without the integration of women in the process of growth. To promote women's emancipation, the State must open doors to women who ought to be adequately trained to use the new information technology. By gaining new skills, Moroccan women can develop their productivity and improve their standards of living and those of their families.*

I. Introduction

This paper discusses current endeavors to integrate Moroccan women in development and attempts to empower women. The global context is the liberalization turn in economic policy, which is characterized by price and trade liberalization, privatization, deregulation of the State, and the growth of unregulated financial markets. Today, Morocco is 'located at a global crossroads of ideas, markets, and development plans; Morocco has experienced transformation not only in the organization of its market and policies but also in the more profound issues of political identity and social structure'.[1] Despite the recent efforts of government and civil society to modernize the country and promote women, the challenges facing women and development remain significant.

Morocco, which is at the cross-roads of Africa and Europe, covers a surface of 750,000 square kilometers for a population of 30 million people (2004 census). It is divided into eight administrative and economic regions. The rural population is estimated at 51% while the urban one represents 49%. Rural exodus has had a great impact since the 1960s when the rural population was estimated at 75%.

---

[1] S. Cohen and L. Jaidi, *Morocco: Globalization and Its Consequences* (New York: Routledge, 2006), p. 149.

The birth rate is 30%, and fertility rate 4.4 children per woman in the rural areas, and 3.5 children per woman in the cities. Life span is estimated at 70 years and death rate at 7%.[2]

Only 50% of the population has access to sanitation, drinkable water, electricity and hygiene, and 79% of the rural population has no water or electricity. So far as education is concerned, the rate of schooling is 72% while the rate of literacy is nearly 54%. Nevertheless, illiteracy rate among urban women is very high 55%, and in the rural areas it is even higher 65%.[3]

The economy is dominated by agriculture, followed by phosphates and the remittances of Moroccan workers abroad. Agriculture represents 49% in the Gross National Product, industry 17% and services 34%.[4] Note that due to a drought of three years (from 1999 to 2001) there is a large gap between the GNP and demographic growth.

Since 1983, Morocco has engaged in a large structural adjustment program to clean or improve the economic environment. This program has had a positive impact on the macro-economy, but some bad consequences on the micro-economic level: increase of unemployment (16%), stagnation of salaries, low level of education and health services.[5]

At the socio-political level, after the political reforms of the 1990s (re-amendment of the constitution and law on elections), which led to more demo-cratization, we notice the emergence of numerous women's associations with a great national and regional impact. As a case in point, we cite the following most well-known women's associations: *Josour, l'Union Féminine Marocaine, l'Organisation Démocratique des Femmes.*[6]

In Morocco, women play a crucial role in socio-economic development despite the fact that there exist large inequalities between men and women so far as access to resources is concerned.

In the rural areas, which are marked by labor and gender division between men and women, women have growing responsibilities in ensuring the survival and well-being of the family, and in doing their share of farming and of production, small trade, and services.

A considerable, though small proportion of women in Morocco are active in jobs related to the public and private sectors. In the formal sector, women are active in the public domain and in social services. The rate of women working in the public sector has been increasing since the 1960s. However, they have had little access to top jobs or decision-making positions, which is due to negative attitudes and prejudices against women. Today a lot of change has occurred as a result of education and of the democratization process that the country is slowly attesting.

State feminism, which may be defined as the government's official policy and intervention that seek to achieve the emancipation of women and gender equity in all walks of life, started to develop in North Africa after the independences in the

[2] M. Ennaji, *Civil Society, Gender, and Development* (Fès: Fès-Saiss Publications, 2004).
[3] *Al-Alam*, 16 September 2000, p. 10.
[4] See R. Mejjati Alami, 'Femmes et Vulnérabilité sur le Marché du Travail' in F. Sadiqi (ed.), *Mouvements Féministes* (Fès: Faculty of Letters Publications, 2000), pp. 15–28.
[5] M. Ennaji, 'Social policy in Morocco' in M. Karshenas and V. Moghadem (eds.), *Social Policy in the Middle East* (New York: Palgrave Macmillan and UNRISD, 2006), pp. 116–127.
[6] See F. Sadiqi (ed.), *Feminist Movements: Origins and Orientations* (Fès: Faculty of Letters Publications, 2000).

late 1950s and the early 1960s. In Egypt, state feminism started to develop along with Nasser's regime, which promised equality of men and women and a better lifestyle for all. But, in the long run, its main beneficiaries were people from the upper and upper middle classes.

In the 1980s, however, with the application of economic reforms (the structural readjustment plan), the economic and social retreat of the State began, which weakened the prospects of a better future for women of the working and the middle classes.

State feminism is considered a historical strategy that has been adopted in different parts of North Africa to improve women's conditions and to contribute to their well-being. Thus, the provision of education, health, and work to women helped to brighten up the image of the State. All North African states, under specific conditions, declare in their constitutions that all citizens are equal under the law, and segregation on the basis of gender is forbidden. Labor laws were amended to ensure women's participation in the labor force, and they entitled women to a reasonable period of maternity leave. As a consequence, people's attitudes to women's problems, education, and employment have gradually changed in favor of women.

By contrast, the conservative forces view women's role to be limited to home, reproduction, and child rearing. As a result, in Egypt, for instance, the personal status laws passed in 1979 are still implemented. However, in Morocco, the personal status laws (The Mudawana) was first amended in 1993. In 2004, new changes were introduced despite opposition from the Islamists. In Egypt, Libya, and Algeria, the personal status laws define women as economically dependent on men, and as minors under the law; they have no say in their personal affairs including marriage, where the need for a matrimonial guardian is compulsory, and divorce which they have no right to claim, except in exceptional cases and under exceptional conditions.

In Algeria, the 1984 personal status laws, known as the Family Code, in which polygamy was maintained and whereby women's rights were violated, especially the right to divorce and to inheritance, have been replaced by the new reform in 2004, in which polygamy is highly restricted and women's rights are guaranteed.

Up until the 1990s, women in North Africa were almost totally excluded from the political scene by their respective governments to the extent that their participation in political life and their representation in parliament and in policy-making was insignificant.

Thus, although state feminism succeeded in giving women access to education, health, and employment in most North African countries, it did not really challenge the negative social attitudes towards women who are still regarded as dependent on men; these conservative views are reflected in the attitudes of the male judges who often refuse to apply the new laws, and persist on applying the old personal status laws.

The economic reforms which were implemented in the 1990s as a result of the adoption of the structural readjustment, which fostered economic liberalization and free trade, led to a reduction of state feminism. The relative retreat of the State from the economic scene as the main agent of change undermined its commitment to gender equality. In general, it is working-class women who have suffered most from these unfair economic and social reforms. This new situation created a vacuum which was soon filled by the Islamists. The Islamists' views on women's education and employment have been to the detriment of the accomplishments realized by women and by state feminism. Islamists have been rather hesitant about women's work. For them, education is good for women so long as it helped them become obedient wives and good mothers. However, non-government organizations have recently taken the lead by stepping in to encourage women to fully take part in development and to mobilize society as a whole to women's role in democratization and development.

As far as employment is concerned, women's rate of unemployment is still remarkably higher than that of men, and kept rising during the 1990s. While the progressive forces assessed the positive economic effects of women's employment on families and society as a whole, Islamists who opposed women's work focused on the negative impact it had on children and families.

Despite criticisms and harassment leveled by Islamists against working women, women kept on clinging to their jobs. In fact, most official studies demonstrate that two incomes in a family are far better than one. Privatization and inflation rates push many women to join the work force. Some women have opted for migration with their husbands in order to improve their living conditions. Many mothers stay behind in order to avoid the disruption of children's education. Although, they generally work for a small salary, they assume their responsibilities as bread-winners and as educators of their children.[7]

The remittances sent by emigrated males have allowed women and their children to live comfortably, although migration provokes emotional suffering and a disruption of families. Many wives and mothers complain of loneliness and broken families; their children often give up school and become a serious problem to their families and society in general.

On the whole, economic adjustment reforms and privatization have had negative effects on working-class and lower-middle-class women across North Africa. These reforms seriously undermined their economic and social well-being as a consequence of the high rate of unemployment among women. Many have to delay their marriage plans for lack of an income or to accept separation from their unemployed husbands who are unable to cater for their families.

A large proportion of these working-class women gave their support to the Islamists, and often donned the veil as a reaction against their poverty and their marginalization in society. Many who wear the veil see it as liberation from objectification and standards of beauty, enabling women to be treated with respect and more like equals to men in society.[8] By contrast, the market economy has given advantages to middle- and upper-class women who have access to top jobs in the public and in the private sectors, or who have made important investments in the world of business.

Economic liberalization has led to political liberalization, as the State has moved slowly from the autocratic system to some form of a democratic system. Despite this important move, women have not benefited from a larger participation in public affairs and in decision-making. Although the state has declared its readiness to share power, it puts conditions that specify which group or party it is ready to work with and which group it is not ready to tolerate.

---

[7] For more details see M. Ennaji, and F. Sadiqi, *Migration and Gender in Morocco* (Trenton: Red Sea Press, 2008).

[8] P.K. Taylor, 'I just want to be me' in Jennifer Heath (ed.), *The Veil: Women Writers on Its History, Lore and Politics* (Berkeley, CA: California University Press, 2008), pp. 119–138.

Moreover, women's issues have been exploited by the states to attain political goals and to show to the world that the process of democratization is being seriously launched. Women have been used also by political parties for purposes of elections (i.e. to gain more votes). State decrees in favor of women, the reforms of the personal status laws and the participation of women in parliament and government were meant to polish the political image of the regimes, and distinguish their social orientations from that of the opposition parties.

In Morocco, the parliament has recently decided to reserve 10% of seats for women; as a result, 34 women were elected members of parliament in September 2007 in the hope of encouraging their involvement in politics and their representation in parliament and government. The aim of this new law is to build a secular anti-Islamist bloc in a new tacit accord with the State. The law would also enhance the positive image of the political system as it asks for economic and political support, especially from the European Union and the United States.

On the whole, economic structural adjustments and liberalization were neither accompanied by a greater emancipation of women nor by gender equity. Rather, they have introduced changes that reinforced gender inequality at the economic and political levels, which enhanced women's dependence on the State to protect their rights and foster their participation in active life.

In Morocco, women in general continue to struggle so that the State can respond to their economic, social, and political needs; nonetheless, they do not yet enjoy a position of strength. They need to have strong lobbying and organizations which will help to exert their influence on the political scene to defend their rights. Indeed, multiple women's organizations are needed to represent women of all social strata and classes given that economic liberalization and globalization have resulted in dividing women into groups with different social needs and interests.

Despite the positive changes and the growing emancipation of women in all domains, there are still obstacles that hamper their full participation in active life like illiteracy, lack of education and information, lack of technical and professional training, weak resources available to them, difficult access to loans, weak participation in public life and weak or lack of representation in the spheres of policy and policy-making, unfavorable legal status, and weakness in the capacity of organization and associations of women.

The economic situation of these women is distressing; women suffer more than men from poverty, which reveals gender discrimination. Additionally, the rate of schooling among girls is low compared to the schooling rate of boys. On the health level, early marriages are more frequent among girls than boys.

The phenomenon of exclusion strikes more women than men; their poverty is noticeable in the rural areas and in the poor urban districts, and in the growing number of beggars amongst women (generally widows, divorced women, sick women, handicapped women, or women with many children). The Moroccan government has recently launched a campaign to fight against poverty and illiteracy among rural women, which had a great impact on the women's welfare and people's attitudes in general.

On the legal and institutional level, we note discrimination in the laws to the disadvantage of women. The situation of women is made worse by: (i) their ignorance, (ii) the sporadic application of these laws and of the international accords on women's rights, and (iii) the relatively reduced intervention of

Table 1. Unemployment Rates in the 1990s

YEAR	MALE	FEMALE	TOTAL
1992	13%	25.3%	16%

government structures and of civil society in favor of women or for the protection of women's rights.

II. The Socio-Economic Situation of Women in Morocco

While Moroccan women contribute to development, their socio-economic situation has hardly improved over the years as a result of their participation. Despite the increasing aid afforded to the country and despite the numerous programs of development financed by world aid organizations, all the indications show that there exists an increase of poverty, particularly among women. The evaluation of projects specific to the improvement of women's conditions has shown the limits of the economic approach.

The economic reforms which were implemented in the 1990s as a result of the adoption of the structural readjustment which fostered economic liberalization and free trade led to a reduction of state feminism. The relative retreat of the state from the economic scene as the main agent of change undermined its commitment to gender equality. In general, it is working-class women who have suffered most from these unfair economic and social reforms.

As far as employment is concerned, women's rate of unemployment is remarkably higher than that of men. Unemployment among women kept rising in the 1990s[9] (see table 1).

Privatization and inflation pushed many women to join the work force. Hence, the feminization of the labor force which began in the 1970s and developed in the 1990s manifested itself in the public sector, industries and services. Since 1990, women became attracted to the private sector, which generally offered them better wages although it did not guarantee social benefits like maternity leave, health care, and transportation.

On another level, State decrees in favor of women, the reforms of the personal status laws and the participation of women in parliament and government were meant to promote the emancipation of women. In Morocco, the parliament has recently passed the new reform of the family law (on 16 January 2004), whereby women are treated as equal to men before the law: divorce is no longer in the hands of the husband, polygamy is drastically restricted, and the woman is free to marry a man of her choice.[10]

Moroccan women represent 51% of the population, 16% of whom live in rural areas. They have a crucial role in socio-economic development despite the fact that there exist large inequalities between men and women so far as access to resources is concerned.[11]

[9] World Bank (1995b) p. 5; ESCWA (1999, 2000) p. 37; ILO (1996); Moghadam (1998).
[10] See Sadiqi and Ennaji, 'The Feminization of Public Space: Women's Activism, the Family Law, and Social Change in Morocco', *Journal of Middle East Women's Studies (JMEWS)*, 2(2) (2006), pp. 86–114.
[11] M. Ennaji and F. Sadiqi, *Migration and Gender in Morocco* (Trenton: Red Sea Press, 2008), Chapter 4.

Table 2. Unemployment by gender, its Evolution from 1990 to 1997

UNEMPLOYMENT BY GENDER	YEAR
Male labor force	13.9% (1990)
	15.8% (1997)
Female labor force	19.6% (1990)
	23% (1997)
Male percentage of total employment	67% (1990)
	65% (1997)
Female percentage of total employment	33% (1990)
	35% (1997)

In the rural areas, which are marked by labor and gender division between men and women, women have growing responsibilities in ensuring the survival and well-being of the family, and in doing their share of farming and of production, small trade, and services.

A small proportion of women in Morocco are active in jobs related to the public and private sectors. In 1994, women represented only 13.5% of salaried people in the formal sector, of which 70% were concentrated in social services. The rate of women working in the public sector was around 25%. However, they had little access to top jobs or decision-making positions, which is due to negative attitudes and taboos against women. Today a lot of change has occurred within the context of democratization that the country is attesting.

The socio-economic situation of women is generally alarming; women seem to be more struck by poverty than men, a fact that indicates inequality of the sexes. Recently, the Moroccan government launched a campaign to fight against poverty and illiteracy among rural women, which had a great impact on the women's welfare and people's attitudes in general (see table 2).[12]

At the educational level, even in present-day Morocco, the soaring percentages of illiteracy amongst women in the country are in the majority of cases composed of rural women. According to official statistics, 65% of rural women and 55% of urban women are illiterate.[13] In spite of the considerable endeavors that are being made at the government and civil society levels to remedy this state of affairs, the specter of illiteracy is still very real. In retrospect, it seems that another vector of discrimination against rural women is the Moroccan educational system, which has till recently favored urban areas to rural ones. Indeed, generalized education has not systematically favored equality between urban and rural women and between men and women. Even in urban areas, girls are generally encouraged to opt for the least prestigious disciplines or for the ones that lead to the least available professional prospects, and dropping out of school is considered less problematic for girls than it is for boys, because they can always find a husband who can provide for them.

The rate of schooling among girls (55%) is low compared to the schooling rate of boys (86%).[14] On the health level, early marriages are more frequent among girls than they are among boys: 16 years for 27% of women against 21 years for 19% of men.

[12] Source: World Bank: http://www.genderstats.worldbank.org
[13] See M. Ennaji and F. Sadiqi (2008), *Migration and Gender in Morocco*, Chapter 4.
[14] See the Moroccan daily *Al-Alam* of 16 September 2000, p. 10.

Rural women contribute considerably to agricultural and rural development. They work in the fields, feed livestock, search for water and wood, participate in artisan activities, and in many cases, actually manage all household operations while also caring for their children. Given this level of female participation, all development programs need to incorporate women in their activities. However, almost all government interventions until just recently were targeted exclusively to men. Statistical indicators such as literacy, primary school attendance, life expectancy, and maternal mortality clearly point to the disenfranchised status of rural Moroccan women. There exist daily constraints upon rural women's productivity. These constraints are tied to their health, time allocated to each activity, and economic, socio-cultural, and institutional obstacles, as well as existing impediments to social and technical services. Measures facilitating the lifting of such constraints must begin by lightening the burden upon rural women so that they may improve their economic situations. Other measures may be implemented, including those in the areas of preventive and reproductive health, other efforts designed to increase incomes, and actions aiming to improve women's status over the long term.

Non-government associations play an important role in the integration of women in development. Many help mostly illiterate rural women to sell the rugs and other textiles they weave on the Internet, which could provide a solution to the perennial problem of marketing the products of isolated rural women. This measure allows women to increase their revenues as well as obtain some degree of empowerment. The profits are at times used to support the family or contribute towards children's education.[15]

Moroccan urban women started to participate in the household economy in the 1930s. Their work was not an act of 'militantism', rather it was dictated by poverty, as most of these women worked as domestics in French or upper-class Moroccan households or were recruited as low-paid workers doing unskilled jobs in the fields or in factories. However, a few Moroccan urban women managed to create their own enterprises in the 1930s and 1940s in cities.[16] After Morocco's independence, a growing number of Moroccan urban women were incorporated in the 'official' labor market. Women's rate of 'economic activity' in urban areas increased from 5.6% in 1960, to 10.8% in 1971, 14.7% in 1982, 17.3% in 1994, and to 27% in 2004, according to the general statistics of the Moroccan Ministry of Population and Housing. Further, the rate of the feminization of the labor force (15 years of age or more) grew during independence and reached 33% in the 1990s.[17] Women's work in industry greatly helped Morocco's economic development. The greatest majority of salaried women has been and is still constituted of the lower and average parts of the job ladder. Very few women have managed to reach top positions in their jobs.

[15] S. Schaefer Davis, 'Women Weavers Online: Rural Moroccan Women on the Internet', in *Gender Technology and Development*, 8(1) (2004), pp. 53–74. Cf. also F. Mernissi, 'Le Tapis Amazigh et les Tisseuses Artistes', in Moha Ennaji (ed.), *La Culture Amazighe et le Développement Humain* (Fès: Publications of Fès-Saiss, 2007), pp. 15–20.

[16] Cf. A. Belarbi, 'La représentation de la femme à travers les livres scolaires', in M. Al Alahyane et al. (eds.), *Portraits De Femmes* (Casablanca: Le Fennec, 1987), pp. 47–68.

[17] cf. United Nations Development Program (UNDP), 1996.

III. Family Strategies

To face the economic crisis and the low family income, many families are mobilized to reduce the effects of this hardship and of unemployment. Many poor families incite women or young children to work in the informal sector (as maids, or as shop assistants or as cheap labor in handicraft). A majority of 79% of Moroccan women in urban centers confirm that their first contact with a job was the result of the family strategy to help surmount their socio-economic difficulties.

Female employees are for the most part confined to commerce and services, but recently women have also gained access to the domain of industry which recruits a young and less qualified workforce. In the latter sector, the rate of women workers increased from 46.5% in 1982 to 50% in 1990 with a strong concentration in the food and textile industries. In the 1990s, however, employment became more important in the area of services. Very few women have access to jobs requiring degrees and diplomas or to administrative jobs (8.9%). Access to technical, scientific, or liberal professions is very limited.[18]

In Morocco, for example, the rate of active women in urban areas increased from 5.6% in 1960, 10.8% in 1971, 14.7% in 1982 to 17.3% in 1994 according to government statistics on population.[19] Women usually work in departments of services and domestic spaces. Every year, this branch of activity occupies the first place.

Recent research has shown that industrial growth is closely linked to women's active place in employment. Women's employment has reached a rate of 9.54% between 1980 and 1993, whereas the rate of global employment reached only 5.38%.[20] Salaried women, generally young and illiterate, are at the bottom of the social ladder and are discriminated against in matters of recruitment and social promotion through their jobs. Women's qualifications remain weak when confronted with the new needs of globalization which constitute a real challenge for women's emancipation. It is hard to imagine how Moroccan economies can integrate world economy which is very competitive at a time when the female work force is both unqualified and underpaid. This is a real challenge because it is hard to guarantee women stable and decent jobs in a context where unemployment is very high (15%), as a result of the economic readjustment implemented since the 1980s. This inequality and economic hardship have hit women more than men.

The main objective of any plan to promote women in society should be centered on finding ways of integrating them into the development and democratization processes. Gender issues are to be included in the social and economic perspectives of the country. This can be done by examining the role of women in economic development, and by assessing the effects of economic transformations on women. Thus, a new culture has to be established which takes into account a gendered agenda, which is generalized to all institutions and organizations as an important component in any development strategy. To implement this culture, all actors of change have to be involved, mainly government institutions and civil society.

Civil society plays a crucial role in sensitizing officials and people alike about the role of women in development and in training them to adopt this new culture,

---

[18] Mejjatti Alami, 'Femmes et Vulnérabilité sur le Marché du Travail', pp. 15–28.

[19] Direction des Statistiques, 1999.

[20] Mejjatti Alami, 'Femmes et Vulnérabilité sur le Marché du Travail', pp. 15–28.

starting by fighting illiteracy among women. Civil society has also a role to play in sensitizing employers to take measures favorable to women by protecting their rights and by being aware of their impact on development and the competitiveness of the economy as a whole.

All this necessitates the training of women and the training of non-government organizations. New information technologies can be helpful in training women and valorizing products made by women and to find new markets for these products. Thus, women and women's organizations have to be initiated to these technologies like the computer, the internet, etc., as well as to the modern techniques of marketing and management.

These objectives cannot be realized without a national policy which seeks to protect women's rights and to valorize their products, and without a research strategy that seeks to enhance the participation of women in the processes of development and democratization. Decision-makers must take into account the gender dimension in all their undertakings and transactions, be they national, bilateral, or international accords. Up until now, men are the first actors on the economic, social, and political levels. Women are often ignored as the gender element has not been considered; many decisions are taken without considering their impact on gender, which reinforces their exclusion.

IV. Conclusion

The role of women in development and growth is crucial. Education and training are so important for women to enable them to meet the new challenges and to help them safeguard their rights and interests. The development of society cannot be achieved without the integration of women in the process of growth.

To promote women's emancipation, the State must open doors to women who ought to be adequately trained to use the new information technology. By gaining new skills, Moroccan women can develop their productivity and improve their standards of living and those of their families.

Women's associations and civil society in general play a major role in sensitizing women, families, and social actors as to the importance of integrating women in economic, social, and cultural development. Further steps in favor of protecting women's rights are badly needed to ensure their strong contribution to sustainable development.

Gender Equality in Tunisia

AMEL GRAMI

ABSTRACT   *Throughout the twentieth century, the status of women in Tunisia has been caught up in political wars fought largely over other issues such as colonialism, nationalism, modernity, and Islamic cultural identity. By taking the decision to reform the family law, the state redefines rights and obligations for all citizens. Behind the promulgation of a new family law there is a vision of a modern society. The purpose of this paper is to highlight the status of Women in Tunisia, to expose the impact of family law reforms on everyday life of Tunisians and to show the challenges Tunisian women are facing today.*

I. Introduction

Modernization movements and efforts were central issues in the regional political discourse of the nineteenth and early twentieth centuries in the Middle East. Over the last decade, most countries have implemented new reforms promoting women's rights and showing increasing sensitivity towards gender issues. Questions of law, gender, women's rights and citizenship become among the most controversial topics of public debate, media coverage, and academic inquiry.[1]

The Middle East shows a great degree of diversity in the formulation of legal codes and their relevance to women's everyday lives. Tunisia, Algeria, and Morocco for example share many cultural characteristics, but the extent of the legal reforms redefining gender relations has varied greatly from one society to another. The elaboration of family laws differed in accord with the differences in the political leverage of kin groupings and the form of central authority in the pre-colonial society. In these three *Maghribi* countries, post independence family law was formulated by their political leadership, which chose either to maintain Islamic law, to oscillate between alternatives or to actively promulgate some radical reforms.[2] The type of family law enacted in each country was in fact an

---

[1] The issue of gender justice and citizenship in the MENA constitutes a challenge to scholars, feminists and policy makers for the foreseeable future. More research on the history of organizations, their structure, their membership, modes of organization and strategies is needed.

[2] In Tunisia, where the power base of the postcolonial state was independent of tribes and lineages, a liberal policy on family law greatly expanded women's rights. In Morocco by contrast, the postcolonial state, which developed in alliance with tribes, promptly promulgated a conservative family law favorable to lineages and unfavorable to women. In Algeria, the government was in partial alliance with forces anchored in kin-based formations and unable to resolve internal divisions. Algerian law was caught in prolonged gridlock until a conservative legal code was eventually adopted. M. Charrad, *States and Women's Rights:The Making of Postcolonial Tunisia, Algeria and Morocco* (Berkeley, CA: University of California Press, 2001).

expression of the model of kinship favored by the political actors in the newly formed national state.

II. Status of Women in Tunisia

The roots of Tunisia's pioneering role in women's issues reach back to the beginning of the twentieth century.[3] Tahar Haddad (1899–1936), a progressive scholar of the *Zitouna* Great Mosque, called for freeing women from their traditional bonds. He wrote a book entitled *Our Women in the Shari'a and Society*, published in 1930, dealing with the importance of women in a modern and flourishing society.

Haddad, examined the position of women in Tunisian society juxtaposing it with Islamic Law. He advocated formal education for women and maintained that over many years Islam had been misinterpreted to such an extent that women were unaware of their duties and the legitimate advantages they could expect in life. In the name of Islam, Haddad denounced all forms of abuses against women such as repudiation, whereby a husband could divorce his wife without any explanation. Refuting assertions that such behavior is permissible for Muslims, Haddad affirmed that religion is innocent of the oft-made accusations that it is an obstacle in the way of modernity. According to Haddad, Islam is a source of progress. The decadence of Muslims is the consequence of traditions and customs, negative attitudes and mentalities. Haddad called for support for social change and, religious respect of identity.[4]

Despite the ban of Haddad's book and the violent reaction of his colleagues from the religious institution *Zeitouna*, he holds an important position in Tunisian history as the inspiration for a new religious, social and political discourse that would influence development and assure success in those early decades.

Tunisia had a history of women's emancipation[5] which led in 1936 to the creation of the important first women's organization. Building upon the positive atmosphere created by Haddad's writing, women advanced their own cause significantly by playing active roles in their country's struggle for independence, which broke into the open in 1938 when leaders of the Destour party, and women who joined in a party demonstration, were arrested. In 1950, as post-war agitation for independence resumed, the Neo-Destour party founded its first official women's section. A large number of women members were arrested in subsequent demonstrations that preceded French withdrawal and the attainment of Tunisia's independence on March 20, 1956. As a result of local practices, the prominent role of women in the new nation's politics, and perhaps most of all the remarkable foresight demonstrated by Habib Bourguiba (1903–2000) leader of the Neo-Destour Party, women benefited almost immediately from the country's independence.

The Code of Personal Status (CPS) was adopted on August 13, 1956, just a few months after Tunisia achieved independence. It is important to note that the CPS was not a response from the state to women's claims and pressures but a political decision taken by political leaders and urban reformists.

[3] Ilhem Marzouki, *Le mouvement des femmes en Tunisie au XX siècl*, (Tunis: CERS production, 1993).

[4] M. Charrad, *States and Women's Rights: The Making of Postcolonial Tunisia, Algeria and Morocco* (Berkeley, CA: University of California Press, 2001), pp. 216–217.

[5] In 1929 a liberal woman, Habiba Al-Menshari attended a meeting in a literary club unveiled and managed to convince many women to drop the veil.

The term of office of Tunisia's first president, Habib Bourguiba (1956–87), was in fact a time of advancement and modernization of the country. Early in his 31-year rule, the president believed that if Tunisians were to build and enjoy the forward-looking society they had been promised, both men and women would be required to play an important role in its construction. Article 6 of the Constitution, which was promulgated on June 1, 1959, provides that 'all citizens have equal rights and duties and are equal before the law', thereby paving the way for subsequent laws that progressively established the fundamental rights of women in all fields: the right to vote and stand for office, the right to work, the right to free and compulsory education, the right to social protection, the right to make their own choices in life, the right to enter into contracts and so forth.

Accordingly, family law reform in Tunisia redefined the rights and responsibilities of citizens by presenting a new concept of gender relationships that not only departed from the model associated with kin groupings, but steered individuals away from the extended kin group. The new Tunisian laws challenged the extended tribal kin grouping.[6]

Since the 1950s, Tunisia was considered a shining example for other Arab countries, because of its social revolution. The new vision of society had been widely disseminated and had gradually been adopted by the majority of women. Equality of opportunity was beginning to emerge[7] and was given considerable impetus through new women's organizations. The state formation was accompanied by the rise of a feminist consciousness. The Tunisian Code of Personal Status does not contain explicit references to Islam, though Islamic values played a role in its crafting. The government has sought to develop a new phase of Islamic interpretation (Ijtihad) distinct from the Islamic law in other Muslim countries. This new thinking has included reforms to create gender equality in the areas of marriage, divorce, child custody, and women's social autonomy. Supporters of the reforms do not see this as an abandonment of Islamic values, but rather as an evolution for the modern period.

Despite the anger of religious leaders, religious courts had been abolished. The government unified the judicial system by integrating all courts into a single national system. This measure aimed to undermine the religious establishment and to limit kin-based tribal groups. The message of the new family law was that the nuclear family would constitute the real and significant locus of solidarity. The dominant discourse assumed a secular society where religion was considered a private affair. The Code of Personal Status banned polygamy (prov. 18) which became a crime punishable by a fine and imprisonment, a unique development in the Arab world. It was inspired by a similar prohibition previously adopted by Turkey. The ban of polygamy strengthened conjugal ties, reinforced women's rights and provided a context of increased security for children.

That and other reforms incorporated in the CPS were presented as a sign of the revival of Islamic jurisprudence. According to reformists, the Code of Personal Status was innovative with respect to Shari'a, but several of the reforms met with serious opposition. The majority of Ulema did not look favorably on the new family law and particularly the ban of polygamy.

---

[6] Indeed it was in the best interest of the state leadership to break kin-based solidarities, and it was possible for it to do so because tribal groups had already lost much of their power and leverage as politically relevant actors. M. Charrad, *States and Women's Rights*, p. 238.

[7] To further facilitate the process of development, less than a year after the introduction of the Personal Status Code, women were given the right to vote on March 14, 1957.

Bourguiba established laws and asked official *muftis* (religious men who often interpreted the Qur'an) to justify them according to tradition and Islamic Law. For example, Tunisian legislation recognizes monogamy only. But the Qur'an speaks explicitly of polygamy, allowing up to four wives plus all the servants that one may have (4, 3). So how can the prohibition of polygamy be justified?

The verse in question goes on to say: 'but if you fear that you will not be equitable (*ta'dilū*), then marry only one'. Verse 129 of the same chapter explicitly says: 'And you have it not in your power to be equitable between wives, even though you may wish (it)'. Thus, the Qur'an authorizes up to four wives, adding however that if a man fears not being fair, he must limit himself to one. And further ahead it states that a man cannot be fair.

Bourguiba concluded: 'In fact, the Qur'an wished to guarantee monogamy. But keeping in mind the weakness of Arabs, their state of mind and the customs of the time, it temporarily authorized polygamy, subordinating it to a practically unattainable condition'.[8]

As can be seen, progressive interpretation can allow for much adaptation. The meaning of the verse on treating wives 'fairly' is not in the sense of 'equal justice' as is the interpretation of many Muslims but in the sense of duty affection and sexuality: polygamy foresaw equal shares of sexual enjoyment, the same number of nights. So it is possible to read verses in a more liberal sense by emphasizing the contexts in which these verses occur. *Bourguiba* encouraged scholars to try to open the gates of interpretation (Ijtihād) and to seek further understanding of the spirit of the Qur'anic text in order to produce jurisprudential texts based on values of equality.

The Tunisian reading of the Qur'an outlaws polygamy while in all other Islamic countries, polygamy is still a man's prerogative. The Tunisian interpretation of the Qur'an shows that Islamic sources are interpreted through two cultural patterns; an Arab cultural base pattern that is patriarchal and a western cultural base pattern that supports gender equality.

Other reforms incorporated in the 1956 CPS abolished the right of a father to force his daughter to marry against her will. Nowadays marriage can only take place with the consent of both parties to the marriage (prov. 22). The code also set the legal age for marriage for men at 20, and for woman at 17, with marriage below those ages permitted only with the consent of both parents and the decision of a judge. It seems that the institution of dowry was maintained symbolically, in order not to break completely with the Islamic Law. The amended Family Code, however, no longer contained a fixed amount.

Unilateral repudiation was equally abolished (prov. 30). It was a practice whereby a husband could simply terminate his marriage without explanation. Now in Tunisia both husband and wife can initiate divorce proceedings. A divorce can be granted only by a judge who has exhausted all efforts to reconcile the two parties. Women also may be granted a financial settlement under the law, and the government has set up a fund to pay the divorced husband's obligations to his former wife if he fails to do so himself (Measures of August 11, 1997)

Whereas Islamic law forbids adoption, Bourguiba promulgated the statute on adoption in 1958. Man or woman, married or not, can adopt a child. The adopted

---

[8] H. Bourguiba, *Discours* (Tunis: Publications du Secrétariat de l'information, 1978), p. 56.

child would become a full member of the family and benefit from all the rights as the right to take the name of the adopting parent and to inheritance.

In 1965, Tunisia became the first largely Muslim country to liberalize its policies on abortion. By 1973, Tunisian women were granted the right to abort in the first three months of pregnancy. Tunisian law also protects the right of a woman to decide whether or not to practice birth control, and whether or not to have an abortion. The fact that families are exercising their legally protected right to choose is manifested by the reduction in the size of the average Tunisian family. Tunisia has succeeded in stabilizing its population growth, another pioneering development in the Arab world.

By establishing reforms, Bourguiba consolidated state institutions in the aftermath of independence as part of his project to build a modern state. Convinced that the CPS was in advance of society and aware of the resistance of people, Bourguiba decided to give many speeches, to explain the reforms to Tunisians and to enforce their application.[9] In many speeches, Bourguiba referred critically to 'archaic' society, 'retrograde' mentalities, and groups 'hostile to change'. Implementation was not always easy. Problems were reported in the enforcement of some reforms when they were contrary to social convention and values. Several additions, clarifications and amendments have been made at different periods since 1956. Now, under the new Tunisian law, men and women alike gain full adult rights at age 20. After that, men and women have exactly the same rights to vote, enter into contracts and buy and sell property and goods. An adult woman is recognized as a full person before the court, and a woman's testimony is considered equal to that of a man.

The new family law was founded on the concept of mutual respect and cooperation between the spouses in all family matters, including the education of their children. A new article 23, further provides that both spouses shall cooperate in managing the family's affairs, the proper education of their children and the conduct of their children's affairs, including education, travel and financial transactions. Two major laws, adopted in 1997 and 1998, substantially strengthened the rights of women as persons, namely the law concerning the patronymic name of natural or abandoned children and the law organizing the regime of the joint estate of husband and wife. The move to eliminate the notion of submission is a fundamental measure which represents a break from the former system of reference based on the treatment of women as inferior beings.

Recent changes in the text of the family code are pointing in the direction of promoting more gender equality. Married couples are allowed to hold property jointly, thus giving women more control over family's assets and their bequeathal. Previously, women were not obliged to contribute monetarily to the maintenance of the family. Now with the reforms they are so obliged.[10] The argument is that the Tunisian woman has not only equal rights with the man but also equal responsibilities in monetary terms.

Contrary to the new Moroccan family law, the present Tunisian Code continues to describe the husband as the head of the family. As women gradually became more independent economically, the role of the husband as economic custodian would certainly disappear.

---

[9] See Mark A. Tessler, Janet Rogers and Daniel Schneider (eds.), *Women's Emancipation in Tunisia* (London: Virago Press, 1976); Lois Beck and Nikki Keddie, *Women in the Muslim World* (Cambridge, MA: Harvard University Press, 1982), pp. 141–158.

[10] The sociological reasons for this change were the protests of men. They were complaining about this form of discrimination against them.

The rights of children from free unions[11] were protected through a system of judicial machinery. The custom of awarding custody of children from the age of seven in the case of boys and nine in the case of girls automatically to the father was banned. Under the terms of the Law of July 12, 1993, certain child custody prerogatives were granted to the mother, such as the right to respect children's education or the right to manage their affairs. Related to the guardianship of children after divorce, other reforms providing for a divorced woman's allowance (July 1993). Similarly, where previously widows did not automatically retain custody of their children, the CPS provides that a surviving parent, regardless of sex, remains the principal guardian of minor children. The Code of private international law November 27, 1998, provides that when one of the spouses is a native of a country where polygamy is permitted, officers in charge of civil status and notaries will conclude marriage only on presentation of an official document certifying that the spouse is not bound by any other marital bond (Art. 46). A Tunisian woman married to a non-Tunisian may legally transmit her nationality to her child, provided the father consents.

Inheritance laws, too, were overhauled to improve protection of the rights of women. Some reforms of the inheritance law have been taken. The state introduced obligatory bequests in favor of orphaned grandchildren through sons or daughters, limited to first generation of grandchildren and to a maximum of one-third of an estate; introduced and extended the doctrine of *radd* (return) to allow the surviving spouse to share in residue of the deceased partner's estate. Another provision made it that if the deceased has surviving daughters only, estate shall go to children and not to paternal uncles.

The penal code, as amended on March 8, 1968, stipulates that adultery is a crime and lays down equal sanctions for a wife or husband judged guilty of adultery. These are up to five years imprisonment and a fine of 500 Tunisian dinars. Penalties for rape also have become increasingly severe. A March 1985 law allows the death penalty in cases of rape where violence and armed threat are used, and where the victim is under 10. The penalty for all other kinds of rape is imprisonment and hard labor. Similarly a law on manners and sexual harassment was promulgated amending Article 226 of the Penal Code. The law extends the definition of sexual harassment to words, gestures or actions that undermine a person's dignity and feelings. It increases penalties for sexual harassment at work or in public places to one year in prison and a fine of 3,000 dinars. This penalty is doubled if the victim is a child or a mentally or physically vulnerable individual.

The Code of Personal Status is widely credited with making Tunisian women among the most liberated in the Muslim world. They are strongly represented in national and local politics, the judiciary, academia, law, medicine, the media and big business. The Code of Personal Status has also inspired activists and lawmakers in countries such as Egypt and Morocco to call for similar empowerment of women. But the questions posed here: does Tunisian family law reflect true gender equality? Do Tunisian women believe that they represent a model for all Muslim women or are they challenging another reality?

---

[11] Concerning prostitution, the legislator declared that regulated prostitution was not banned because it curtailed clandestine prostitution and protected minors from abuses. Clandestine prostitution is severely punished in Tunisia.

III. Claiming Full Equality and Facing New Challenges

No one can speak about the status of women in Tunisia without taking into account changes that occur over time in society. It is evident that the major change for women was the government's recognition of a family model in which women were the foundation and accordingly granted new rights. The second factor which contributed to change the status of women was the urbanization of society witch enabled women to progress beyond the production function that they had served under an agrarian system in traditional society. Since then, women have pushed for greater economic power and independence.

Literacy has also proven vital to women asserting their rights under the reformed personal status code. Access to education had an impact on women's perception of themselves, their reproductive and sex roles, and their social mobility expectations. Women in Tunisia are active participants in shaping their own definition of need. Not only feminism, but the practices of everyday life offered spaces for women to plot out their own lives. Tunisian women give greater priority to careers because they are responsible for their own survival. Many of them now feel greater responsibility to take care of their parents, a domain once reserved for sons.

Although the role of women has expanded outside the home into the economic sphere, most Tunisian men think that husbands are not obliged to help women in the house, and that their role should reflect their superior status as family heads. Men are experiencing disturbance in two spheres simultaneously provoked by changes in women's economic and domestic behavior. The first is that wives and mothers are leaving the home in increasing numbers for at least part of their day. Woman becomes more self-assertive, less ready to accept a husband's authority. Secondly, women represent a growing source of competition for men in the workplace and in other fields.

On the one hand women have increased access to birth control, and they are more involved in the public sphere and in family discussions. On the other hand we notice a worsening of family relations and detrimental changes in family eating habits. At the same time, each spouse has been expecting something more important from the other: men expect women to make a greater financial contribution to the household and to promote their children's happiness, and maintain a balance between their private and professional lives, and women expect men to play a greater role in the children's socialization and at home. In a country praised as a standard-bearer of women's rights in the Muslim world, some men had shown resistance fuelled by the growth of fundamentalist trends and their increasing impact on the common consciousness. The majority of men want to preserve their traditional gender roles. They believe that they lost their power and their exclusive role as breadwinners.

Today, most men refuse to support women's rights movement in family law and even the application of rules. Some men are worried about the emancipation of women with no clear landmarks ahead. They don't have the family and workplace privileges by right of their gender that they see in other Arab countries. Can we speak about a masculinity crisis in Tunisia?

In spite of the global commitment to achieve gender equality, much remains to be achieved. Key obstacles are related to inattention to appropriate theoretical and political issues. The example of Tunisia shows that a legislation empowering women is necessary but insufficient to guarantee them a real promotion. The gap remains large between the legal framework and the lived reality on the one hand, and between law and mentalities on the other. We notice a dualism between the 'public' social, economic, and political rights women are guaranteed under family law and the restrictions placed on their 'private' home lives by cultural norms. Recently, cultural heritage has become for some Tunisians the symbol of their Islamic identity.

Although the gender ideology is an important part of the Tunisian regime's message, women continue to face gender-based obstacles to receiving full realization of their rights as equal participants in society. No doubt the family continues to be the first social institution that reproduces patriarchal relationships, values and pressures through gender discrimination. As more women gain access to education, the pool of women's rights advocates expands and more women are becoming active in demanding reforms of the law. During the past few years some parliamentarians, including female members, have called for mandatory military service for Tunisian women. The Minister of Defense declared that women's recruitment would be gradually enforced.

According to feminists and activists,[12] Tunisia is not a wholly egalitarian state today, as its women still face discrimination. It is evident that discrimination violates the principles of equality of rights and respect for human dignity. It is an obstacle to the participation of women, on equal terms with men, in the political, social, economic and cultural life of the country. This hampers the growth of the prosperity of society and the family and makes more difficult the full development of the potentialities of women in the service of their country.

Indeed, Tunisian women have made progress and are appreciative of their special status, but they are convinced that they must push for change in the personal status code, which still favors men with regard to issues of marriage age, dowry, sexual harassment, rape, and inheritance.

Activists criticize the position of the state concerning CEDAW which was ratified by Tunisia in 1985, but reserved the provisions that contradict the Tunisian Constitution, the Personal Status Code, or the Tunisian Nationality Code.i [8] more specifically, articles 9(2), 16 (c), (d), (f), (g), and (h), and 29(2) have reservations, and 15(4) has a declaration. Indeed the state has taken significant strides to implement the standards of CEDAW and to ensure that Tunisian laws are in compliance with international standards on women's rights. But according to activists it is time for the government to remove all reservations to CEDAW and take steps to implement full equality, in other words: Equality without reservations.[13]

As Tunisia celebrated the 50th anniversary (in August 2006) of a revolutionary family law, many women's rights activists[14] are criticizing the authorities over the

---

[12] Hafidha Chekir, Sana Ben Achour, Khedija Cherif, Khedija Arfaoui, Ilhem Marzouki, Latifa Lakhdar, Kalthoum Meziou, Saida Garrache, Sihem Ben Sedrine and others. For further reading see Ilhem Marzouki and Khedija Cherif, 'Les facteurs socioculturels défavorisant les femmes en matière de succession', in Actes du colloque, *La non-discrimination à l'égard des femmes* (Paris: CERP-UNESCO, 1989); A. Chérif Chamari, *La femme et la loi en Tunisie* Casablanca: Le Fennec, 1991; Hafidha Chekir, 'Women, the Law, and the Family in Tunisia', *Gender & Development*, 4(2) (1996), pp. 43–46.

[13] Khadija Cherif, Report of the action of lobbying of the coalition 'Equality without reservation' during the first Session of the Universal Periodic Review – April 2008.

[14] Only in the 1990s did women's agency emerge on the political scene, as women's rights advocates seized an opening created by conflicts in national politics.

fact that the country's laws of inheritance remain inequitable, favoring sons over daughters. They declared that inheritance laws contribute in some way to the consolidation of patriarchal values and claim that the 1956 text needs urgent updating.

The resulting reforms of the law combined with the opinion of public morality that the dowry should be limited to a symbolic value have now fueled a debate on whether such a change in the obligations of the woman requires an interpretation of the inheritance laws that would conform to the situation foreseen in the Qur'anic text of a woman foregoing a high dowry. Activists criticize the institution of dowry because it is one of the manifestations of subordination of women.

Feminist scholars find that a non-Muslim wife is discriminated against in the private sphere. When married to a Muslim husband, she is not entitled to inherit from her husband, nor will her children inherit from her. The Inheritance legislation bears therefore an attempt against women's freedom of religion. Women's organizations invite the state to reaffirm the supremacy of the freedom of religion of all women over inheritance law.

Feminist scholars have studied the historic texts and point out that women were allowed to inherit half of that of men in the seventh century. The rationale for unequal inheritance was that men, unlike women, had legal financial obligations. Given the likelihood that today's women earn incomes, scholars have urged a reinterpretation of the appropriate Qur'anic verse to ensure inheritance is equally shared between men and women.[15]

Despite the claim of feminist NGO's such as AFTURD (Tunisian women association for research and development) and the Tunisian Democratic Women's Association to reform inheritance law, the government argues that any radical, quick changes could bring instability, reform should take place over time. Tunisian society was concerned with following the principles of religion without sacrificing progress. The issue of inheritance law is under examination by legal and religious scholars.

The Tunisian elites controlling the state pursued the policy of splitting the difference between the demands of women activists pushing for liberal feminist reforms and those of a conservative religious intelligentsia that was antagonistic to these reforms. It is clear that the discourses of tradition and modernity should be taken as political constructs and the question which should be asked is: who benefits from each discourse in given political, social and religious contexts?

Indeed, the government attempts to fight discrimination in employment by making equal opportunity a mandatory part of investigation within audits of governmental institutions and state-owned enterprises. However, these standards have only limited effect, as these requirements do not apply to the private sector. Women working in the textile, manufacturing, and agricultural sectors still suffer from discrimination.

Although the Tunisian Penal Code has made domestic assault a punishable crime, violence against women is still pervasive and prosecution is infrequent.

---

[15] Collectif, 2006, 'Egalité dans l'héritage: Pour une citoyenneté pleine et entière', Vols. 1 & 2, AFTURD, Tunis, *La Revue Réalités*, No. 810, 05/07/2001, pp. 16–17 and No. 814 –815, 02/8/2001, p. 10, No. 816, 16/8/2001, pp. 20–22.

Women in their families have been victims of lingering injustice. NGO's surveys[16] demonstrate that violence is deeply rooted in societal norms including gender roles and expectations and codified in legal systems that discriminate against women. Violence is often sanctioned by patriarchal interpretations of the Qur'an, including the belief in male authority over women. Most women do not officially report abuse because of the social stigma and the lack of intervention and code enforcement by authorities such as the police and courts. Yet the law does not recognize marital rape or consider it a crime, despite the existence of Tunisia's other laws and policies that emphasize women's rights to dignity and bodily integrity. The feminist movement began to challenge the concept of family privacy that shielded wife abuse. Many activists demand more protective laws.[17] Studies shows that lack of education, unemployment, weak financial conditions, corruption and lack of freedom make men insecure and more liable to turn oppressive, violent and dominant, proving to themselves and others that they are still 'Man enough'.[18]

Another point raised by activists is sexual harassment. They welcomed the law concerning sexual harassment but expressed concern that it linked sexual harassment to safeguarding manners, lacked an adequate definition of harassment and did not contain adequate provisions for investigating allegations.[19]

According to women's rights activists, family law shows another aspect of gender inequality. A Muslim Tunisian woman is not allowed to marry a non-Muslim man. If she marries a non-Muslim outside Tunisia, the marriage would be classified as common law, which, under the revision of the Personal Status Code, is illegal.[20]

Despite the positive impact of all modern legal educational, and economic reforms of the position of women and the work of feminist NGOs, a growing number of girls have not benefited from the opportunities created, especially in the economic and political spheres. Women are still the minority in decision-making positions due mostly to prejudices and lack of attention to women's issues on

[16] The Centre of Listening to Women victims of Violence has progressively developed its activities. Between 1990 and June 2000, the Centre has filed 789 cases of violence against women. The vast majority of them are cases of domestic violence. In the second position, come cases of sexual harassment or violence at work. Other cases include rape, incest, family violence (detention of young women), and violence in the street. Beyond this, the Centre has encountered or witnessed a great number of difficulties in bringing the cases to Court, and obtaining legal remedy for the victims. If legal remedies are available in principle, they often meet the resistance of the judge to be practically pursued. Pressure, in some cases, has been exerted on the judge, for him not to take up the case, not to mention sometimes critical attitudes towards women within the Court. In some cases, non-application of a law or discriminatory application of the law is also reported. Cases of rape are inadequately investigated without the use of objective means of evidence, such as through genetic proof (while this modern tool is used for the recognition of fatherhood). In alleged cases of incest, the father remains free until the pronouncement of a judgment, without precautionary measures being decided upon, such as the physical separation from the child. Sexual violence is insufficiently covered by the law, preventing adequate redress, but more importantly, from raising social awareness on its different forms.
[17] Tunisia has one shelter for battered women in operation. It is run by the Tunisian Democratic Women's Association. About twenty women per month seek services at the shelter. The National Union of Tunisian Women (UNFT), a government sponsored association, also provides support and services to women in crisis. The majority of UNFT's clients are victims of domestic violence and sexual assault.
[18] Sous la direction de Christiane Veauvy, Marguerite Rollinde et Mireille Azzoug, *Les Femmes entre violences et stratégies de liberté. Maghreb, Europe du Sud* (Paris: Editions Bouchène, 2004).
[19] Sexual harassment is not recognized by law, and therefore remains very badly documented or prevented.
[20] Amel Grami, 'L'interdiction du mariage de la musulmane avec le non musulman: une forme d'exclusion', in Vincent Feroldi (ed.), *Chrétiens et Musulmans en dialogue: Les Identités en devenir* (Paris: L'Harmattan, 2003), pp. 343–356.

the part of the predominantly male 'leaders'; some of whom viewed patriarchal traditions as integral components of Arab identity and culture.

Most women in the parliament don't play a greater role in political decision-making. Their roles remain restricted and cosmetic. According to many activists, the issue of women's political rights is a type of 'democratic façade'.

Many scholars point out that the state has an instrumentalist approach toward women, gender, and the family: Policies and laws that strengthen the position of the state itself are the ones that will be enacted. Women's lack of political power, results in their plight being taken lightly by decision-makers and their rights being used as political commodities to be traded and exchanged between male leaders of various political groups.[21]

Women's status has occupied a central place in the modernization efforts in Tunisia. For decades, the modernist thinkers argued that reforms in the position of women in the economic, educational, political and legal spheres would lead to more 'modernization', and consequently, to greater gender equality in all spheres. However, women are among the first who recognize the complex and contradictory nature of modernity. In fact modernization projects did not necessarily lead to real gender equality for all or in every sphere.

Progressive thinkers and activists call for educational reform to correct stereotypes through presenting a more positive image of women in school textbooks, the media and through human rights education. It is evident that the struggle to realize full equality is not only legal, but social as well. Major concerns were illiteracy and the resurgence of backward models under the influence of current fundamentalism. Many feminists notice that there are changes in attitudes toward women across Tunisian society. The resistance to change is also on the part of women themselves.

After the emergence of political Islam in Tunisia there have been many positions regarding women's rights and beliefs about their appropriate roles. Some feel that equality has been achieved and it is time to move on from gender issues. Others have lost their desire to battle and realized that there is no hope. Many women see feminism as old-fashioned and think the term carries a stigma. Others believe that feminism had become a 'dirty word'. In fact there is a lack of transfer of knowledge and awareness. Many younger women ignore the history of feminism in Tunisia and in Arab countries. No definition of feminism has been provided and women were left to make their own judgment about their rights and their self perceptions.

As in Arab Muslim countries during the past ten years, Islamic discourse has become dominant in Tunisia.[22] More Tunisian women are beginning to wear the headscarf, apparently under the influence of Tele-preachers on Arab satellite channels whose influence bypasses national boundaries. According to feminists the increasing number of veiled women reinforces traditional stereotypes and prejudices and strengthens patriarchal ideology. It creates an intimidating environment. Some groups of veiled women are developing a new discourse; they want equity not full gender equality.

---

[21] Ilhem Marzouki, 'La subjectivité fait-elle le sujet féminin? Une lecture sociologique de l'expérience tunisienne' in *Les femmes entre violences et stratégies de liberté*, pp. 105–120.

[22] We should keep in mind that after the late President Habib Bourguiba was deposed, fundamentalists called for a referendum on the PSC in order to change it. The second Republic chose to continue the policy of the first, and brought the women's movement into association with other Tunisian political forces in a 'National Pact' to safeguard the PSC, thereby turning the majority of Tunisian women into protectors of the state.

The discourse of most of the new generation of Tunisian women, which emerged in a specific context wherein they benefited from an oft-amended CPS, required that they don't demand for new rights. Today, some girls confess that they are ready to accept polygamy. Referring to pressure exercised by religious extremist groups in neighboring countries and whether there was any long-term plan that would guarantee women their full rights and avoid any set-backs,[23] human rights activists think that the rise of political Islam represents an acute threat to the rights and freedoms of Tunisian women. They consider that women are facing traditional interpretations of the Qur'an that hold them back from full participation in their societies. According to some feminist activists, Tunisia is turning its back on its secular traditions. The new behavioral modes and religious practices that are foreign to Tunisian society's traditions and values are disseminated by the modern means of information and communication, especially certain Islamist satellite channels. Religious programs are deeply affecting the upbringing of people. Islamists are using religion as a means to swallow up women's rights.

Many activists stressed the need to separate religion from the state as an essential approach to realize gender equality.[24] They believe that the promotion of women's rights is the key to the gate of freedom for women and the best safeguard against extremist and retrograde movements.[25] It is important to note that feminists who advocate reform of Tunisian family law particularly inheritance law are often charged with supporting changes that are un-Islamic. According to religious fundamentalists, women's rights are perceived as another Western export being imposed on Arab society. The term gender itself is now seen as going against religion. The difference in affiliation with an Islamic movement or feminist group produces, in fact, a difference in attitudes towards gender.

Today Tunisian women are facing new challenges. The idea of being 'a model' pushes activists to struggle in order to spread awareness.[26] They refuse to forfeit their position and their rights because they believe that their present status is not a gift. They have worked for it and still do. Gender equality in Tunisia offers new Islamic cultural images to the contemporary Islamic world. Also, it carries a specific message regarding the perception of modernity as envisaged by political leaders, the place accorded to women in the society and the conception of gender equality. Tunisia shows that in the absence of women's agency, the state handles women's rights in a variety of ways, depending on its own source of support, its projects for the future society, and the nature of other contenders to power within historical context.

IV. Conclusion

Change in family law is considered as a significant index of social change in the Middle East. It is a barometer of the internal debate within Islam, and an

[23] The growing influence of the Islamic revival movement was curbed in the late 1980s by a regime change that also worked to further improve women's legal status.

[24] Jamel Arfaoui, 'Women's rights activists stress the need to separate religion from the state', http://www. magharebia.com/cocoon/awi/xhtml1/en_GB/features/awi/features/2007/12/04/feature-01.

[25] It is important to note that, the Tunisian government places restrictions on women's organizations and their ability to advocate for their rights, particularly groups that call for greater democratic freedoms and civil liberties. The work of most NGOs is closely monitored by state security agencies.

[26] A government survey in 1991 found that 70% of illiterate women were unaware of their rights under the code.

illustration of the capacity for Islamic reform. It is also highly indicative of the role of the state's legal policy in matters of gender and the family. Historically it was men who acted as commentators of the religious texts as well as legislators, jurists and judges and political actors. Men determine the rights or the lack of rights for women. There are, however, a number of social, psychological, and economic traditions which govern the thinking of most Muslims and which are particularly effective of woman's status and role in Islamic society. Understanding these, can help us understand the issues which affect male and female status and roles, and how we should react to movements which seek to improve the situation of women in MENA.

Throughout the region, women's organizations have placed priority on changing personal status laws to grant women full equality. Arab women activists who have long been dealing with patriarchy are deconstructing history and religious texts to find spaces of empowerment for women. While some are joining Islamist groups and are working within their logic, others are resolutely rejecting any association within such movements. All, however, are learning how to situate themselves and how to interact with different ideologies.

No doubt women activists are making great efforts to promote gender equality in the context of the increased politicization of Islam.[27] They want to break the monopoly on patriarchal religious interpretation to challenge legal discrimination, defy many taboos and to work to address social and economic disparities. More cooperative activities should be encouraged to consolidate women's rights that had been gained so far and to prevent any set-back as a result of the threat of religious extremist trends. A consideration of gender policy in any specific country of MENA today must take into consideration the role of women's rights advocates.[28]

---

[27] Leila Hessini, 'Women contesting Islamist movements in the Arab world', http://www.whrnet.org/fundamentalisms/docs/issue-arab-0606.html
[28] Mounira Maya Charrad, 'Unequal Citizenship: Issues of Gender Justice in the Middle East and North Africa', http://www.idrc.ca/en/ev-111820-201-1-DO_TOPIC.html

Party Politics of the AKP (2002–2007) and the Predicaments of Women at the Intersection of the Westernist, Islamist and Feminist Discourses in Turkey[1]

AYŞE GUNES AYATA and FATMA TÜTÜNCÜ

ABSTRACT *Celebrating the World Women's Day and initiating a conference for promoting Turkey's integration to Europe on the one hand, and discussing the discrimination against women on the ground of human rights and even harbouring the radical protest from left-wing as well as the Islamist women on the other, the women auxiliaries of AKP* (Adalet ve Kalkınma Partisi, Justice and Development Party) *seemingly position themselves at the very intersection of various political discourses including Westernism, feminism, liberalism and Islamism. Articulating these disparate discourses, however, requires a meticulous selectivity and a specific political strategy. Is this discursive selectivity inevitable for an overtly religious party in a modern nation-state where secularism and integration into the European civilisation have dominated the state ideology since its foundation? What are the reactions of outsiders, especially of European countries? More specifically, what are the repercussions of this strategic mentality in terms of the women's question? Does it attract various women's groups and thus create solidarity among different voices? Or on the contrary does it not truncate or even silence the demands of women? This paper discusses the women politicians in the AKP as well as its policies on gender equality and relations. It aims to analyze the party on three angles: women's representations and visibility, changes in political ideology and rhetoric, and the adaptation of party organization to the demands of women.*

I. Introduction

On March 8, 2005, the women's auxiliaries of the Justice and Development Party (Adalet ve Kalkınma Partisi, AKP) organized a conference entitled 'Fighting against Gender Discrimination in the Process of European Union' at Bilkent Hotel, Ankara.

---

[1] This paper reflects AKP politics during its first period in power, 2002–2007. The second period has not been analysed.

The talk of the most prominent invited-speaker, Emine Erdoğan, the veiled wife of Prime Minister Recep Tayyip Erdoğan, was interrupted twice by different female political activists. The first interruption was by two young women having apparently a left-wing tendency, shouting, 'March 8 is not your day, it belongs to the women workers'. After a short time the second group, four-veiled young women, began their protest asking with the fliers at hand: 'Is 70 percent not enough for social consensus?',[2] evoking here, Prime Minister Erdoğan's promise that the head-cover problem will be solved as soon as social consensus is reached. There were questions exposed in the written handbills that they yelled across the conference room: 'Ask me what discrimination means', 'How will you pay for our lost lives?', 'Which discrimination? Gender discrimination or veiled-not veiled discrimination?' The young women demanded their right to education with wearing headscarves, and criticized the Erdoğan family who could easily send their veiled daughters to the US to get an education. They were then thrown out of the conference room in tears by the gendarmes.[3]

The women's auxiliaries of the AKP seemingly position themselves at the very intersection of various political discourses, including Westernism, feminism, liberalism and Islamism, by celebrating the World Women's Day and initiating a conference for promoting Turkey's integration to Europe.

The conference discussed the discrimination against women on the ground of human rights, and there even was the harbouring of radical protest from left-wing as well as Islamist women. Articulating these disparate discourses, however, requires a meticulous selectivity and a specific political strategy. This could be witnessed, first, in the timing of the first national congress of the women's auxiliaries of the AKP on Mother's Day [read the cliché: women-mother]. Secondly, the composition of the members of the administrative unit proves the same mentality: six veiled and six unveiled administering women are neither a mere coincidence, nor a result of democratic election. In fact, such a selective and strategic mentality appears not only in the activities of the women's auxiliaries, but is pursued by the AKP in other political and cultural issues. Is this discursive selectivity inevitable for an overtly religious party in a modern nation-state, where secularism and integration into European civilization have dominated the state ideology since its foundation? Apart from the effects from within, what are the reactions of outsiders, especially of European countries to the AKP government? More specifically, what are the repercussions of this strategic mentality in terms of the women's question? Does it attract various women's groups to organize under the AKP and thus create solidarity among different voices? Or, on the contrary, does it not truncate, even silence the demands of women?

Keeping these questions in mind, we shall briefly sketch and base this discussion on the socio-political and cultural transformation in Turkey following the 1980 coup d'état, which can be seen as an era of a liberal turn. Apart from the other liberal awakenings, this era witnessed the rise of feminism and Islamism as powerful movements. Simultaneously in this period, Turkey's integration into Europe turned into a more concrete goal. The AKP came to power in this particular atmosphere. It would be erroneous, however, to ignore their enormous political efforts to gain power. Their political success at the local level, especially in

[2] The Justice and Development Party has two-thirds of the seats in the parliament, with 34% of popular vote, and some polls say that approximately 70% of the population supports the option of wearing headscarves.
[3] *Milliyet Daily* (March 9, 2005).

municipal elections is significant, mostly thanks to their women members.[4] How does the AKP pay its debt to women? The answer to this question can best be investigated in the structure of the organization of the women under the AKP, and the debates between the feminist groups and the AKP leadership, while accompanying recent legal amendments of the Turkish Civil and Penal Codes according to the requirements of harmonization with the European Union. In analyzing the structures of the women's political adherence to the AKP and the debates revolving around the 'quota', 'positive discrimination', 'adultery', and the general repercussions of the legal amendments on the women question in Turkey, we shall specifically expose the predicaments of the women who are organized in the AKP in general and in the women's auxiliaries in particular, who are silenced on the very basic matters which directly concern them as women. The very predicaments and reactions of these women will give us indicators regarding the quality of the merger amongst Westernist, Islamist and feminist discourses.

The rise of the visibility of women in the AKP has led to the revival of a very familiar discussion regarding gender and politics. A significant part of this discussion relates to 'classical' theories of political participation of women: since the suffragettes, as is quite well known, actualization of women's demands in political participation has had its theoretical and practical problems. The feminist objective in this endeavour has been to render women visible and to empower them. In principle, in a democratic country women should be represented in proportion to their populations and their interests should be taken into account. However, the problem of representation is a widely discussed issue, having political as well as philosophical consequences.[5] In the last couple of decades, the feminist movement has not only come up with a new set of demands, but has largely infiltrated into the political parties and other political movements, trying to create a gender awareness and create changes towards the gender inequalities in the society.[6] Political parties do not necessarily constitute one of the primary targets of feminism. Nevertheless, there have been some concerted efforts to integrate women into formal means of representation. Lovenduski argues that, in addition to representation, such political efforts may lead to changes in party programmes and policies, as well as altering the organizational structure.[7] We also know that such a change is not easy, even though most political parties find it very difficult to resist the feminist pressures and women's demands. They rarely take structural precautions, such as affirmative action to integrate them into politics. However, in many countries and political situations women make at least half of the votes. As a response, some parties tend to make rhetorical changes; for example, this method is common amongst right-wing parties, which tend to overemphasize women's motherhood roles as opposed to their public visibility; another issue that is widely discussed in the impact of women in politics. Even though women's political entry is very difficult, we may also experience problems with the women who are elected. Many women politicians may realize the

[4] J.B. White, *Islamist Mobilization in Turkey: A Study in Vernacular Politics* (Seattle and London: University of Washington Press, 2002); Yeşim Arat, *Political Islam in Turkey and Women's Organizations* (Istanbul: TESEV, 1999).

[5] Carole Pateman, 'The Fraternal Social Contract', in J. Keane (ed.) *Civil Society and the State* (London: Verso, 1988).

[6] Vicky Randal, 'Gender and Power: Women Engage the State', in V. Randal and G. Waylen (eds.) *Gender, Politics and the State* (London: Routledge, 1998).

[7] Joni Lovenduski, 'Dynamics of Gender and Party', in J. Lovenduski and P. Norris (eds.) *Gender and Party Politics* (London: SAGE, 1993).

reluctance of political parties to adapt feminist demands, and to avoid 'unnecessary' problems of resistance, they may resort to conventional male discourses with career expectations. In countries where a critical mass of women's representation does not exist, women may tend to be more conformist to patriarchal norms.

We argue that even though there has been an increased visibility of women in the AKP politics, this has not lead to an increased representation of women, or any other kind of structural change. Gender issues have been subsumed under ideological debates on Islam, secularism and westernization.

This study covers the politics of the AKP from 2002 to 2007 and is based upon four different types of data. The first set of data was collected in August 2005 when the Second Congress on the Women in Local Governments was held at the Bilkent Hotel, Ankara. By using a participatory observation and conducting interviews the local experience of the women organized under the AKP was received. More than 300 AKP women participated in the Second Congress. We used every opportunity to receive the AKP women's ideas, who came from different regions of Turkey. We talked with them in the public buses, while going to and coming back from Bilkent Hotel. We shared the same lunch table while chit-chatting on politics, on the direction of Mecca (kıble) in Ankara, and on insipid rice pudding, *sütlaç*.

In restrooms, there were ablution rituals, gossips and complaints, which we noted. After the speeches and discussions, there was a tea-party where we directly asked our questions about what it meant to be a politically active woman in the AKP.

The second set of data was based upon the interviews conducted in October and November 2005, with the women at the head office of the women's auxiliaries and the main office of the AKP in Ankara. We interviewed 15 women and that required incessant insistence.

While our first data were based upon informal and short interviews, the second were formal: we distributed our questionnaire before the meeting and visited the women in their offices at the appointed time. However, we were allowed to ask different questions, since we had enough time and our interviewees were willing. In this sense, our second data were semi-structured. The difficulty of making an appointment with some women led us to search dailies and journals which would retain special interviews. Thirdly, we systematically read the dailies, namely, *Yeni Şafak, Zaman, Sabah, Milliyet* and *Radikal*, especially during September 2004 when the discussions initiated by the AKP leadership on adultery were at their peak. Yet our search covers a larger time-span. In our readings, we paid special attention to the construction of events in news articles, and the arguments and justification of the columnists supporting or criticizing the AKP government. To supplement these data, lastly, we used the AKP monthly, *Türkiye Bülteni*, its web sources and the various pamphlets and documents published by the AKP, disseminating their political perspectives and activities especially on European integration and on the women issue.

II. The Rise of the AKP

The general elections held on November 3, 2002 had serious consequences for Turkish politics. First of all, none of the parties constituting the coalition government before the election could gain significant power. Instead, a newly established party reached victory. Second, since Turkey was on the eve of starting negotiations with the European Union on full membership, the rise of a religiously oriented party, AKP,[8] caused a heated debate on whether the AKP would halt, threaten or question Turkey's long-lasting march toward Europe. Such a question was not irrelevant, considering the politics of the previous religious parties which had an overt opposition to Turkish membership in the EU. In their expressions, calling pro-EU political parties 'European imitators', was an essential part of the religious parties' critique.[9] Thus, when AKP began to utter pro-European Union statements, secular groups often referred to this as dissimulation (*takiyye*).[10]

The first response of the AKP leaders to counter the dissimulation argument was to put a distance between their new party and the previous religious parties.[11] From the beginning, the AKP claimed that their party is not Islamist; they even rejected the use of the label 'Muslim democrats' as an analogy to the Christian democrats[12] in Western Europe. In rejecting the label 'Muslim democrat', Erdoğan stated that: 'These attributions are not correct, not because we are not Muslims or democrats; but because these two [identities] should be considered on different planes'.[13] Rather, the AKP based its policies on the 'conservative democracy' program. Instead of emphasizing their Muslim identity, they preferred to ground their moral and religious values within the confines of 'conservatism'. Concomitantly, their search for democratization in Turkey was repeatedly disseminated in almost all of their public speeches. Underlining that search for democracy was diminishing the role of the military in the political sphere. In a similar vein, certain liberal and left-wing figures claimed that the general elections on November 3, 2002, would contribute to democracy, and would expand the 'restricted political sphere' created by the authoritarian military regime following the September 12, 1980, military coup in Turkey.[14]

In the 1980s, Turkey witnessed the rise and the proliferation of *Islamism* and *feminism* as independent political movements. As a matter of fact, Islamism had begun to search for a legitimate representation in the secular and modern political field as early as the 1950s. Since then, various right-wing and/or religious parties have harboured Islamists. On the other hand, when the military regime harshly

---

[8] The AKP began its political life from the ashes of the Islamist Welfare Party. The Welfare Party was banned by the Constitutional Court for threatening the secular basis of the national social order. For a detailed evaluation on the process of the Welfare Party's dissolution, please see Dicle Kogacioglu, 'Progress, Unity, and Democracy: Dissolving Political Parties in Turkey', *Law and Society Review*, 38(3), (2004).

[9] Sencer Ayata, 'Changes in Domestic Politics and the Foreign Policy Orientation of the AKP Party' in L. Martin and D. Keridis (eds.) *The Future of Turkish Foreign Policy* (Cambridge, MA: MIT Press, 2004).

[10] *Takiyye* is a method of concealing one's real ideas and beliefs in order to save Muslim and Islamic beliefs; or it is to gain some practical advantages that would eventually serve the Islamist cause. This method is based upon *Āl-'Imrān* and *Al-Nahl* Suras in the Qur'an. In the Turkish political context, the AKP's *takiyye* means, as Heper explains, to hide its 'true intention of bringing to Turkey a state based on Islam, or Shari'a rule' (Metin Heper, 'Turkey Between 'East' and 'West'', *Institute of European Studies* (Berkeley, CA: University of California, Paper no: 40516, 2004), p. 13.

[11] Metin Heper finds the dissimulation thesis totally inappropriate in evaluating the AKP leaders and states that, 'As a Sufi, Erdoğan did not favour using Islam for political gain'. Please see 'The Justice and Development Party Government and the Military', *Turkish Studies*, 6(2), (2005), pp. 215–231.

[12] William Hale compares the AKP to the Christian Democracy tradition in Europe, and comes to the conclusion that although there are some similarities in terms of moral, cultural and educational issues, the historical and religious differences made the analogy between the AKP and the Western Christian Democrats difficult. 'Christian Democracy and the AKP: Parallels and Contrasts', *Turkish Studies*, 6(2) (2005), pp. 293–310.

[13] Cited by Simten Coşar and Aylin Özman, 'Centre-right Politics in Turkey after the November 2002 General Election: Neo-liberalism with a Muslim Face', *Contemporary Politics*, 10(1) (2004), pp. 57–74.

[14] Among others please see Ahmet İnsel, 'The AKP and Normalizing Democracy in Turkey', *The South Atlantic Quarterly*, 102(2/3) (2003).

suppressed left-wing movements, women found a niche to express their feminist concerns. Although the women's existence in, and concern with, politics has a longer history[15] – and some scholars have even talked of a 'state feminism' with respect to the republican reforms[16] – Turkish women had enjoyed only public and legal equality since the foundation of modern Turkey. The inequalities in the private realm were widely disregarded. In this connection, the feminist women in the 1980s focused primarily, but not exclusively, on the private sphere issues, including domestic violence, sexual harassment, control over women's bodies, and the like. Both Islamist and feminist movements in the 1980s were anti-establishment movements.

The second common point of the Islamist and feminist movement is that they both reflect heterogeneous structures. As the feminist movement embraces different colours and ideas, the Islamist movement also articulates various groups and discourses. Some Islamists are liberal, others radical; some are open to a dialogue with the West, others are anti-Western. Some of the Islamists support the equality between men and women; others emphasize the essential difference between women and men.

The third point is that both Islamists and feminists concern themselves with and participate in the debate over the women who demand wearing the headscarf in the universities. Until the 1980s, there were no laws or statutes regulating women's clothing, except for government employees; however, Turkish women were encouraged to appear in public in their Westernized outlook. Educated and professional women were willingly following that way. It was only after women wearing headscarves began to appear in the universities[17] in increasing numbers that the Council of Ministers in 1981 initiated the prohibition of the headscarf in the educational institutions, and a year later the Council of Higher Education began to enforce this prohibition in universities.[18] Underlying such prohibition is the neutrality principle of public services in a secular state modelled on the French understanding. Although women are free and have been so since the foundation of modern Turkey in covering their heads in the private as well as the public realms, when they become affiliated with public service, they are expected to strip off their engaged political disposition.

After the 1980s, the headscarf controversy has become the focal point of Turkish politics. Is it an individual right, or an expression of freedom of religion and conscience? Is it an assault on public neutrality, or a symbol of the Islamist agenda which aims at abolishing the secular and modern establishment in Turkey? These are the significant questions attached to the headscarves of women.

[15] Serpil Çakır, *Osmanlı Kadın Hareketi*, (İstanbul: Metis, 1994); Yaprak Zihnioğlu, *Kadınsız İnkılap: Nezihe Muhiddin, Kadınlar Halk Fırkası, Kadın Birliği* (İstanbul: Metis, 1993).

[16] Jenny B. White, 'State Feminism, Modernization, and the Turkish Republican Woman', *National Women's Studies Association Journal*, 5(3) (2003), pp.145–159.

[17] Nilüfer Göle detects an irony in the visibility of women wearing headscarf in the universities. The republican understanding has considered the visibility of women in the public life as a shift from an Islamic way of life to a secular and modern one; however, the very visibility of veiled female students in the universities in the 1980s led to the rise of Islamism and the Islamic way of life against the established understanding of politics and modernity in Turkey. Please see her article 'Secularism and Islamism in Turkey: The Making of Elites and Counter-Elites', *Middle East Journal*, 51(1) (1997), p. 51.

[18] Yeşim Arat, 'Group-Differentiated Rights and the Liberal Democratic State: Rethinking the Headscarf Controversy in Turkey', *New Perspectives on Turkey*, 25 (2001), pp. 31–46.

The rise of the AKP, a party rooted in political Islam, into power on the eve of Turkey's integration into the EU, gave the situation a new twist. First of all, expressing loyalty to the long-lasting desire for European integration of the country, the AKP launched several legal amendments for harmonization with the EU, including significant legal transformation for equality between women and men. Secondly, the AKP, appreciating the role of women in their rise to power, established nationwide women's auxiliaries, consisting of veiled as well as unveiled women. It promised to realize and increase the 'political literacy' of women and, hence, seemed to encourage their political participation. This process, nonetheless, witnessed an encounter between the feminists and the Islamist AKP government.

III. Women in Islamist Parties and the AKP's Women's Auxiliaries

It is a well-known fact that the Welfare Party (Refah Partisi, RP) preceding the AKP, had used its women's auxiliaries most effectively for its efficient party organization nationwide. Women members of the Welfare Party were very active in reaching potential voters in their homes. Sharing similar behaviour patterns with poor people residing in the shanty towns of the big cities, the RP women promised that they would be with them in good as well as in bad days by participating in the organization of weddings and circumcision ceremonies, as well as visiting the sick and the elderly.[19] In fact, Recep Tayyip Erdoğan personally benefited from women's work when he was running for the position of mayor of Istanbul in 1994; his campaign manager was Sibel Eraslan, a veiled woman and a columnist of an Islamist daily. She was at that time, named by daily newspapers as 'the Welfare Party woman who carried Tayyip to the position of Mayor'. Heper claims that it was Erdoğan, not Erbakan, who had encouraged and made it possible for women to participate more actively in party politics.[20] In fact, studying the women's auxiliaries of the Welfare Party in detail, Yeşim Arat also comes to the conclusion that 'the idea of organizing women within the party and trying to reach other women was most closely associated with Tayyip Erdoğan who was, at the time, head of the Welfare Party's Istanbul organization'.[21]

After the establishment of the AKP, Erdoğan retained his appreciation of women's contribution to his political success. He attributed great significance to their work, and demanded continuation of their support. Concomitantly, for AKP's success in the November 2003 elections, the AKP women decided to reactivate their method and knocked on the doors of neighbourhood women to demand votes. Among others, the head of the AKP women's auxiliaries of Konya, 27-year-old Leyla Betül Küçük, the vice chair of the Women's Auxiliary Head Office, stated on October 2, 2002 that:

> We are going to introduce the AKP to the ladies in Konya. We selected female representatives in most neighbourhoods. We are going to train them as trainers to tell about the missions and deeds of the AKP. The administrative unit of our women's auxiliaries and our candidates for Parliament are going to participate in home meetings.

[19] Gareth Jenkins, 'Muslim Democrats in Turkey?', *Survival*, 45(1) (2003), pp. 45–66.
[20] Metin Heper, 'The Justice and Development Party, Government and the Military in Turkey', *Turkish Studies*, 6(2) (2005), pp. 215–231.
[21] Yeşim Arat, *Political Islam in Turkey and Women's Organizations* (İstanbul: TESEV, 1999), p. 14.

These homes will be determined by our neighbourhood representatives. *The meetings targeting women will generally be held during daytime when husbands are at work.*[22] [emphasis added]

The efficient political work of the AKP women caught the attention of other political parties as well. Nuray Bayat Usta, the head of women's auxiliaries of Iğdır, explained: 'We established women's auxiliaries and empowered them to work regularly. For the first time, in our province, we celebrated the Mother's Day with our women's auxiliaries. In the local elections, our rivals considered our women's auxiliaries as our most important asset and were worried about that'.[23]

Women's auxiliaries of the AKP were officially established on February 19, 2003. They were quickly organized in 81 provinces, 923 sub-provinces and 55% of all small municipalities in Turkey. An outstanding event of the devoted efforts of the AKP women is the Babaeski experience. At a dinner party for celebrating their success and strengthening solidarity among the AKP women, it was underlined that they began their work with three women and within three years their members have reached 600. Their obvious success in organization is considered as the promise of their future accomplishment: as the AKP women from Babaeski said together: 'We shall be the voice and words of all women in politics', and Yusuf Vehbi Tamerol, the head of sub-provincial administration of AKP in Babaeski added 'May God make our two worlds illuminated' (*iki dünyamız da aydınlık olsun*).[24]

Knowing the importance of the local organization and women's great contribution in local governments, Erdoğan initiated some provincial congresses of the women's auxiliaries. In Trabzon, when delivering the opening speech to women's auxiliaries, Erdoğan underlined the temporality of this world and the importance of leaving 'a pleasant voice under the sky' (*gökkubbede hoş bir seda bırakmak*).The pleasant voice is that of *serving the people*. These words of Erdoğan reflect a common play of words often used by Islamists arguing that 'the representatives of *Hak* [God] and the representatives of *Halk* [the people] have converged'.[25] Serving the people amounts to serving God, Erdoğan added that 'the year 2005 will be the year of women in the AKP' in order to stimulate their political activism. The chair of the Trabzon women's auxiliary explained that, 'We deem it our duty to jollify the meal of the poor and caress the head of the orphan'.[26]

One of the most salient activities of the women's auxiliaries is the social assistance to the poor, the elderly, and the handicapped. The intensity of the support increases during Ramadan. In Ankara for instance, the women's auxiliaries visited 20 families a day during Ramadan, approximating 600 families in a month. They shared the same *iftar* (breaking of the fast) meal with the poor people and listened to their problems and promised to help. Similar initiatives were undertaken in Samsun by the women's auxiliaries: poor families and the sick people were visited

---

[22] A news by Osman Başeğmez, October 2, 2002, ntv.com.tr.

[23] *Türkiye Bülteni*, October 2004, no. 17.

[24] *Gazete Trakya*, May 2, 2005.

[25] Cihan Tuğal, 'Islamism in Turkey: Beyond Instrument and Meaning', *Economy and Society*, 31(1) (2002), pp. 85–111.

[26] *Türkiye Bülteni*, February 2005, no. 21.

and in-kind aid was offered. Poor students were supported financially, and 200 of them were given free *iftar* meals. Another exemplary activity was made by the women's auxiliary of Ordu, where the elderly were visited in their retirement homes.[27]

In the Second Congress of Women in Local Government, Erdoğan asked the AKP women to find the poor and needy in the remotest corners of the country, and added that, 'Even the poorest member of this society is proud and does not ask for help'. That is why Erdoğan wanted the women of the AKP to be in ready response to people's needs and to go and find the needy in their homes. Considering the feminization of poverty in Turkey, the efforts of the female party workers become very meaningful and effective indeed. Erdoğan also wanted women to enlighten people on their rights, as the Turkish state supports the needy. As part of the state's direct cash transfer to the poor,[28] Erdoğan mentioned the allowance given to the poor families' children until the age of six, and said that, 'We give this allowance to the mother, in case the father would spend it on cigarettes. This is *our* positive discrimination for women'. Here Erdoğan reiterates the cliché on the poor families: the self-sacrificing mother and the drunk-father. His skipping the word 'drunk' and replacing it with the 'smoker' is quite symptomatic of the Islamic ban on alcohol.[29] Erdoğan's reference to positive discrimination highlights another contested issue. Feminists harshly criticize the AKP government for neglecting widespread gender discrimination in Turkish society. We shall mention these problems in the following part.

All in all, however, Islamist mayors and local governors, in the absence of good state-run welfare policies and with a philanthropic motivation, have launched social assistance programs, including the distribution of free meals, health-centre services, and in-kind aid to the poor. In addition, since the redistribution of the resources from the rich to the poor is important in their belief system, they have encouraged businessmen to provide goods, buildings and money.[30] As Keyder expressed, such engagement requires large numbers of party activists establishing networks, linking with the populace, and the young AKP women have especially been quite active in that.[31] It is significant to note here that although Islamist parties including the AKP have seemed to act, to use Jenny White's phrase, 'as the champion of the poor and disadvantaged', they have no concern over a total eradication of economic inequalities in the society; on the contrary, they have concealed economic inequalities by categorizing all people attached to

---

[27] *Türkiye Bülteni*, November 2005.

[28] The direct cash transfer to the poor was initiated before the AKP government in line with the World Bank policies.

[29] Erdoğan banned alcoholic beverages in the public cafes and restaurants belonging to the municipality of Istanbul when he was the mayor. The same tendency, causing a public debate, becomes dominant in the municipalities governed by the AKP today.

[30] A very recent enlargement of this understanding nationwide has been mentioned by the AKP leadership in their 'food-banking project' for fighting against increasing 'new' poverty in Turkey. Many scholars argue that the AKP has created a new form of machine politics, where the municipalities favor companies owned by their supporters in their contracts. The contractors are required to pay dues and contributions towards the Party who then partly distributes the funds as aid to the poor.

[31] Çağlar Keyder, 'The Turkish Bell Jar', *New Left Review*, 28 (2004).

their movement, regardless of their class and status, as 'Islamist elite', who have superior life-styles only because of practicing certain Islamist cultural rituals.[32]

IV. Organizational Structure of Women's Auxiliaries

The AKP has a centralized structure in its women's auxiliaries. At the top of the hierarchy there is Selma Kavaf, an unveiled schoolteacher, appointed by Erdoğan first, then elected. When we asked our interviewees from the women's auxiliaries why she was appointed by Erdoğan, a woman stated that 'it is Prime Minister's loyalty'. Selma Kavaf is the sister of Sema Ramazanoğlu, a veiled, founding-member of the AKP. She has worked a lot for the success of the AKP since its inception. Although Selma Kavaf was not active at the beginning, she became the deputy candidate from Denizli and could not win the election. She says she has always dealt with politics, but her father did not permit her to be engaged in politics when she was younger. She reflects a more 'systemic' and 'European' face of the AKP: a tall and slim, blonde lady.[33]

Under Selma Kavaf's leadership, there are 12 vice-chairs. Although the AKP leadership insists on their democratic election mechanism in their party organizations, leadership positions are strictly controlled. Some assume that the headscarf is the main criteria in determining the membership of significant administrative and executive boards. When the Mother's Day was celebrated in 2004 at the residence of the Chief of Staff of the Turkish Armed Forces, where the mothers of the martyrs were allowed to don bonnet and scarves, a general opinion appeared in public that 'soldiers are against the turban only'.[34] And when the first bonnet-donned woman, Ayşe Keşir, was chosen as the vice-chair of the women's auxiliaries, this event was linked to the opinion that soldiers are not against the bonnet. In fact, when we asked for an interview from her, Ayşe Keşir curiously asked us the question why she was chosen, instead of other vice-chairs. After we conducted our interview, she confessed that she thought she was chosen because of her bonnet. But our main aim in choosing her is her position: she directs the social charity affairs, in addition, we also asked for others, but she was the first person affirming our request. Apart from Ayşe Keşir, other vice-chairs are as follows: Ülkü Taş, not veiled, of media and promotion affairs; Tuğba Oral, not veiled, of economic affairs; Habibe Yıldız, not veiled, of public relation affairs; Fatma Şahin, not veiled, of political and legal affairs; Leyla Betül Küçük, veiled, of organizational affairs; Meral Kirişçioğlu, not veiled, of election affairs; Sema Özdemir, veiled, of foreign relations; and Nur Özkaya, veiled, of local government affairs.

Because of the headscarf controversy in Turkey, the AKP leadership is more careful in their decisions. For example, they had no veiled candidate for the parliament. However, this does not mean that democratic mechanism intrinsic to the party is precluded by merely external factors. As Selma Kavaf explained, 'in

---

[32] Jenny B. White, *Islamist Mobilization in Turkey: A Study in Vernacular Politics*, (Seattle and London: University of Washington Press, 2002), pp. 233–234. For a critical analysis on changing consumption patterns of Islamist upper middle-class, the Islamist elite proper, please see Mücahit Bilici, 'İslam'ın Bronzlaşan Yüzü: Caprice Hotel Örnek Olayı', in Nilüfer Göle (ed.) *İslamın Yeni Kamusal Yüzleri* (İstanbul: Metis, 1999).

[33] In underlining such qualities of Selma Kavaf, we have in mind the comparison made between 'white Turks' symbolizing the secular elite of the dominant system and the 'black Turks' symbolizing the Islamists as the excluded, stated by M. Hakan Yavuz, 'Cleansing Islam from the Public Sphere', *Journal of International Affairs*, 54(1), (2000). After the AKPs coming to power, however, his arguments required re-evaluation.

[34] *Milliyet Daily* (June 24, 2005).

our provincial and sub-provincial congress, we are trying to nominate a 'single' candidate in order to prevent competitions and disputes among our members'. In addition, when coming to the leadership of the women's auxiliary, she was first appointed and then elected on May 8, 2005, when she was the single candidate for leadership.

All vice chairs have their differentiated work definitions and support staff. The most significant work of the political and legal affairs department is based on the EU harmonization. It watches the domestic as well as the international political developments in line with the EU requirements, it educates the AKP's female members on party politics and general ideology of the AKP, and it cooperates with other women's organizations such as KA-DER.[35]

In a similar vein, the department of foreign relations concentrates on EU affairs, visits various European and other foreign embassies, and spreads information on AKP's gender policies.[36] The department of organizational affairs made possible for the AKP to establish women's organizations in 81 provinces and 933 sub-provinces, and 55% of the small municipalities. The department of election affairs conducted its first activity for the March 28, 2004, municipality elections. It worked with the local organizations and appointed women as the ballot box observers and chief observers.[37] The basic work of the department of promotion and media affairs is to disseminate AKP's missions among women. For this purpose, it prepares booklets and organizes conferences and public speeches.[38] The department of Social Charity Affairs conducts significant work in line with AKP's general policies on social welfare, including the support for needy, elderly, lonely women and students.[39]

The department of local government works for increasing the representation of women in local government, and it encourages women to be candidates for the position of mayor and members of provincial and sub-provincial municipality assemblies.[40] Despite the established division of labour amongst AKP women, their work definition is not strict in practice, and they work in cooperation to increase the AKP's power and effectiveness nationwide.

V. 'Out Of' The Home 'into' Politics?

The political under-representation of women in the parliament as well as in the local governments is obvious. Another obvious fact is that women as voters and party workers have a great potential in shaping politics. The AKP leadership knows well the power of women; the AKP women have disseminated the mission of the party in the remotest corners of the country, and carried the party into power with their tremendous efforts. If so, does the AKP leadership detect a problem in terms of women's participation and representation? Does it have a determination in solving this problem? How does it conceive of the social and political position of women? And more significantly, how does the AKP itself position women? In

---

[35] KA-DER (Kadın Adayları Destekleme Derneği, or, in English, Association of Support for Women Candidates) is an important women organization in Turkey. It was established in 1997 to support, educate and promote women for decision-making positions in politics.

[36] AKP Head Office Women's Auxiliaries Activity Report (2005), p. 5.

[37] Ibid., p. 7.

[38] Ibid., p. 10.

[39] Ibid., p. 11.

[40] Ibid., p. 12.

answering these questions, we observed that, at the organizational level, the AKP strives for a home-based politics, yet at the institutional level, it disqualifies the home-orientation as the ground of politics. In what follows, we shall clarify the contradictory discourses of the AKP in the organization and the institutionalization of politics.

Selma Kavaf comments on the women's auxiliaries' first national congress on May 8, 2005, in these terms, 'This congress will be the political awakening of women .... The women who have set their hearts on the AKP, who have worked for the AKP, will be the potential holders of all positions to be held by elections. Although women and men together shape the world, in politics one side's weight is uneven'.[41]

Erdoğan argues that women are under-represented because, 'They [Turkish women] do not participate in politics; they are shy. We should encourage women to participate in political and social life. Not only in big cities but in all 81 provinces, women should be active', and that 'Turkish women could not grasp the meaning of political participation'.[42]

Erdoğan's vice-chair, Nükhet Hotar, the İzmir deputy, stated, 'It seems that women voluntarily leave politics to men, because their identification with home and mothering becomes more significant than their political identity. Women should deal with politics not only for politicizing their feminine identity, but also as citizens they have to participate in politics in general and the parliamentary politics in particular'.[43] And Selma Kavaf explains that the basic aim of the AKP's women's auxiliaries is 'making women go out from their homes'[44] to participate in politics.

Underlining women's shyness, indifference, motherhood and the home-orientation, the AKP leadership deems it is the personal life of women that precludes their political activity and that causes the feminine under-representation. This understanding is paradoxical. First of all, as a basic political strategy for women the AKP leadership in line with the larger experience of Islamist parties has made the home-setting 'political', and mobilized the women into politics through a seemingly 'apolitical' process.[45] The party women organized informal chats at homes; while participating in wedding, birth and circumcision ceremonies they propagated the party ideology. Thus, the AKP leadership knows well that their success is directly related to their 'home politics'. Why do they see it as an obstacle now? One of the female deputies of the AKP, Fatma Şahin, while emphasizing the difficulty of women in making politics, explained: 'For women, it is hard to compete in the *coffee-houses* at midnight'[46][emphasis added]. If half the population is female, as Erdoğan also highlighted, why is the coffee-house as the male domain privileged over the female domains?

On the other hand, the women of the AKP have done quite well in participating in the public domains without leaving aside their home responsibilities. When we asked them about how they come to Ankara for the Congress on Women in the Local Governments, where there were women from all over the country in our interviewees, all of whom were married with children except one, explained that

[41] www.akparti.org.tr
[42] www.akparti.org.tr
[43] *Türkiye Bülteni*, February 2005, no. 21.
[44] A press meeting held on June 9, 2005.
[45] Arat, *Political Islam in Turkey*, p. 23.
[46] An interview with Fatma Şahin, 'Politics makes women masculine', March 21, 2005, *Aksiyon*, no. 537.

they left their children to their relatives or friends. The unmarried one stated that she had to close her shop to come. In addition, they paid for their own accommodation. Another woman we interviewed at the head office of the women's auxiliaries came to meet us with her two-year-old daughter, and she left her to the secretary when we began our talk. A young pregnant woman working at the head office of the AKP said that at times she works until midnight, but since her husband is a journalist dealing with the AKP politics, her late-coming does not create problems at home.

Obviously, it is not the women's shyness or indifference or the home responsibilities that explain their under-representation in politics. One of the means of overcoming such an under-representation could have been establishing 'gender quotas'. However, this has become an important dispute between the AKP leadership, feminists and the party's auxiliaries as well as the present government.

VI. The Quota Debate

In line of the harmonization with the EU, certain amendments were made in the legal structure of Turkey. Thanks to these amendments in the civil as well as the penal code, various gender discriminations were removed. In 2004, a clause was added to Article 10 of the Turkish constitution, which stipulates that women and men equally enjoy the same rights, and the state is responsible for the implementation of these equal rights in the life of its citizens. The AKP considered these legal amendments, and especially Article 10 of the constitution, as adequate for gender equality in each and every sphere of life including politics. However, the feminist organizations demanded gender quota for removing the long-lasting male domination, especially in politics. They asked for an equal representation of women in the Parliament and Local Governments, especially KA-DER, while organized a campaign entitled 'Gender Quota: From Male Democracy to Real Democracy', to pressurize the AKP government. Feminists in general emphasized that it is not the political indifference of women that leads to their under-representation, but the male domination in politics is the basic obstacle. Feminist groups argued that at least 30% of the female quota is necessary for breaking the male domination in the political decision-making mechanism. The AKP government initially seemed positive for gender quota and then left this understanding and came to the conclusion that the quota is an insult to women. The counter-quota sentiment has spread among male as well as the female deputies of the AKP.

Fatma Şahin, a female deputy of the AKP, stated that 'Women should not demand ready-made positions for them. Instead of concentrating on tea-soup parties and charity, they should learn the internal dynamics of politics'.[47] Instead of quota, she explained that they should resort to political education: 'We are using our Women's auxiliaries as the school of politics'.[48] In our interviews, some AKP women underlined the importance of improving 'political literacy of women'. Nükhet Hotar, the İzmir deputy and vice chair of the AKP, stated similarly, that 'Instead of quota, the women who are educated and qualified should be encouraged for politics'.[49] Nimet Çubukçu, the state minister responsible for women and family, argued that:

[47] Ibid.
[48] Ibid.
[49] *Milliyet daily* (January 5, 2004).

In the EU countries there is no such article as 'women's quota' in the political party laws. Some of the political parties have certain rules in their party regulations. This issue in Turkey must be left to the goodwill of political parties'. The problem cannot be solved by compulsory rules and regulations. This does not mean, however, that I am happy with the number of women in the Parliament'.[50]

Furthermore, she said elsewhere that 'in Rwanda the rate of the women's representation is 54 percent. Can you say that Rwanda is a democratic society?'[51] Dengir Mir Mehmet Fırat, the vice-chair of the AKP, underlined that, 'Quota is an insult to our women; it is belittling them; putting them under protection. Women do not need protection'.[52] Salih Kapusuz added, 'Politics is a matter of love, not of law. Politics has its own rules. If the demands are high enough, then the representation comes'.[53]

Yet women's organizations objected to the gender-blind arguments of the AKP leadership. They underlined the patriarchal structure precluding women's participation and representation. For breaking male domination and creating a genuine democracy, they demanded equal opportunities for women. They worked hard to add a clause concerning positive discrimination for women in the democratization package, which includes the implementation of capital punishment, State Security Courts, and the role of the military in politics. During the discussion of the democratization package in Parliament, feminist groups were there to lobby for gender equality. The government and opposition parties chose the female deputies to maintain the discussion. The women's concerns on the democratization and discrimination were obvious. The opposition party deputies supported the idea of affirmative action. Oya Araslı, in her speech, asked the male deputies: 'Do you not need women outside the home?' As a response, Nimet Çubukçu, the Istanbul deputy of the AKP, in rejecting the necessity of putting a clause on positive discrimination, reminded us that in the proposed package for equality, there exist clauses guaranteeing gender equality, and she wished women to enjoy their rights without being subjected to further discrimination among women themselves; her implication was about the discrimination against veiled women.[54] The only female deputy of the AKP supporting positive discrimination was Serpil Yıldız. She stated that she is not a feminist, but she has connections with women's organizations and NGOs, and that she greatly appreciates their activities.[55]

When we asked about quota to our interviewees, all of them at the outset repeated the same arguments developed by the AKP leadership: 'quota is an insult', 'women do not need quota'. However, when we asked about the difficulties they met in their political lives, they stated that in their local areas they could not break the male domination. One of the women from the AKP's Kırklareli provincial organization stated that, she initiated and empowered the local organization; however, she is leaving politics to the young. She further stated that women have the responsibility but have no authority in the AKP. And she even wanted us to transmit her messages to the leadership of the AKP. All of the women in the municipality assemblies demanded that being a member does not mean

[50] An interview with Nimet Çubukçu, *Radikal daily* (August 14, 2005).
[51] *Kazete Independent Woman's Journal*, September–October 2005, no. 49.
[52] *Milliyet Daily* (January 5, 2004).
[53] Ibid.
[54] *Sabah Daily* (May 5, 2004).
[55] An interview with Serpil Yıldız, *Sabah Daily* (June 12, 2004).

anything, they need to be appointed to the position of vice-mayor; they need to have the authority to act in the name of the institutions. As a protest, one of the women from Bursa asked the women in the conference room if they have the authority to act in the name of their institutions, and only a handful of women from at least 300 women replied affirmatively. One of the women from Maraş explained that: 'The most significant difficulty I met is that we have to ask everything to our seniors. Even the simplest things cannot be done by us alone. Before being a member of the political party, I was much more active in life. I feel quite passive after entering politics'.

When we conducted interviews with the women working at the main office of AKP, some women rejected to be interviewed on the ground that they are actually not interested in politics. Some explained that they principally do not answer political questions; one who has a doctoral degree in engineering and worked as a university assistant professor for a while, explained that she is in the MKYK (Central Decision-Making Council), but she does not have much experience in politics. One of the interviewees explained that although she got a Master's degree in politics, she has no political aspirations, rather she wants to direct her energy to home domain and gardening; she is only considering another degree in landscaping. She explained that perhaps because of her veil, she unconsciously feels handicapped. Another young mother explained that she does not aspire for a political career. She graduated from Open University, and she felt that she is not qualified enough for a political position. When we asked about the main reasons of the under-representation of women, the women in Ankara have a tendency to say that politics has no relation with gender, but women should develop their own political qualities to be part of politics. One of the women explained that women compete with other women, instead of working together harmoniously. That is to say, some of the women explained the female under-representation with female hostility among women.

We observed that AKP leadership demands unconditional devotion from women in the local organizations as well as at the head offices, underlining that there is no 'me' understanding but there is 'we' in the party, and offers very little encouragement to women in politics. Underlining such discouragement is its conservatism revolving around the family friendly policies, blended with religious patriarchy.

Selma Kavaf explains the predicament of women who are divided between politics, work and family life as follows:

> We are women, who want to increase our number in the work life and demand to be in politics. However, we do not want to sacrifice our husbands, children and families for work and politics. That is why, all the members of the family should get their share from the transformation and change in Turkey. We were running a congress in Erzurum, which, as you know is a very conservative eastern province. In the congress hall, women gave speeches and politics was getting harsh (kıran kırana); their husbands outside were looking after their children, feeding them with chocolates. This is when there occurred a positive transformation and change in men's mentality. Men recognized the idea that their wives would be in politics, and that if their wives were in politics, they should ease the burdens of their wives in sharing the burdens of life, child care and house chores.[56]

[56] An interveiw with Selma Kavaf, *Zaman Daily* (October 23, 2005).

The very idea of participating in child-care and house chores annoyed the patriarchal Islamists, among whom Ali Bulaç, one of the most significant Islamists in Turkey, harshly criticized Selma Kavaf, in his column, entitled 'Fathers should look after their children'. Bulaç stated that Western modernity with its Enlightenment ideals had eliminated the thousands of years–age-old world order where customs, religious and moral values had commonly shaped humanity. However, the West abolished all the customs and values apart from its own. Now our 'women' and 'family' are under attack,

> What do we understand from Ms Kavaf's words? This: Woman and man come together and marry. For the survival of humankind they make children. The woman gets pregnant and delivers the baby. According to the genuine convention of humanity, it is the woman who breastfeeds the baby, raises it in her arms, gives the baby love, tender and strength. However, with modernity women are forced to give up their basic duty with such understanding as: women should be in economic, social and political life; women should have an autonomous mind and free body and should be subject, instead of object. In terms of children, Kavaf sees the most significant change in Turkish family structure is that, while women are making politics, their husbands should look after the children, feed them and should change their nappy.[57]

Then, what are the proper roles and duties drawn for women within AKP in particular and the Islamist circle in general? Does Bulaç simply voice his own idiosyncratic understanding on women? Or is it a larger reflection of Islamist patriarchy having a ground in AKP politics as well? Does the AKP leadership sincerely support the political participation of women?

VII. Public Discourse in the Private

The most sensitive issues of patriarchy are manifest in discourses on private life. For this purpose, we shall analyze the 'My Family Turkey' project and the 'adultery debate'. In fact, religious patriarchy shaping the conservative politics of AKP can best be observed in these projects and debates, both of which indicate how women are positioned in the private sphere. In the AKP programme, it is claimed that, 'Not only because women make up half of our population, but also because they are primarily effective for raising healthy generations, they should be considered as individuals before everything else'.

Associating women directly with their maternal function reflects the AKP's conservative politics toward women. Within the religio-conservative world of AKP, women are simply, basically and most crucially mothers. In this connection, the women in the AKP are not confined to the women's auxiliaries. Apart from the female deputies, and a female State Minister responsible for Family and State, the AKP also has an expert and advisor on women and family. For instance, Ayşenur Kurtoğlu, a veiled woman with a PhD in sociology, is a founding member of the AKP. Since July 2003, when she was appointed by Erdoğan as an advisor responsible for the family and women, she has been producing projects on women, family and marriage, while contributing to AKP journal, *Türkiye Bülteni*. As she sidestepped our interview request, we conducted an interview with her assistant, as a first step to reach her. We gave her our questionnaire in advance and her assistants explained that in principle she does not answer all questions in the interviews (she skipped political ones). Considering the predicament women face

[57] Ali Bulaç, 'Fathers Should Look after their Children', *Zaman Daily*, November 14, 2005.

86

in balancing their responsibility in politics and family, Ayşenur Kurtoğlu symbolizes the family side in the AKP politics. Publishing books and articles on etiquette and rules of conduct, she explained to a religious journal,[58] that she was inspired by her elder sisters who went to the Girls' Institute, where they learnt how an ideal woman would arrange her conducts in life. As a matter of fact, Girls' Institutes were established in the early republican period for educating young women in accordance with the republican ideals and Western civilization in daily life.[59] For breaking up Turkish women's ties with traditional life-styles in domestic setting, the republican elite encouraged a scientific and rational home management and counselled young women about modern daily manners including how to look fashionable, how to dance, how to make a smart hat, how to cook a healthy meal, how to entertain guests over the weekend, and so on. What differentiates Ayşenur Kurtoğlu's advice from those of the republican elite as reflected in the Girls' Institutes is that the former is mingled with religious values. For instance, young people are advised on how long they should stay at a home-meeting organized to celebrate 'one's memorizing the Qur'an'.[60]

Ayşenur Kurtoğlu expresses similar themes with Ali Bulaç on the importance of the family and the women's leading role in it. In her projects, she suggests that she wants to 'consolidate the Turkish family structure'. Kurtoğlu stated that,

> Our greatest and not yet spoiled value is our family system. We should be protective to our families. We should mostly protect and greatly care for the family institution … Today, technology, television and internet are threats against the family structure. In the last three or four years the rate of divorce has increased because of economic conditions and the family life has been shaken. Economic crisis has negative influences on the family. We should talk about them. Universities, government, NGOs and local governments should cooperate and do something for solving these problems.[61]

In accordance with her anxieties on the family values, she initiated a project, namely, 'My Family Turkey' and prepared a series of books, including the books on daily life. These guide books aimed to remove the superstitious beliefs on marriage and family life; they are sent to the AKP municipalities and are given as a gift to the marrying couples on the wedding day. The books contain quite detailed advice on different facets of family life including sexual life. For example, advice on the first night of the wedding is as follows:

> The man should psychologically prepare his partner for sexual intercourse. He should encourage and explain the futility of her anxieties. The man should not be in a rush or rude. He should not say that 'we are married now; I can have her as I wish'. Both parties, physically and psychologically, should be ready for sexual intercourse. The man should successfully arouse the feelings of his wife. In these conditions, the woman does not feel pain. Lastly, it is stated, that: 'Your marriage life is the most proper place to live your sexuality'.[62]

[58] *Zaman Daily* (November 17, 2002).
[59] Dilek Cindoğlu and Şule Toktaş, 'Empowerment and Resistance Strategies of Working Women in Turkey: The Case of 1960–1970 Graduates of the Girls' Institutes', *The European Journal of Women's Studies*, 9(1) (2002), pp. 31–48; Elif Ekin Akşit, *Kızların Sessizliği: Kız Enstitülerinin Uzun Tarihi* (İstanbul: İletişim, 2005).
[60] Ayşenur Kurtoğlu, *Günlük Hayatımızda Görgü ve Nezaket* (İstanbul:Timaş, 2002).
[61] *Zaman Daily* (August 21, 2003).
[62] Esma Sarıkaya and Zeynep Yeşim Özcan, *Aile Sağlık Rehberi* (Çankaya Belediyesi: Ankara, 2005). Apart from *Aile Sağlık Rehberi* there are also other books *Aile Hukuk Rehberi, Bir Yastıkta Bir Ömür and Aile Ev Rehberi* are also given to newly married couples.

VIII. The Adultery Debate

Should people be put into prison if they have sex out of wedlock? This is a question that dominated the debates in September 2004. Initiated by the Prime Minister who explained his demand for punishment of adultery, as: 'We should take all precautions to protect the Turkish family'. The adultery debate came as a surprise to many in Turkey as well as to the EU authorities. This also brought to the surface the ongoing debate between the AKP government and women's platforms and feminist groups in Turkey.

Before their annulment by the Constitutional Court, the adultery of husbands and wives were defined, respectively, in Articles 441 and 440 of the Turkish Penal Code, and required unequal punishment discriminating against women in marriage.

The Constitutional Court annulled first Article 441 in 1996 for eliminating discrimination of women in marriage. Thanks to the campaign organized by the women's groups, Article 440 of the Penal Code regulating adultery of wives was also annulled by the same court in 1998.[63] Since then adultery is no longer a crime under the Turkish Penal Code. However, all of a sudden, the AKP leadership attempted to add a clause to the draft Turkish Penal Code, which was being discussed in the Justice Commission of the Parliament. What is more interesting in the debate is that the adultery question is strictly tied to the women's question as Nimet Çubukçu, now the state minister responsible for women and family, stated: 'The disloyal husbands are the most crucial problem for Turkish women'. She even added that, 'if we had a survey on that, you would understand my point'.[64] As a matter of fact, the AKP leadership conducted a public survey on adultery to sound the opinions of the people. According to ANAR's survey[65] conducted in the first week of September 2004 in 12 provinces, it was found that 83% of the people supported an article to be added to the Penal Code for punishing adultery, and that 54.7% of them demand an imprisonment for the adulterous actor. The survey also indicated that although the debate on adultery is widespread in public, many people (52%) have no idea about the debate; among the ones who are familiar with the debate, some have no information on the proposed article by the AKP, and only 37% knew the content of the proposed regulation on adultery. Even the religious groups evaluated the adultery debate created by the AKP leadership as a 'miscalculation' according to the 'mathematics of politics'.[66] Political mathematics requires a rational calculation before introducing a new agenda to society. And the timing in this regard is very crucial.

In spite of the harsh criticism arising from various groups in society, the AKP leadership seemed to be recalcitrant on the adultery question as 'a problem of wives' and the Prime Minister commanded AKP's women's auxiliaries to enlighten people on why adultery was to be criminalized by initiating a campaign. In explaining their activities on the adultery question at the MKYK (Central Decision-Making Council) meeting of the women's auxiliaries, Selma Kavaf's words were interrupted by Erdoğan himself, who stated: 'As the Women's

[63] Feride Acar, 'Country Papers: Turkey' in Marilou McPhedran et al. (eds.), *The First CEDAW Impact Study, Final Report* (Toronto: The Centre for Feminist Research, York University and the International Women's Rights Project, 2000).

[64] An interview with Nimet Çubukçu, *Radikal Daily* (August 14, 2005).

[65] *Yeni Şafak Daily* (September 23, 2004).

[66] Fehmi Koru, 'The Mathematics of the Politics', *Yeni Şafak Daily* (September 21, 2004).

Auxiliaries, you did not do your job well on this matter. Now, you must explain this problem to the people in detail. It is your task to enlighten people'. He added that such criminalization of adultery aims at 'protecting the rights of women who suffer from the infidelity of their husbands'.[67]

Feminist groups were already involved with the discussion of the Turkish Penal Code proposal, which was monitored in the Parliament by seven women's platforms and 80 women's organizations from various regions of Turkey. They had a very strong objection to the criminalization of adultery, but they were not welcomed by the AKP leadership. After the debate on adultery, and during the discussion of the new Penal Code in the Parliament, Erdoğan went to Brussels to convince the EU leaders on the concern of their government on adultery, and then participated in the First Congress of Women in the Local Government-2004 organized by his party in Ankara. In his speech, Erdoğan reflected his reaction against the TCK Platform (Turkish Penal Code Platform) and other feminist groups watching the debates on the new Penal Code, as follows:

> I see certain handbills held by some vociferous women [against the punishment on adultery]. In the name of democracy, some women hold certain handbills which are not harmonious with our traditions and our moral values, I feel sad for Turkish women. I cannot applaud the words that cannot fit to our moral norms, because Turkish women are powerful with these norms. There is no such understanding that a certain marginal group [feminists], would assume to represent Turkish women's strength. In Turkey, 52 percent of the population are women, among them there are the women who have set their hearts on the AKP.[68]

Clearly, AKP women in particular and the Turkish women in general (but not the feminist women), occupy a special position within the religio-conservative discourse of the AKP. This special position reflects a moral and cultural essence attached to the women, who resist the hegemony of Western culture, which balances the material adoption of Western civilization and which keeps the purity of the tradition.

Similar themes attached to the women can be witnessed in the words of certain Islamists. Among others, Davut Dursun stated, that 'I could not understand those women who criticize the punishment on adultery. Men's objection can be figured out. But why do women object to it? It is really hard to comprehend it. Adultery is a moral question, not a concern of human rights and freedom'.[69] Ahmet Taşgetiren elsewhere explained that the demand for punishing adultery reflects 'our moral difference' from the EU, and added that:

> I went to Europe and saw that they have no family life. There is sexual promiscuity. Marriage as an institution does not function. The population does not increase...Promiscuity and sexual liberation is not something to be accepted by Turkish society.[70]

Sami Uslu[71] resorted to a joke, which he suggests is based upon realities of the West: 'Western family includes three parties, wife, husband and the wife's lover'. Another columnist from Zaman explained that the adultery concern of the AKP

[67] *Sabah Daily* (September 10, 2004).
[68] *Radikal Daily* (September 25, 2004), 'Erdoğan'ı Zina Pankartı Üzdü' (The Adultery Banner Saddened Erdoğan).
[69] Davut Dursun, 'Adultery is a Moral Question', *Yeni Şafak Daily* (September 23, 2004).
[70] An interveiw with Ahmet Taşgetiren, *Radikal Daily* (September 13, 2004).
[71] Sami Uslu, 'Is It Too Unjust to Punish Adultery?', *Zaman Daily* (September 22, 2004).

should not be an obstacle for EU integration, as the AKP's reaction is a typical reaction of a conservative party; it has no connection with its Islamist root. He further explained that the demand for the punishment on adultery came from a woman who is not an Islamist, and such demand was supported by a signature campaign. Thus, the AKP's attempt for punishing adultery is a response to a democratic demand, rather than bringing Islam into legal affairs.[72] Others supported Alpay's idea that adultery has no connection with Islam on the ground that in Islam the punishment for adultery is totally different from what the AKP government proposed.

When we asked our interviewees whether they support the punishment for adultery, most of them reacted affirmatively. However, some argued that God will punish us for our faults; there is no reason to bring punishment in the name of God in this world. None of them accepted that their main problem is their wandering husbands. They did not question the permission for polygamy in the Qur'an; however, they explained that polygamy is not an option in their own marriages. One of them explained, off record, that in the Qur'an, adultery is mentioned only once, while social charity is recommended many times.

IX. Conclusion

Analyzing the discourses and characteristics of the women organized in the AKP, we came to the conclusion that women are important interlocutors of the Islamist populism as it is expressed by the AKP. Islamist populism in Turkey depends on its double-sided criticism of material as well as cultural and/or civilizational aspect of modernity, and on successful articulation of the conflicting demands of people in economic and moral terms in their daily lives. While certain scholars tend to evaluate this populism as an anti-systemic movement or as counter-hegemonic politics, we observe a more systemic populist tendency in the politics of the AKP as being the government party. This is not to suggest, however, that we evaluate the AKP as 'only' a centre-right party; on the contrary, in spite of its repetitive rejection of the label Islamism and some other scholars' emphasis on the AKP's docility in the sense that 'it separates Islam from politics', we suggest that the AKP has been a party that often resorts to using Islamic motives in its discourses. However, it is important to note, that the AKP as a legal party constitutes only one of the matrices of Islamism in Turkey; amongst others, there are Islamic capital, religious communities and radical Islamist organizations.[73] These different groups share some common traits, while they may also vary significantly in their ideologies and practices.

Unlike the women in the National Outlook tradition,[74] the women in the AKP are politically more assertive. While the AKP demands an unconditional devotion from the women as the previous Islamic parties did, now the women expect more politically. This is partly because of AKP's position such as being a single-party government, and having the support of various segments of society as well as the external forces such as the EU countries and the US. In addition, the political

---

[72] Şahin Alpay, 'On Sexual and Political Disloyalty', *Zaman Daily* (September 18, 2004).

[73] For a more detailed analysis on Turkish Islam, please see CihanTuğal, 'Islamism in Turkey: Beyond Instrument and Meaning', *Economy and Society*, 31(1) (2002), pp. 85–111.

[74] 'National Outlook' (Milli Görüş) understanding was developed by the National Salvation Party (Milli Selamet Partisi, MSP) of Erbakan in the 1970s and it aimed at differentiating Islamist party from other systemic parties which were all positioned as Westernist.

discourse of the AKP in seeking legitimacy underlines democratization, equality and human rights. Accordingly, women consider that they are entitled to use their democratic rights in the political sphere. On the other hand, a significant proportion of women in AKP do not come from an Islamist tradition; instead, most of these unveiled women have been invited to the AKP by its leadership. These women are educated, strong, and are conscious of their qualifications for holding political offices. However, the AKP leadership incessantly emphasizes the political 'ignorance' of women and directs them to a harsh competition with men; it also creates a competition between the veiled and unveiled women, between the women who have set their hearts into the AKP and the Islamist tradition for a long time and the new women who come to an already strong government party. Underlining the attitude of the AKP leadership towards women is religious patriarchy, which also explains AKP's family and mothering-oriented emphasis and adultery concern. In terms of the 'meaning' dimension of the Islamist populism, AKP leadership places women at the heart of the culture, which is deemed essentially different from European civilization. Thus, it invites women to return to the family nest, instead of seeking political status and power in the public sphere.

Arising in the 1980s, two separate political movements, feminism and Islamism initially expressed more anti-systemic characteristics of the politico-social movements. In twenty years, however, both of them have turned out to be more 'systemic' political movements.[75] In the 1980s, Turkish feminists showed significant diversities amongst themselves. This was reflected in their relationship with the state and their criticism of patriarchy in society. Moreover, there has been shifting alliances through time, not only amongst themselves, but also with the different sections of the state and society. Some have retained their anti-systemic characteristics, such as the Islamic feminists, initiating street protests, campus sit-ins, publishing alternative journals and delivering them especially among the university youth, organizing various campaigns in order to enlarge the strictly controlled public sphere to alternative voices, emphasizing respectively 'women', and 'Muslims' as the 'other' of the existing political system.

Within Turkish feminism there have been those who have been very critical of Islam, but also have been able to distance themselves from the state and its perception of women. They have initiated proposals to change the legal structure and demanded a more egalitarian public order. Within these groups, there have been lobbyists that resorted to conventional means, but also radicals that propagated through non-conventional forms of action. Turkish feminism, since the 1980s has clustered its relationship to politics as well, even though a common denominator for all feminist groups was the problem of integrating women into politics and increasing female representation. There has never been any attempt at creating a feminist party with a full-fledged program.

Islamists, on the contrary, have always retained their claims of political domination. Islam having strong roots in society has had an all-encompassing claim in the politics and economy. The compatibility of these claims with western democracy has been a controversial issue that has been discussed by all groups

---

[75] For a more detailed analysis on systemic, anti-systemic and radical characteristics of Islamist and feminist movements in Turkey, please see Sefa Şimşek, 'New Social Movements in Turkey Since 1980', *Turkish Studies*, 5(2) (2004) and Gül Aldıkaçtı Marshall, 'Ideology, Progress and Dialogue: A Comparison of Feminist and Islamist Women's Approaches to the Issues of Headcovering and Work in Turkey', *Gender and Society*, 19(1) (2005).

from Muslim theologians to politicians from Western societies. The Justice and Development Party, the AKP, has had a very clear stance in this issue. They have discharged the questions all together by arguing that they would not allow for a doctrinaire discussion of the problem. So the party has deliberately avoided issues of Islam in democracy (e.g. that of Shar'ia) or in economy (such as bank-interest).

However, when faced with challenges in gender issues, the AKP government and its leadership did not refrain from Islamic references; on the contrary, they argued for Muslim consent and solutions. For example, when the European Human Rights Court's decision was to approve Turkey's ban on the headscarf, the prime minister argued that the decision was void, because the Muslim theologians were not consulted. In short, the gender issue has been the 'Muslim face' of the AKP.

It is through the gender issue that the AKP leadership has tried to overcome the difficulty of articulating the Westernist and the Islamist discourse. In this context, the AKP government 'has found itself in a quandary of contradictions'[76] between Western human rights norms, Islamic community pressures, European Union ideals, secularization, demands from their own members and feminists, as well as between the republican establishment and their own ideological supporters and roots. It has reiterated the common motto of the non-Western countries vis-à-vis modernity: 'Let us take the techniques of the West, but keep our own culture and civilization'. This understanding has provided the AKP with a selective adaptation of the Western procedures, legal and constitutional requirements as the technique of the West. This explains the success of the AKP in pursuing the EU ideal of Turkey. However, whenever the procedural and legal requirements are extended to the gender issue, the AKP resorts to the arguments lying at the core of the Islamist patriarchy. In the name of preserving culture, the AKP positions the women as the cultural essence. It attaches all cultural differences, moral values and religious sentiments to the women, and their 'uncontested status in the private realm'. This also explains why it frequently has entered into harsh debates with feminist groups.

The AKP increased the visibility of conservative and Islamist women in politics. However, this was almost an introduction to politics through the headscarf debate and as an auxiliary for vote mobilization. We see that the women in the AKP have had very little impact on increasing representation, or changing the rhetoric and programme, as well as not being close to power positions in the organizational structure.

---

[76] Nüket Kardam, *Turkey's Engagement with Global Women's Human Rights* (Ashgate: Aldershot, 2005).

Women and Media in Saudi Arabia: Rhetoric, Reductionism and Realities

NAOMI SAKR

ABSTRACT *Contradictions inherent in restrictions on women in Saudi Arabia have been shown to create space for renegotiation of women's personal and political status in the kingdom. The Saudi media offer a window onto this renegotiation process, not because there is any automatic correlation between women's visibility in the media and their status in other areas of public life, but because analysis of media institutions can shed light on the contingent and historically specific nature of legal and social constraints on women. This paper, by examining multiple developments in women-media interaction during the period 2004–06, uncovers an uneven picture, whereby heightened visibility for women in the media was accompanied by rather little change in promotion of female media professionals to decision-making positions. Nevertheless, modest breakthroughs occurred due in part to initiatives driven by the domestic and foreign policy interests of influential elements in the Saudi ruling establishment. Beside these was a parallel process of renegotiation for the status of all citizens, male and female, vis-à-vis government and the state.*

I. Introduction

Saudi Arabian public discourse about women's status is puzzling. On one hand official statements are replete with rigid essentialist rhetoric about 'women's nature' and limitations on what women may do and where they may go. On the other, government policies have produced significant change in women's education, employment and legal standing in recent years. Professions and university courses that were once barred to women have been opened up; women have been authorized to apply for identity cards without a male guardian's consent; in 2005 they were promised the vote in municipal elections in 2009. Do these measures signify that constructions of womanhood prevailing in Saudi Arabian society are being revised in response to the exigencies of an economy in which women's material assets, purchasing power and earning potential carry increased weight? Do they mean that interpretations of Islam promulgated by the kingdom's unbending religious establishment are being gradually modified or set aside?

II. Renegotiation as a Process: Spaces and Constraints

Several scholars who have probed these questions have concluded that contradictions inherent in strict ideas about acceptable behaviour for women in Saudi Arabia create space, albeit limited, for renegotiation. Soraya Altorki found that 'ambiguities and contradictions' within 'key concepts of the belief system' make it possible for members of the Saudi elite to modify 'patterns of meaning featured in the established ideology'.[1] Mai Yamani found that her young respondents experienced a 'clash between a national, rigorous socialization and the uncertainties and promises stemming from wider access to different cultural influences'. While young Saudis saw Islam as the 'stable and unchallenged base of their identity', the majority revealed 'discomfort' with a rigid conception of gender roles and were searching for a compromise between their personal expectations and the demands of family and society.[2] Eleanor Doumato noted a 'certain hypocrisy' built into the sex segregation system. She concluded that women in the new industrial, landed and merchant elites were taking initiatives behind a façade of discretion, whereby the pretence was maintained that strict rules on segregation were being fully observed.[3] Michaela Prokop pointed out that renegotiation had also taken place between different wings of the establishment over girls' education.[4] A public outcry that followed the death of 15 girls in a Makkah school fire, in 2002, blamed the religious police for obstructing evacuation and resulted in responsibility for girls' education being transferred from the *Ulema* (clergy) to the Ministry of Education. The loss of life in the fire called into question the bargain whereby princes of the Al-Saud legitimize their hold on government by ceding control over many aspects of daily life to the religious authorities.

The present paper examines the process of renegotiating women's personal and political status in the kingdom as it has been played out in recent years in the Saudi media. It is tempting to regard media representations of women and the hiring of women for media jobs as indicators of shifting public attitudes towards gender roles, especially in the Saudi context, where women's visibility in the media began to increase very noticeably in 2004. This temptation undoubtedly explains high levels of Western press interest in such outward aspects of Saudi public life. However, although a quantitative increase in women's media presence in the kingdom is not in doubt, the factors contributing to it and the precise forms it took merit closer scrutiny. One reason is that research on other Arab countries demonstrates that there is no automatic correlation between women's visibility in Arab media and their status in other areas of public life.[5] In Egypt, for example, the large number of female managers and presenters in television reveals little about where in the television hierarchy editorial decisions are actually taken. It also contrasted sharply for many years with vanishingly few seats for women in parliament or on the judiciary. Developments in Qatar, meanwhile, demonstrate

[1] Soraya Altorki, *Women in Saudi Arabia: Ideology and Behavior Among the Elite* (New York: Columbia University Press, 1986), pp. 150–151.

[2] Mai Yamani, *Changed Identities: The Challenge of the New Generation in Saudi Arabia* (London: Royal Institute of International Affairs, 2000), pp. 133–134.

[3] Eleanor Abdella Doumato, 'Education in Saudi Arabia: gender, jobs and religion', in E. Doumato and M. Pripstein Posusney (eds.), *Women and Globalization in the Arab Middle East: Gender, Economy and Society* (Boulder, CO: Lynne Rienner Publishers, 2003), p. 253.

[4] Michaela Prokop, 'The War of Ideas: education in Saudi Arabia', in P. Aarts and G. Nonneman (eds.), *Saudi Arabia in the Balance* (London: Hurst & Company, 2005), pp. 63–64.

[5] Naomi Sakr, *Arab Television Today* (London: I.B. Tauris, 2007), p. 105.

that social norms may militate against the brandishing of women's personal identities without preventing them from being appointed or elected to public office.[6] A second reason for peering behind the presence or absence of women in media output has to do with assumptions often made about the social impact of so-called 'positive' or 'negative' representations of women in film, on television or in the press. Commentators on media everywhere, including Arab countries, often deplore or commend certain depictions of women in terms of their alignment with strategies for national development or women's advancement. Such assumptions, which one scholar has termed the 'role-model' approach,[7] have more influence than they deserve. Media research shows that meanings cannot be fixed: the meanings that audiences derive from a media text may well be at odds with those intended by the originator of the text or those inferred by commentators. This undermines the notion that images can be self-evidently either positive or negative. As Amanda Lotz has shown in relation to women's media activism in the US, for anyone wanting to 'intervene in a dominant meaning system', the task is not to try to fix meanings but the reverse: to foster a multiplicity of images such that stereotypes become altogether 'uninhabitable' and the practice of media 'representation' is revealed for what it is.[8]

In other words, practices and processes behind media portrayals are not only as important as the portrayals themselves, but possibly even more so. On that basis the aim here is to explore institutional structures and the production of texts in order to try to understand the processes that underlie apparent changes in Saudi women's presence in local media, rather than to try to evaluate outcomes. The idea is not simply to see whether women were incorporated, or 'added in', to 'constructions that are *constituted* as masculine',[9] but to gain some insight into whether the constructions themselves were in any way transformed. In this sense, 'gender' is not mere shorthand for social constructions of 'man' or 'woman' but a conceptual invitation to grasp how thinking, knowledge and values are shaped, how 'knowledge claims are legitimated', and hence how culture and materiality are mutually produced or co-constituted.[10] For, while knowledge claims in the context of Saudi Arabia or anywhere else may be legitimated through ahistorical references to religion or tradition, this does not mean the claims themselves cannot be inserted into history. On the contrary, an historical perspective would note, for example, that the Iranian leader Ayatollah Khomeini took diametrically opposite positions on women's political rights before and after the Iranian revolution, from declaring voting rights for women to be against Islam in 1962 to declaring in 1979 that women have a duty in Islam to intervene in politics.[11] Hanna Papanek has shown that groups who are doubtful about their cohesion, but who want to present a united front to others, are inclined to exert heightened pressures for conformity on group members with the least power. Many societies undergoing periods of rapid change make women the 'carriers of tradition' or 'centre of the family'.

---

[6] Ibid., pp. 89–94.

[7] Amanda Lotz, *Redesigning Women: Television after the Network Era* (Urbana, IL: University of Illinois Press, 2006), pp. 11–17.

[8] Ibid., p 17.

[9] V. Spike Peterson, 'How (the Meaning of) Gender Matters in Political Economy', in A. Payne (ed.), *Key Debates in New Political Economy* (London: Routledge, 2006), p. 82, emphasis in original.

[10] Ibid., and p. 86.

[11] Azadeh Kian, 'Women and Politics in Post-Islamist Iran: the gender conscious drive to change', *British Journal of Middle Eastern Studies*, 24(1, May) (1997), p. 76.

These identifications, being 'selective reincarnations of particular visions of the past', are usually called 'traditions'. In fact, Papanek writes, 'they are no such thing'. Instead, they 'embody the hopes for future power and domination by those who manufacture them against the perceived threats of a pluralistic world that requires accommodation and compromise'.[12]

By recognizing the work of manufacture that is invested in so-called traditions it becomes possible to step aside from reductive value judgments about women and religion or women and democracy. Indeed, it becomes possible to see that any such judgments, irrespective of whether they are supposedly liberal or illiberal, are themselves deployed to 'serve the interests of different sources of power'.[13] A dialectical approach, as advocated by Shahrzad Mojab, considers religious claims and counter-claims 'in the context in which they are expressed' since all such claims 'express contemporary interests in this world'.[14] Thus the opposing notions of 'pure religion' and 'wrong Islam', which Arab ruling elites commonly use to de-legitimize Islamist political trends, are not useful in their own right to an exercise of scientific analysis, since religion has always been practiced in a 'social and historical context that influences the understanding of the religious message'.[15] The particular historical context of Saudi Arabia is one that has given its people reason to differ over whether it is a civil or a theocratic state, but has also ensured that their differences can only be discussed by reference to interpretations of Islam. When asked about the Saudi government's commitment to reform in 2004, a senior prince who is often credited with liberal views conceded that 'the Islamists hold a "card"', because the kingdom, despite being a civil state, was founded on the basis of Islamic canon law.[16] As Madawi al-Rasheed puts it, the 'official legitimation formula' of the Al-Saud is a 'double-edged sword'. 'To use Islam to legitimize a political system is to invite opposition groups to debate the degree to which Islam has been incorporated in politics'.[17]

As for correspondences sometimes drawn between examples of women's empowerment and efforts at democratization, here again it may be a question of who is making the connection and why. That point is made by authors of the 2005 edition of the *Arab Human Development Report*, which is subtitled 'Towards the Rise of Women in the Arab World'. They take a dim view of cosmetic measures on women's political rights that have been adopted in some Arab countries as a 'type of democratic façade', whereby women become an 'easily manipulated symbol for countries that wanted to escape political criticism of their undemocratic conditions'.[18] Hence, for example, governments appointing women as ambassadors may be more interested in avoiding democratization than in pursuing it. But the *Arab Human Development Report* itself demonstrates how constructions of

---

[12] Hanna Papanek, 'The Ideal Woman and the Ideal Society: control and autonomy in the construction of identity', in V. Moghadam (ed.), *Identity Politics and Women: Cultural Reassertions and Feminisms in International Perspective* (Boulder, CO: Westview Press, 1994), pp. 45–47, 70.
[13] Shahrzad Mojab, 'Gender, Political Islam and Imperialism', in C. Mooers (ed.), *The New Imperialists: Ideologies of Empire* (Oxford: Oneworld, 2006), p. 79.
[14] Ibid., p. 73.
[15] Marc Lavergne, 'The 2003 Arab Human Development Report: A Critical Approach', *Arab Studies Quarterly*, 26(2, Spring) (2004), p. 30.
[16] Prince Talal bin Abdel-Aziz al-Saud, interviewed by Ahmad Adnan for *elaph.com*, August 17–18, 2004.
[17] Madawi al-Rasheed, 'God, the King and the Nation: political rhetoric in Saudi Arabia in the 1990s', *Middle East Journal*, 50(3, Summer) (1996), p. 371.
[18] United Nations Development Programme (UNDP), *Arab Human Development Report 2005*, New York: UNDP Regional Bureau for Arab States, p. 22.

gender roles can short-circuit discussion about women as citizens. Among the forewords to the 2005 edition is one by Prince Talal bin Abdel-Aziz, brother of the king of Saudi Arabia, president of the Arab Gulf Programme for United Nations Development Organizations (Agfund) and a self-professed supporter of internal reform and codification of laws that can enable Saudi Arabia to 'develop itself into a modern state'.[19] In the foreword, he appears to deny women any persona other than that of family member. 'We have always believed', he states, 'that Arab women (as mothers, sisters, wives, daughters) are not less, in any way, than women in societies that have preceded us on the ladder of development'.[20]

The remainder of this paper probes women-media interactions in Saudi Arabia as potential instances of renegotiation of the social and political order, bearing in mind that insights may emerge if these interactions are studied with a sense of historical perspective that is alert to the manufacture of tradition and tries to discover who takes the lead in constructing and legitimizing 'knowledge' and ideas. The category 'Saudi media', discussed in relation to women's representation, raises questions of its own about ownership, control and areas of overlap between media institutions and government. In situations where political parties are banned and political interests are denied means of formal organisation, media institutions take on particular importance in the negotiation of change. It has been suggested that initiatives such as the formation of a Saudi Journalists Association and a National Human Rights Association, both of which have implications for the way Saudi media representation of women is negotiated, indicate that the 'regime has essentially embarked upon a modernization of Saudi authoritarianism by attempting to institutionalize important aspects of the political debate'.[21] The possibility of a modernized authoritarianism draws attention to media ownership structures, and to the question of whether or not these remain the 'very same power structures that excluded women for so long'.[22]

Since a study of this kind calls for examination of processes involved in news production, in building media institutions and in employing media personnel, the present paper is forced to adopt some selection criteria to limit the quantity of data for reasons of space. Hence, all examples discussed relate to a specific three-year period in the very recent past, but with some historical comparisons where relevant. The recent period begins at the start of 2004, with the launch of *Al-Ekhbariya*, a 24-hour news channel complete with female newsreaders and presenters, set up as part of Saudi state-owned television. It ends in late 2006. By this time, a popular Saudi TV entertainment programme had broken new ground by satirizing sex segregation and the *mutawa'īn* (religious police), and a woman had been appointed as editor-in-chief of *Rotana* magazine, published by the Rotana Audio and Video Company in Riyadh. Landmark events taking place in Saudi Arabian national politics during these three years included municipal elections, sessions of the National Dialogue, and the accession of a new king in 2005.

[19] See the interview published in *elaph.com*, referred to in note 16.
[20] UNDP, *Arab Human Development Report* 2005, p. viii.
[21] Steffen Hertog, 'The new corporatism in Saudi Arabia: limits of formal politics', in A. Khalaf and G. Luciani (eds.), *Constitutional Reform and Political Participation in the Gulf* (Dubai: Gulf Research Centre, 2006), pp. 241–242.
[22] Naomi Sakr, 'Women-media interaction in the Middle East: an introductory overview', in N. Sakr (ed.), *Women and Media in the Middle East: Power through Self-Expression* (London: I.B. Tauris, 2004), p. 3.

III. Media Transformations: Encouraging or Enabling?

It was half way through 2006, towards the latter part of the period under review, that Sultan al-Qahtani, writing for the Saudi-owned website *Elaph*, declared that the Saudi media had undergone a 'remarkable' and 'unprecedented' transformation over the past two years. The peg for his story was an announcement in the daily *Al-Riyadh*, to the effect that Al-Yamama Press Company had appointed five women to senior positions. Qahtani said women were now appearing daily on the front pages of all eight official newspapers, which had previously been 'monopolized' by men. Official television channels, which had once 'minimized' the presence of women in newscasts and other programmes had now, according to Qahtani, turned into 'advocates' for an *iqtihām* (invasion) of the media by Saudi women.[23] While not everyone would have used Qahtani's militaristic terminology to describe this phenomenon, most people in Saudi Arabia concurred with his observation that Saudi women's faces could now be widely seen in public, where only a short time ago they were barely seen at all.

If the sudden upsurge in women's visibility, both as producers and subjects of Saudi news, had itself become a news story by 2006, it was at least partly because of its apparent incompatibility with officially sanctioned norms of sex segregation and restrictions on women's travel. Disseminating pictures of women's faces, in broadcast or print, directly contradicts the very taboo on images of women that was invoked by opponents of women having their own individual ID. A woman working as a journalist can hardly do her job without travelling independently or speaking to unrelated men. Here, then, was what appeared to be a challenge to those members of the Saudi religious establishment for whom 'Islamic teaching' meant that there is something called 'women's nature', which strictly limits what they are allowed to do. The former Grand Mufti, Sheikh Abdel-Aziz ibn Baz, once warned that 'removing a woman from her home, which is her kingdom, means removing her from what her natural state and her character require'.[24] Abdel-Aziz ibn Baz died in 1999 but similar references to 'women's nature' persist in official policies on media and education. If a woman works outside the home, 'Islamic teaching' is said to require that she should only undertake activities that are 'compatible with her nature'[25] and avoid mixing with men. Officially, all Saudi media are directly instructed to observe these norms. The Media Charter adopted by the Council of Ministers in 1982, which remained in force in 2006 even though the media licensing and regulation system was changed in 2001, calls on editors and journalists to observe 'the nature of women and the role she is called to play in society without that role conflicting with such nature'.[26]

For many Saudis, the logical response to increasingly obvious contradictions between media realities and strictures on women was to point out that, set against the backdrop of Saudi Arabian culture and history, the strictures were actually relatively new. Qahtani's article in *Elaph* did this in a muted way. He wrote of a significant change in a 'methodology' that had been used for 'over a quarter of a century', implying that anyone who looked back more than 25 years

[23] Sultan al-Qahtani, 'Saudi Women invade News Broadcasts and Newspaper Headlines' [in Arabic], *elaph.com* June 27, 2006.
[24] Quoted in Eleanor Doumato, 'Women and Work in Saudi Arabia: How Flexible are Islamic Margins?' *Middle East Journal* 53 (4, Autumn) (1999), p. 578.
[25] Saudi Ministry of Education document quoted in Prokop, 'The war of ideas', p. 63.
[26] Semi-official translation kindly supplied to the author by staff at *Saudi Gazette*.

would find a different 'methodology' in force. In fact, anyone caring to look back would find that 1979 had been a watershed year for the Saudi government's approach to media and women. That was the year when Juhayman ibn Mohammed al-Otaibi led a siege of the mosque in Makkah during the annual pilgrimage, in protest at what he and his followers described as the 'religious and moral laxity and degeneration' of Saudi rulers.[27] As a political protest couched in religious terms, the siege prompted the government to shore up its religious credentials. Saudi Arabian women with experience of working in the media before and after the siege regard it as having triggered the 'first wave of anti-woman activity',[28] something they attribute in particular to the religious police, the Committee to Protect Virtue and Prevent Vice, or *hai'a* as it is known for short. Other sources testify that, after the Makkah siege, Saudi women were banned from television altogether for a short time, after which written rules for Saudi television continued to include a ban on women appearing on screen during the month of Ramadan.[29]

Before the siege, in contrast, women's media presence had been established for many years. Their writing was to be found in the printed press since the 1950s[30] and their work in broadcasting grew in the 1960s in parallel with expansion of local Saudi broadcast media, which was driven in that decade by electrification and efforts to confront anti-monarchist media messages emanating from Nasser's Egypt. Where the broadcast media were concerned, compromises were negotiated between King Faisal, who ruled from 1962 to 1975, and members and supporters of the religious police. When a deputation of religious leaders and lawyers had protested to Faisal about a woman's voice being heard on Radio Makkah for the first time in 1963, his answer was that the Prophet Mohammed had enjoyed hearing the voice of the poetess Al-Khansā'.[31] Television was introduced in 1965, in the face of violent opposition by a small group of extremists, after which women and girls were involved in television plays and children's programmes. One account tells of a decline in women' television appearances after 1968,[32] but they continued working in radio. The kingdom's press in the 1970s is said to have been 'replete with articles arguing the pros and cons of an enlarged role for women' in social and economic life.[33] When Dalal Aziz Dia started her career with Saudi radio in 1980 she followed in the footsteps of her mother and her mother's female colleagues who had worked there in the 1960s.[34] Educational opportunities for girls inside Saudi Arabia developed in tandem with the media. Dar al-Hanan, opened and initially financed by King Faisal's wife Iffat bint Ahmad al-Thunayan, grew from a girls' elementary to a secondary school and

[27] Madawi al-Rasheed, *A History of Saudi Arabia* (Cambridge: Cambridge University Press, 2002), p. 144.

[28] Author's interview with Nawal Bakhsh, a director of programmes at Riyadh Radio, Amman, September 19, 2006.

[29] Douglas Boyd, *Broadcasting in the Arab World: A Survey of the Electronic Media in the Middle East* (Ames, IA: Iowa State University Press, 1999), pp. 163–165.

[30] Saddeka Arebi, *Women and Words in Saudi Arabia: The Politics of Literary Discourse* (New York: Columbia University Press, 1994), pp. 30–35.

[31] David Holden and Richard Johns, *The House of Saud* (Sidgwick and Jackson, London, 1981), p. 261.

[32] William A. Rugh, 'Saudi Mass Media and Society in the Faisal Era', in W. A. Beling (ed.), *King Faisal and the Modernisation of Saudi Arabia* (London: Croom Helm, 1980), p. 140.

[33] Catherine Parssinen, 'The changing role of women', in W. A. Beling (ed.), *King Faisal and the Modernisation of Saudi Arabia* (London: Croom Helm, 1980), p. 166.

[34] Mona Almunajjed, *Saudi Women Speak* (Beirut: Arab Institute for Research and Publishing, 2006), pp. 119–122.

graduated its first female secondary school students in 1965. These graduates went on to join teaching training colleges and the University of Riyadh.

Today's professionals are often aware that previous generations of women in the kingdom were subject to fewer restrictions than are in force today. When an episode of the popular Saudi TV series *Tash ma Tash*[35] satirized strict sex segregation in October 2006, in an episode entitled *Sour al-Harīm* (Women's Fence), Maha al-Hujailan, a medical researcher at King Khaled University Hospital, wrote a newspaper column about issues raised in the show. In it she referred to 'earlier times – when our grandparents were young' and 'there was no such rigid separation between men and women'.[36] Abeer Mishkhas, a journalist with *Asharq al-Awsat*, recalls open-air film screenings run by the state company Petromin in the 1970s, where segregation was not enforced.[37] Mixing of the sexes and cinema were both subsequently banned. It seems, therefore, that the same kinds of accommodation between different attitudes and interest groups that led to the bans may also play a part in efforts aimed at relaxing them. Local explanations vary as to where the leverage for relaxation has come from. Most, including Qahtani in the *Elaph* article mentioned above, highlight the role of King Abdullah, whose reputation as a supporter of moderate domestic political and social reform was earned before he acceded to the throne in August 2005. The urgency of reform became irrefutable after the 9/11 hijackings in the US in 2001 and two suicide bombings in Riyadh in 2003 put the inner workings of the Saudi Arabian state in the international spotlight.[38] But initial measures predated these events by some years, spurred in part by negotiations for membership of the World Trade Organisation (WTO) and the economic liberalization this implied. Regarding women's status, the Saudi government had signed the UN Convention Against all forms of Discrimination Against Women (CEDAW), albeit with multiple reservations, in 2000. June 2003 saw the first exploratory session of the government-sponsored National Dialogue, a small gathering of representatives from different sections of Saudi society, which subsequently convened twice yearly to debate pressing national concerns. October 2003 saw the government announce its intention to hold municipal elections within a year, as the country's first elections for any tier of government.

As to the precise link between these reform initiatives and a breakthrough in press coverage of conflict over women's status, the link was clearly drawn by Abeer Mishkhas in an article published in April 2004. She wrote that, 'ever since January', when the government announced that the third session of the National Dialogue would discuss domestic policies affecting women,

> ... newspapers have been warming up for the event by giving unprecedented coverage to the clash of conservative and liberal views over whether women should play a larger role in society and politics. In the process, issues from which editors usually avert their eyes – whether women should vote, work where they please, drive and play sports – have finally

[35] Meaning roughly 'What comes, comes'. For alternative translations see John Bradley, *Saudi Arabia Exposed: Inside a Kingdom in Crisis* (New York: Palgrave Macmillan, 2005), p. 7, or Pascal Ménoret, 'Saudi TV's dangerous hit', *Le monde diplomatique*, September 2004, p. 13.
[36] Maha al-Hujailan, 'Nurturing a climate of social criticism', *Arab News*, October 20, 2006.
[37] Personal communication to the author. London: August 23, 2007.
[38] The first, in May, killed 35 people, including nine suspected bombers, and wounded 194, most of whom were non-Arab. The second, in November, at the Al-Muhaya residential compound, killed 18 people and wounded 122 others, most of them Arab workers and their families, during Ramadan.

been laid out in newspaper pages. Many of us here have been overjoyed to see a long-closeted debate go public.[39]

Mishkhas went on to report how news of impending elections had inspired women with the hope that they would be able to vote or run for office and sparked a 'war of words' between those for and against women's political participation. She cited outspoken pieces in local dailies, including one by Muram Abdel-Rahman in *Al-Watan*, demanding women's inclusion in the elections.[40] It later emerged that women would not be permitted to vote or stand for municipal councils in 2005, allegedly due to the difficulty of organising segregated voting booths, and nor would they be appointed. Nevertheless, the public exchanges of early 2004 could hardly have contrasted more sharply with January 2001, when the daily *Al-Riyadh* had reported Prince Nayef bin Abdel-Aziz, the interior minister, as ruling out any possibility of public debate about women's rights. According to *Al-Riyadh*, the prince had said that such a debate would be 'useless and produce a hollow exchange of ideas'.[41]

Looking first in more detail at the National Dialogue, it should be noted that the process of holding these meetings prompted debate not only about the chosen themes; extremism, youth, women, 'We and the Other', but also about whether the debates should be shared with the wider public or held behind closed doors. The first meeting, in June 2003, had involved no more than 30 people, who reported in person to Abdullah (then Crown Prince) on their deliberations. According to one participant, speaking three days later, these had covered national unity and external relations, including issues of freedom of expression, women's civic rights and duties, and intellectual diversity.[42] When the second round of the dialogue took place in December 2003, the secretary-general of the newly created King Abdel-Aziz Centre for National Dialogue argued that the dialogue was experimental and should be conducted in private. But voices in the press and Majlis al-Shoura (Consultative Council) disagreed. When the third meeting followed in Medina in June 2004 under the title 'Women: Their Rights and Duties', it was fully covered in Saudi newspapers with verbatim reporting of exchanges and photographs of men and women involved in the debates,[43] even though these had been conducted between separate rooms for men and women via closed-circuit TV. As a result, two precedents were set. One was numerical equality between men and women participants, since half the 60 participants in the June 2004 session were women. In the previous round there had been only 10 women out of 75 participants and seven of the 10 were holders of PhDs. The second precedent was that of publicising the content of discussions. Attempts at secrecy for the second session, 'so as not to influence attitudes',[44] had been undermined by publication of the session's recommendations on the website of the daily *Al-Watan* and coverage in Saudi Arabia's two English-language newspapers, *Saudi Gazette*

---

[39] Abeer Mishkhas, 'Women's rights will benefit all Saudis', IPS News/Global Information Network, Jeddah, April 8, 2004.
[40] Ibid.
[41] BBC, ''No debate' over Saudi women', *BBC News Online*, January 25, 2001.
[42] Ihsan Buhlaigah, economist and Shoura Council member, addressing the Royal United Services Institute, London, June 24, 2003. Author's transcript.
[43] Charles Radin, 'Saudi Women Ask if Economic Development, not Political Rights, Holds the Key to Liberation', *Boston Globe*, October 3, 2004.
[44] Suha al-Ansari, 'Women Address Issues Boldly at National Dialogue Summit', *Saudi Gazette* website, January 3, 2004.

and *Arab News*. *Arab News* reports of the third session were particularly graphic on the clash of views about equality for women, with both men and women speaking for and against.[45] Because the session was closed, however, a participant who was later questioned on television about his contribution could dismiss press reports as lies.[46]

During the year after the Medina conference on women many things were to change. On his accession in August 2005, King Abdullah broke with precedent by meeting with two groups of about 40 women who came to swear a *bay'a* (oath of allegiance), in a ceremony that was partly televised.[47] At the same time, women journalists, professors and businesswomen were recruited to join Saudi delegations on official visits overseas. In September 2005, Channel 1 of the official state television network carried a programme on preparations for the fifth round of the National Dialogue in which it broadcast numerous phone calls from viewers, including nine women.[48] All of which makes it seem quite logical that, when it came to the December 2005 round of the National Dialogue in Abha, the proceedings were not only televised but the final session was broadcast live. Viewers of the state-owned news channel, *Al-Ikhbariya*, were consequently able to witness women proposing amendments to the conference recommendations. Instead of encouraging women to take part in 'international bodies and societies interested in women's affairs', one urged that the word 'encouraging' should be replaced with 'enabling'. Another proposed 'enabling women to assume senior posts'.[49]

The difference between 'encouraging' and 'enabling' is crucial because it encapsulates the difference between superficial and structural change. Although mounting media attention to women's 'rights and duties' certainly encouraged heightened expectations, changes outside the media, in votes and jobs for women, tell a story of intensifying inconsistencies and contradictions. TV reporting of King Abdullah's meetings with groups of women, organised by the Ministry of Education and the Ministry of Culture and Information, revealed little about what was actually agreed. It is known that female delegates raised specific points about such things as restrictions on travel and difficulties in pursuing higher university degrees.[50] It is reported that spokeswomen were appointed to represent specific groups and that Dalal Dia of Saudi radio (mentioned earlier) spoke for media women.[51] But it also appears that the king's main message, influenced by powerful opponents of public roles for women, was to urge the delegations to take a 'softly softly' approach to avoid rocking the boat.[52] Given this advice it is perhaps unsurprising that significant breakthroughs did not always make top headlines in domestic Saudi media, even when they attracted attention abroad. For example, when two women were elected to the board of directors of Jeddah's

[45] Abdul Wahab Bashir, 'Madina Forum on Women Calls for Respecting Tradition', *Arab News*, June 14, 2004.

[46] Omar al-Midwahi, 'Remarks on Women's Rights Cause Uproar', *Arab News* June 15, 2004.

[47] Alain Gresh, 'Saudi Arabia: Reality Check', *Le Monde Diplomatique*, February 2006, p. 2.

[48] Saudi TV1 programme presented by Jibril Abu-Diyyah and broadcast on September 24, 2005.

[49] World News Connection transcription, entitled '*Al-Ikhbariya* airs Saudi National Dialogue Conference Session, Final Statement', December 27, 2007. The participants who made these points were Dr Badriyah al-Bishr and Dr Thurayya al-Urayd.

[50] For an insight into these difficulties see Abu Bakr Ahmad Ba Kader, 'Women, Higher Education and Society: a Gender Perspective. Case Study of the Kingdom of Saudi Arabia', *Al-Raida*, 23–24(114–115, Summer/Fall) (2006), p. 26.

[51] Report in *Al-Quds al-Arabi*, September 29, 2005.

[52] Personal communication to the author by a participant, September 19, 2006.

Chamber of Commerce and Industry (JCCI) in December 2005, in the first chamber elections to be contested by women, Manal al-Sharif, an editor at *Al-Watan*, told a foreign reporter that she kept the story off the front page to avoid the misogynist backlash experienced by others who had openly broken taboos.[53] Even so, images of women continued to proliferate in Saudi media in the following months, to the point where King Abdullah met with local editors in May 2006 and told them that photographs published in some newspapers were provocative and unsuitable. The daily *Okaz* quoted the king as saying: 'One must think, do they want their daughter, sister or wife to appear like that? Of course no-one would'.[54] His comments reinforced a circular from the Ministry of Information to advertising agencies and media owners, reminding them that any pictures used in editorial material or magazines should be respectful and expose no more of a woman than her face, hands, neck and feet.[55] With newspapers and women's leaders under instructions to downplay the rising profile of women in the public domain, at a time when women were getting elected to the boards of bodies such as the JCCI and the Engineers Syndicate and more female consultants were being appointed to the Shoura Council, it seems that newspaper columns and the airwaves in Saudi Arabia may not always offer the most transparent window onto changes affecting women. Despite the women's 'invasion' of press and broadcasting alleged by Sultan al-Qahtani, and despite the inspiration drawn by Abeer Mishkhas from seeing issues of gender inequality broached in public after a long silence, these phenomena are ultimately only indicators of encouragement. Signs of any media involvement in the structural 'enabling' of Saudi women need to be sought elsewhere.

IV. Behind the Scenes: Shifts in the Media Workplace?

While some Saudi journalists were commenting on women's growing visibility in the media, others were looking behind the scenes, at trends in training and employment, and finding much less to get excited about. Maha Akeel, surveying the scene at the end of 2006, concluded that little had changed either quantitatively or qualitatively since she gathered data for her master's thesis in 2004. Far from documenting an 'invasion' by women, Akeel's findings showed that women account for less than 8% of the total staff on any of the country's newspapers and around 5% of the total in radio and television.[56] She found that the majority of women in the press worked only part-time, that none worked in administration, production or technical fields, and that the highest position a women could hope to achieve was that of head or managing editor in the 'women's department', which only applied of course to those newspapers where such a department exists. Despite reaching high positions in local radio and television stations, run by the Ministry of Information, women had not been promoted to administrative or executive levels in the ministry. In her thesis Akeel had identified obstacles to women's advancement in media careers, which remained valid two years later.

[53] Hassan Fattah, 'Evolution, not Revolution, for Saudi Women', *International Herald Tribune*, December 22, 2005.
[54] After Associated Press reported that King Abdullah had ordered Saudi editors to stop publishing pictures of women (AP, May 18, 2006), *Arab News* corrected the information in an article by Somayya Jabarti, 'Abdullah did not ban women's pictures', May 18, 2006.
[55] Tim Addington, 'Saudi gets tough on images of women', *Campaign Middle East*, June 15, 2006.
[56] Maha Akeel, 'Empowering women in Saudi media', *Arab News*, January 6, 2007.

They included the lack of college places for girls to gain degrees in journalism and media, compounded by discriminatory treatment in salaries and career opportunities.[57] A lack of qualifications puts women journalists at a double disadvantage vis-à-vis male colleagues, since 'unqualified' is also taken to mean 'unprofessional'. Akeel's assessment was later corroborated by Sabriya Jawhar, head of the women's department at *Saudi Gazette*, who told the Second Women's Media Forum in Riyadh that women journalists often work without contracts or rights, on low pay and at permanent risk of losing their job. She said that even women who had been working as full-time journalists for many years often had to pay their own expenses.[58]

Degrees in journalism and media were off limits to female students until 2005, when the first undergraduate course in Mass Communication was formally opened to girls at King Abdel-Aziz University. No-one had yet graduated from this programme by September 2007,[59] and a programme promised for King Saud University had not started by this point. It was not until the end of 2007 that the Ministry of Higher Education announced plans to open a Mass Communications College for girls in Jeddah. The announcement came two years after the Shoura Council had called for expansion of women's technical education and vocational training to enable them to branch into jobs beyond the traditional sectors of teaching and health. It also followed repeated calls by women writers irked by the unprofessional image surrounding women working as journalists without media degrees. Al-Jawhara al-Anqari had addressed one of her weekly columns in *Okaz* to the minister of higher education, 'on behalf of Saudi women', urging the creation of information and journalism schools for women in Jeddah and Riyadh.[60] Maha Akeel, commenting ruefully on low attendance at a workshop on women in the media organized by *Al-Jazirah* newspaper in 2003, reported that participants had called for a role in making decisions about women's involvement in the media. Without that role, she wrote, 'they will continue to be marginalized and ignored'.[61] How marginalization works on a day-to-day basis was demonstrated at a three-day forum on Media Education and Training in Riyadh, organised by the Saudi Association for Media and Communication, based at King Saud University. The association, founded in 2002 with a membership of over 1200, organizes training courses and conferences for journalists. Female participants at its forum in Riyadh in December 2005 were frustrated that it overlooked the burning issue of media training for women. They tried to put the point to male colleagues by means of the usual video link but were ignored because, as far as the men at the event were concerned, they were literally invisible.[62]

Mounting pressure for local training in journalism and media during this period can also be attributed to rapid expansion of Saudi-owned media, affecting both state organizations based inside the kingdom and private bodies with their main offices outside. Public and private ownership systems in Saudi media reflect the

---

[57] Ibid.

[58] Sheikha al-Dosary and Najah Alosaimi, 'Rights of women journalists discussed', *Arab News*, May 4, 2007.

[59] According to Ibrahim Beayeyz, then Chair of the Mass Communication Department at King Saud University, speaking at the University of Westminster, September 5, 2007.

[60] Almunajjed, *Saudi Women Speak*, p. 77.

[61] Maha Akeel, 'Women Yearning for a Role', *Arab News*, March 4, 2003.

[62] Suzan Zawawi, 'Media Forum Fails to Mention the Lack of Training for Women in the Field', *Saudi Gazette*, December 4, 2005.

way the alliance between princes and the religious authorities works in practice: by investing in media operations beyond the kingdom's borders, senior princes gain a say in national and regional affairs that would not be possible within the confines of Saudi Arabia's own strict media laws, even though these are issued by royal decree. Thus MBC, a satellite channel launched in London and later moved to Dubai, belongs to a brother-in-law of the late King Fahd. Rotana, with offices in Lebanon as well as Saudi Arabia, belongs to the multibillionaire global investor Prince Alwaleed bin Talal, son of Prince Talal bin Abdel-Aziz (mentioned earlier in this paper) and a nephew of King Fahd and King Abdullah. The owners of MBC and Rotana expanded their satellite networks after 2001 with the avowed intention of de-radicalising young audiences by offering youth-oriented entertainment and news that would compete with Al-Jazeera.[63] MBC2 and MBC4, introduced in 2003-05, featured non-stop Hollywood films and subtitled US lifestyle reality series and talk shows. Rotana featured Arabic films and music video. In March 2006 Alwaleed started a general channel called Al-Resalah (The Message) promoting what its managers called 'Islamic entertainment'. Saudi Radio and Television also expanded at this time, with the addition of a sports channel and a satellite news channel at the start of January 2004.[64] The news channel, Al-Ekhbariya, was created to improve the flow of favourable information about Saudi Arabia's part in fighting armed attacks by religious militants at home and abroad.[65] MBC group supplied training and equipment to Al-Ekhbariya through the same structures serving its own 24-hour news channel, Al-Arabiya. The latter hired many female production staff.

Expansion of television entertainment under Saudi sponsorship intensified contradictions with the traditionalist message. In 2004, with music video on Arab satellite channels challenging social norms, Princess Al-Jawhara bint Ibrahim, a wife of King Fahd, urged women in the kingdom to stick to 'Islamic' values and traditions. Addressing female graduates at King Abdel-Aziz University in Jeddah she accused satellite channels of waging 'frenzied campaigns against Muslim women in general, and Saudi women in particular'. 'Islam's enemies and the fainthearted women who follow in their footsteps do not tire of waging war against our Muslim traditions, trying to incite Muslim women to shed those norms on grounds that they restrict their freedom'.[66] Compared with the glitz of satellite channels, however, even Saudi officials in charge of media affairs found Saudi TV's Channel 1 lacking in the kind of vision that could attract young viewers and Channel 2 failing in its mission to introduce the country's non-Saudi population to Saudi society.[67] By creating Al-Ekhbariya, the government gave itself an alternative means to strive for these objectives. The new channel's director, Mohammed Barayan, told Reuters that foreign media were saying things that 'aren't right', about the position of women in Saudi Arabia and whether or not the country was 'fighting fundamentalists'. 'We want to tell the world about our country', he said, to 'give a new image'.[68] As part of this approach, three female news anchors appeared on Al-Ekhbariya at its launch and programmes were

---

[63] Sakr, *Arab Television Today*, pp. 169–176, 200. See also Naomi Sakr 'Oil, arms and media: how US interventionism shapes Arab TV', *Journal für Entwicklungspolitik* 24(1, May) (2008), pp. 57–81.

[64] Saudi Press Agency Website, December 22, 2003.

[65] Quoted in BBC Monitoring Research, 'Saudi rulers ease their grip on the media', May 28, 2004.

[66] Saudi Press Agency report carried by *Arab News*, May 18, 2004.

[67] Nagah El Eseimy, 'Saudi TV versus satellite TV', *Asharq al-Awsat* English website, May 24, 2005.

[68] Raid Qusti, 'Al-Ikhbariya makes waves', *Arab News*, January 13, 2004.

designed to tackle controversy. According to Khaled al-Maenna, editor-in-chief of *Arab News*, part of the Saudi Research and Marketing Group (SRMG) part owned by the family of Riyadh Governor Prince Salman bin Abdel-Aziz, this was part of a deliberate bid to use television to promote internal dialogue. The September 2001 attacks had made people realise, he explained later, that Saudi media had to face world-class competitors; this meant moving from the defensive to critiquing one's own society, because people in Saudi Arabia were no longer content to wait for foreign media like the BBC to tell them what is happening in Jeddah and Riyadh.[69] Evidence that Al-Ekhbariya was pursuing such an approach came with programmes like a September 2005 episode of *Al-Bu'd al-Jādd* (The Serious Aspect), presented by Wafa Shamma, which discussed the move to allow businesswomen to stand for election to the JCCI board. This programme, like others, allowed male and female speakers from the business and policy elite to situate domestic changes in a global context, including Saudi Arabia's ongoing negotiations to join the WTO.[70] In December 2005, as mentioned in the previous section, Al-Ekhbariya broke with precedent by arranging live broadcasts from the fifth meeting of the National Dialogue.

The hiring of women in state television came some years after the print media had taken similar steps. Here, however, there were differences between the Arabic-language and English-language press. The latter, apparently oriented towards foreign opinion, often took a more liberal line than the former, although members of staff on *Arab News*, a sister paper of *Asharq al-Awsat*, say they could tell from readers' letters that they were also cultivating a Saudi readership. As editor-in-chief of *Arab News*, Al-Maenna is credited by female staff on the paper with having taken the initiative not only to hire women but to offer them tenure, in contrast to the mainly freelance status forced on women in other newspapers. The paper's practice of publishing photographs of female columnists began on a voluntary basis[71] in 2002, at a time when it was doubling its full-time Saudi female staff and sending more female reporters into the field.[72] The editorial line at *Arab News* firmly supported women's right to political participation and freedom to drive. When additional female consultants were appointed to advise the Shoura Council in 2006, Mishkhas argued that it was time for women to be included 'as citizens, not merely as women'. We are told, she wrote, that these women will be consulted on matters related to women. 'Fine. How about other issues? Don't women live in the same country as men and don't they have a right to express their views on all issues concerning their country?[73] Al-Maenna's leader on driving licences for women was headed 'Let them be at the helm'.[74] At the *Arab News* offices in Jeddah, women had an office inside the main building. Those working at *Saudi Gazette* had a separate building. According to Salwa Khamis, working at

---

[69] Remarks to London Middle East Institute conference on 'Popular Culture in the Gulf', February 8, 2007. Paraphrase of author's transcript.
[70] Episode screened at 17:10 GMT on September 20, 2005. Translation from BBC International Reports (Middle East) September 21, 2005.
[71] The first picture of a female columnist was that of Abeer Mishkhas.
[72] Afshin Molavi, 'Young and Restless', *Smithsonian Magazine* online, April 2006.
[73] Abeer Mishkhas, 'Shoura role for Women shouldn't be Ornamental', *Arab News*, July 20, 2006.
[74] *Arab News*, June 6, 2005.

Saudi Gazette's sister paper *Okaz*, this physical separation distanced women from daily meetings and decision making.[75]

In theory, women journalists gained a forum from which to press for improvements in their professional standing when the Saudi Journalists Association (SJA) was formed in 2004 and two women, Nawal al-Rashed of *Al-Riyadh* and Nahed Bashatah, were voted onto the wholly-elected nine-member board. The SJA had a slow start, having been promised in December 2001 and formed in March 2003, with elections to the SJA board initially scheduled for January 2004. At that point voting arrangements for municipal councils were still under discussion and votes for women had not been ruled out. The process of actually holding the SJA elections took until June 2004, being postponed twice because of differences over procedures, nominations and voting methods. During that time, however, five women managed to get themselves included in the final list of 31 nominees. The two eventually elected were quick to pledge that they would use their position to address the main issues facing women journalists in the kingdom, which Bashatah identified as contracts, training and job security. But there was also a groundswell of skepticism about how committed the SJA would prove to be in practice to protecting the interests of journalists, given that five out of the nine board members were newspaper editors, whose appointments are ultimately in government hands. Many questioned whether it would have any powers beyond that of a talking shop. Nabila Mahjoob, one of three unsuccessful women candidates, appreciated the election as a 'learning process', but regretted the delay in counting votes. She had been obliged to fly back to Jeddah before knowing how many votes she received.[76] Two years later, well informed local observers of the media scene were still waiting for evidence that the SJA was achieving results.

Mixed signals like those emerging from the formation and performance of SJA, can also be seen in other institutions set up at the government's behest. The National Human Rights Association (NHRA), formed in March 2004, numbered 10 women among its 41 members. They included Al-Jawhara al-Anqari, known for her media work. They also included Suhaila Zain Al Abideen Hammad, an expert on Islamic jurisprudence and supporter of codifying personal status, who has highlighted the media's role in promoting rights observance.[77] Overseas visits by NHRA delegations raised visibility for the association's female experts. But when it came to defending citizens who alleged that their rights had been abused, the NHRA was cautious.[78] Thus, the plea by women activists for a role in decision making, whether inside or outside the media, has to be seen in the context of wider political structures in Saudi Arabia and the concentration of decision-making powers. Thus, also, any assessment of media contributions to structural change in women's status should not ignore events taking place in other media spheres, from book publishing to the Internet. *Banat Al-Riyadh* (Girls of Riyadh), written by King Saud University graduate Rajaa Al-Sanea and published in Beirut, was allowed to circulate in Saudi Arabia after winning a court case in which it was accused of being 'an outrage to the

---

[75] Quoted by Maha Akeel in 'A female perspective on the Saudi Journalists Association', *Arab News* May 26, 2003.
[76] Quoted in Maha Akeel, 'Hundreds Take Part in Elections for Saudi Journalists Association', *Arab News*, June 9, 2004.
[77] Quoted in Lydia George, 'Legal Battles can be Bruising for Women', *Jordan Times*, July 18, 2005.
[78] Hertog, 'The new corporatism in Saudi Arabia', pp. 254–255.

norms of Saudi society'.[79] While the number of Saudi women novelists reportedly increased dramatically in the wake of *Banat al-Riyadh*,[80] the number of female bloggers was also rising, especially among young women in their twenties. Whatever their individual impact, the net outcome of all these developments was a major expansion in the number of platforms for Saudi women's life experiences and opinions to be shared and discussed.

IV. Saudi Arabian Media Women: Personalities and Patronage

The previous sections gave some indication that systems of patronage and supervision emanating from within ruling family circles helped to engineer breakthroughs such as those on display at Al-Ekhbariya, in the SJA and NHRA, and in women's access to new university courses in mass communication. A closer look at the positions of Saudi women who rose to prominence by being the first in a particular field of Saudi media can illustrate further how those systems work. Pioneers to choose from in 2004–06 include Mona Abu Sulayman, one of four hosts on the MBC talk show *Kalam Nawaem* (Soft Talk), Hind Mohammed, who made her acting debut in the first full-length Saudi-made feature film *Keif al-Hal?*, and Hala al-Nasser, author of the book *Shahrazād fī-l-Sahāfa al-Sa'ūdiya* (Scheherazade in the Saudi Press) and first female editor-in-chief of *Rotana* magazine after its move to Riyadh. Another possible candidate is Rania al-Baz, the first female announcer on Saudi TV in 2001 who made headlines in 2004 by exposing her own experience of domestic abuse and thereby forcing it onto the public agenda.

The first three names on this list are all linked to Saudi media mogul Prince Alwaleed bin Talal as well as to such bastions of the Saudi media establishment as MBC, Saudi Radio and SRMG, the owner of *Asharq al-Awsat*, *Arab News* and a large array of publications including the women's magazine *Sayidati*. Mona Abu Sulayman heads Alwaleed's philanthropic organization, Kingdom Foundation, in addition to her work on MBC's *Kalam Nawaem*. This programme, modelled on ABC's *The View*, features four women of different ages and from different Arab countries hosting a weekly talk show that tackles questions of social conduct and social justice. Born in Philadelphia and a faculty member at King Saud University, Abu Sulayman says she feels that her 'most important accomplishment' as 'a Saudi woman' was to 'break into the international arena', to 'help defend ourselves against international attacks on our identity'.[81] Being involved in the programme was also a nice way of 'enabling a Saudi to get into the preparation' of the issues addressed on the show. 'I've tried to highlight a lot of things that are going on', she told a reporter in 2007, including 'forced divorces, women pursuing scientific majors, the effects of segregating male and female students'.[82] Writing in 2006, Abu Sulayman expressed her aim as that of asking for 'laws that make sense', not as a public relations ploy or out of an abstract sense of justice but 'because we want a better world for our very real children. And we want it now'.[83]

[79] Raid Qusti, 'Court Rejects Case against Rajaa Al-Sanea', *Arab News*, October 9, 2006.
[80] Andrew Hammond, ''Girls of Riyadh' Spurs Rush of Saudi Novels', *Reuters*, July 23, 2007.
[81] Joelle Hatem, 'The Power of Soft Talk', *Middle East Broadcasters Journal*, 12(May–June) (2007), p. 37.
[82] Ibid.
[83] Mona Abu Sulayman, 'Tough Talk in a Soft Voice', *Middle East Broadcasters Journal*, September–October 2006, Online only. Available HTTP: www.mebjournal.com/content/view/207/172 (accessed August 22, 2008).

A few months later she stressed that she was only interested in tackling issues that are 'religiously' and 'socially acceptable in the Arab world'.[84]

Redrawing the boundaries of the socially acceptable is something that Alwaleed did through various arms of his business empire during the three-year period under review. In 2004, while the debate about driving licences for women in Saudi Arabia was raging, he sponsored Hanadi Hindi to study for a pilot's licence in Jordan, reportedly promising to make her Saudi Arabia's first female airline pilot by giving her a job on his own private aircraft.[85] In 2006 Alwaleed's media company Rotana produced *Keif al-Hal?* as the first Saudi feature film in a country where cinemas are banned. *Keif al-Hal?* went into circulation in the Arab world at a time when controversy over modification of the Saudi ban was at its height. Opponents of cinema in the kingdom claimed the ban was sanctioned by a royal decree dating from 1964 and religious rulings issued after the 1979 mosque siege.[86] Supporters of cinema countered this resistance by introducing public screenings of children's cartoons in November 2005 and by holding a Saudi film festival in Jeddah in July 2006, taking care to avoid using the word 'cinema' in publicity material about the event.[87] An Abu Dhabi film festival in 2006 featured *Nissā bilā Dhil* (Women with No Shadow) by Saudi Arabia's best-known female film director, Haifaa al-Mansour. At around the same moment a prominent Saudi religious commentator, Shaikh Salman al-Odeh, said on MBC that cinema deserved support because it could promote Islam.[88] *Keif al-Hal?* contributed its own pro-cinema signal by featuring Saudi Arabia's first film actress, 25-year-old Hind Muhammad.

Before taking on the film role of Duniya, Muhammad was mainly known for her work in drama serials on Saudi radio and as a voice on television cartoons.[89] Since Saudi actresses did not previously feature in Saudi television drama, Muhammad was seen as taking a brave step in accepting the part in *Keif al-Hal?* and one that would set an important precedent for the future of Saudi film. In the judgment of Ayman Halawani, general manager of film production for Rotana group, she had 'shown that a Saudi film actress can both be attractive and dignified'. 'We think', he said, that 'she will be the first Saudi superstar'.[90] Muhammad herself highlighted the fine line she had to tread; when commenting on media portrayals of women for a Lebanese publication, she expressed her belief that Arab women 'should present a positive image to society because the screen is the shortest way into people's homes'.[91] Released in 2006, *Keif al-Hal?* did what a new wave of Saudi novels were also doing, casting light on previously non-discussed aspects of Saudi life. Such exposure could not fail to raise questions about family influences and women's rights. Written by an Egyptian and filmed by a Canadian in Dubai, the film is set in a Riyadh home where different members of one family are trying to get along despite their varied outlooks on life. It begins with the college

---

[84] Hatem, 'The Power of Soft Talk', p. 38.

[85] BBC, 'Saudi Women Take to the Skies', *BBC News Online*, November 26, 2004.

[86] Sabriya Jawhar, 'Media, Conservatives Impede Progress in Opening Theatres', *Saudi Gazette*, November 16, 2005.

[87] Andrew Hammond, 'First Saudi Film Festival Opens Despite Clerics', *Middle East Online*, July 14, 2006.

[88] Reuters, 'Saudis put Cinema Ban in the Frame', *aljazeera.net*, February 23, 2006.

[89] Hassan Fattah, 'Daring to Use the Silver Screen to Reflect Saudi Society', *The New York Times*, April 28, 2006.

[90] Quoted by Vincent Dowd in ''First' Saudi Feature Film Aims High', *BBC News Online*, May 26, 2006.

[91] Hind Mohammed, 'Are Women Portrayed Fairly on Arab TV?', *Middle East Broadcasters Journal*, 10(January–February) (2007), p. 41.

graduation ceremony of a character named Sahar, who has professional ambitions but is urged by her family to marry and stay at home. Sahar is played by a Jordanian. Duniya, played by Hind Muhammad, is Sahar's best friend.

A few months after releasing *Keif al-Hal?*, Rotana group moved the publishing operation behind its *Rotana* magazine to Riyadh and appointed Hala al-Nasser as editor-in-chief, in what company publicity said was an 'an effort to attract new ideas'.[92] This was recognition for someone whose career in Saudi media had started in 1991 with a position as associate editor at *Asharq al-Awsat* and included several years as editor of *Sayidati*. Nasser researched the history of women's journalism in the kingdom for her book *Shahrazād fī-l-Sahāfa al-Sa'ūdiya*. Published in 2005, after Nasser decided that Internet discussions about the topic had reached such a pitch that she could put it off no longer,[93] Nasser's book attracted attention on several counts. Her choice of title did not go unnoticed, given its implication that women journalists are under constant threat of being silenced, just like the legendary Scheherazade.[94] She was also by turns resented and admired for pointing out how some women journalists are reduced to gathering second-hand news at social events and by telephoning each other.

Finally, the experience of Rania al-Baz helps to demonstrate how several recent changes in the Saudi media landscape were able to produce outcomes in 2004–05 that might not have been possible in earlier years. Rania al-Baz was beaten almost to death by her husband in April 2004 after he objected to her answering the telephone. After undergoing extensive surgery, Al-Baz, helped by her mother, provided local media with information about her ordeal and a picture showing the extent of her facial injuries was published, having apparently been taken on a cameraphone. Al-Baz was visited in hospital by Al-Jawhara al-Anqari, of the newly formed NHRA, and by the wife of the governor of Makkah.[95] Her story did not evoke universal sympathy in Saudi circles. But it coincided with the introduction of the NHRA as a mechanism for responding to rights abuse, and contributed to spreading an unfamiliar discourse. As radio journalist Samar Fatany pointed out 15 months later: 'After many years of denying abuse, our society is now exposing the guilty every day'.[96] Importantly, this exposure did not take place through local media alone. In late 2004 MBC launched a new channel, MBC4, and included in its schedules subtitled imports of *Oprah*, the US-made talk show in which Oprah Winfrey coaxes studio guests to disclose their personal stories on the grounds that this can help society confront injustice and taboos. *Oprah* was reportedly such a hit with Saudi women viewers, covering issues that they could not find discussed elsewhere, that MBC made the series the centrepiece of MBC4.[97] In 2005 Rania al-Baz appeared as a guest on *Oprah*, and thus also appeared on MBC4.

[92] *Al-Jazirah* Report, November 8, 2006.
[93] Samar al-Muqrin, 'Review of Shahrazād fī-l-Sahāfa al-Sa'ūdiya', *Al-Watan*, October 11, 2005.
[94] See the review by Fawzia Salama in *Asharq al-Awsat*, March 20, 2006.
[95] Bradley, *Saudi Arabia Exposed*, pp. 185–186.
[96] Samar Fatany writing in *Arab News*, June 14, 2005.
[97] Yasmine el-Rashidi, ''Oprah' is Attracting Young, Female Viewers to TV in Saudi Arabia', *The Wall Street Journal*, December 1, 2005.

V. Conclusion

This account has made only brief and intermittent allusion to the actions and opinions of those members of Saudi society, male and female, who strongly oppose gender equality in principle and practice. An alternative account, with a different focus, could have marshalled ample evidence that these opinions continued to be strongly held, forcefully expressed and, in some cases, imposed on the rest of society in 2004–06. Ultimately, however, that alternative account would lead to a conclusion similar to one that can be drawn here. That is to say, following the argument about stereotypes made in the introduction to this paper, the aim of analysis is not to weigh media interventions in terms of the particular images of women that they promote. Instead, it is to gauge whether a multiplicity of images is emerging that can help to demolish stereotypes. If women and men with widely differing views about women's personal and political status find that their views are better reflected in the media, then the media diversification that produces such an outcome is noteworthy as such. Evidence in this paper suggests that a quantitative increase in Saudi media content addressing women's status did widen the margins of debate. The wider the range of visions presented, the more feasible it was for participants in the exchanges to keep their options open. In that sense, notions about 'positive' or 'negative' in relation to media images of women were shown to fall outside the scope of the analysis. Such notions mean something different to every individual who refers to them and their meanings for each of those individuals may alter over time. What emerges from the present study is a process whereby possible meanings of 'positive' and 'negative' as applied to media portrayals of women were amplified and diversified.

The extent of diversification should not be over-estimated. Mechanisms of political legitimization in Saudi Arabia are such that religious texts enjoy virtual exclusivity as a point of reference in the renegotiation of gender boundaries in and through the Saudi media. But the study showed how the use of texts changed in response to exigencies of the moment, whether internal ones such as the 1979 siege of the Grand Mosque or the Riyadh bombings in 2003, or external ones such as Saudi Arabia's bid for WTO membership or the atrocities of 9/11. Maintaining the status quo in the face of these challenges called for varying sets of alleged 'traditions' and norms to be invoked, and that is how the rules came to change back and forth between the 1960s, 1980s and 2000s with regard to women's visibility on television and the acceptability of forms of entertainment such as cinema. Hence the renegotiation process was seen to have a long history and, despite periodic media silences, to be continuous. The ruling establishment relied on one set of norms to deny women access to public life after 1979. In the same way, reformist elements of a new generation of the same establishment relied on another set when they sought to 'use' women, via MBC, Al-Ekhbariya, Rotana or the SJA, as an emblem of more liberal policies in the wake of 2001. Given the ulterior motives behind this repositioning of Saudi women, it is reasonable to ask whether it could transform the thinking about gender that underlies the profession of journalism in Saudi Arabia. The answer seemed to be that it eventually might. Journalism training and senior editorial jobs, which were once off limits to Saudi women, were coming within their reach by 2006. But evidence also indicated that any reconstruction of media professions would be extremely uncertain and slow.

It would be slow, in part, because of the way decision making works in Saudi Arabia. Initiatives discussed in this study were mostly of the top-down variety, carried out under the sponsorship of powerful princes. Low expectations were expressed in some parts of the media about the impact of new channels of representation like the SJA or NHRA. These further highlighted the extent to which the top-down approach was basically geared to preserving key aspects of the political status quo. In this situation, those princes who patronized the repositioning of women vis-à-vis channels of public communication and cultural expression seemed to be trying primarily to modernize an authoritarian system. Media attention attracted by their high profile support for women's public role tends to overshadow a parallel process, in which individual Saudis seek to renegotiate the status of all citizens, both male and female, vis-à-vis government and the state. This study distinguished between high profile appearances and low profile restructuring of professions and representative organizations. Its findings indicated that the latter process is the one to watch.

Iraqi Women and Gender Relations: Redefining Difference

NADJE AL-ALI

ABSTRACT *The proposed paper will explore the changing role of women and gender in Iraq from the 1950s pre-revolutionary period, throughout 35 years of Ba'th regime, economic sanctions to the current post 2003 period. Against the historic background of both state repression and state feminism, gender relations changed rapidly during the period of economic sanctions (1990–2003) which was marked by a drastic turn towards greater social conservatism. But it is in the current context of occupation and the rising influence of Islamist political parties and militias that gender ideologies and relations are at the centre of political contestations, increasing violence and the instrumentalization of human rights issues. This paper aims to challenge the notion of diversity in the context of Iraqi women as represented in the prevailing political and media discourses which focus on ethnic and religious differences. Historically, as the paper will argue, social class, place of origin and political orientation cut across ethnic and religious boundaries and present the main markers of difference.*

I. Introduction

In current media and political discourses, Iraqi women represent the epitome of oppressed Middle Eastern women. Images of heavily veiled women, stories of violence against women, sectarian killings and honour-killings are frequently interpreted as 'just another Muslim country oppressing its women'. Over the past decade, I have worked both as an academic and as an activist to challenge these stereotypical images of Iraqi women by documenting the various ways in which Iraqi women and gender relations have been changing in the context of political repression under the Ba'th regime, changing state policies towards women, a series of wars as well as economic sanctions. Challenging neo-orientalist frames of explanations of the situation of Iraqi women in terms of culture (Muslim, Middle Eastern or Iraq which are often used interchangeably) or religion (namely Islam), I have been exploring economic, political, and social changes in historical context taking local, national, regional and international factors into account.

In the aftermath of the invasion of Iraq in 2003, I decided to build on my earlier work which had focused on the impact of dictatorship and economic sanctions on women and gender relations in Iraq. I extended the historical frame to include the period before the 35 years of the Ba'th regime (1968–2003), looking back to the transition from monarchy to republic (late 1940s through the revolution of 1958 to the early 1960s), and to deepen my understanding by interviewing almost 200 Iraqi women in Erbil, Sulaymaniya, London, Amman, Detroit and San Diego. This paper is based on this wider project which was published as *Iraqi Women: Untold Stories from 1948 to the Present* (2007, Zed Publishers).

The women I talked to were of different generations, varying ethnic and religious backgrounds: some were more secular, others more religious. I talked to those who have been politically active and those who were not, women associated with different political orientations and parties, professional women, housewives, mothers, happily married women, divorced women, women in unhappy relationships, women who had settled fairly comfortably in their new home countries and those who were eternally homesick for Iraq. Yet, the majority of the women I talked to were educated middle class women of urban backgrounds. It is important to stress the limitations of this specific sample in terms of its representativeness. Hence while there has been a relatively large urban middle class in Iraq since the economic boom of the 1970s, my research does not explore the lives of women of the poorest strata of society nor women who were living in the countryside. In terms of places of origin, the majority of the women I interviewed were from the capital, Baghdad, but I also spoke to women from other major cities and towns such as Basra, Najaf, Karbala, Mosul, Babylon, Kirkuk, Irbil, and Dohuk.

Rather than providing a linear chronological account of the political, social and economic changes that Iraqi women have experienced from the late 1940s until today, I have been trying to show how different women have experienced specific historical periods. And difference, as has been one of my central arguments, is not necessarily defined in ethnic and religious terms, that is whether a woman is Shi'i, Sunni, Kurd or Christian. It is important to emphasise that these are relatively new paradigms for classifying Iraqis. For until very recently, difference has been experienced largely in relation to social class, place of residence, urban or rural identity, professional background, political orientation and generation.[1] This is not to argue that there did not exist sectarian sentiments or tensions, and that all problems started with the invasion in 2003, especially in light of Saddam Hussein's divide and rule tactics and systematic repression of the Iraqi Kurdish and Shi'i populations.

In doing my research, I recognized that while some women might have experienced a certain historical period as 'the golden age', for others it might have been a rather different story. Whether it was the pre-revolutionary era, the years immediately following the revolution in 1958, or the period of economic boom and the expanding middle class in the 1970s, the time of the Iran–Iraq war (1980–1988) or even the 13 years of economic sanctions (1990–2003), there were always diverse experiences and so were the memories surrounding them. These memories contain both accounts of harmonious living together within a multi-ethnic and multi-cultural national entity, a prospering economy and rapid modernization as well as histories of repression, discrimination, the deterioration in living conditions, sectarian tensions, and divide and rule tactics by the government.

---

[1] Nadje Al-Ali, *Iraqi Women: Untold Stories from 1948 to the Present* (London and New York: Zed Books, 2007), p. 2.

II. Experiencing the Monarchy

The narratives of women focusing on the 1950s and 1960s demonstrate that political divisions were not solely or even substantially based on sectarian or ethnic affiliation. Women of all backgrounds were attracted to either of the two main political trends: Communism or Arab nationalism. Of course, Kurdish nationalism is more clearly linked to Kurdish ethnicity, but Kurds were also attracted to Communism and played an important role within the Iraqi Communist party. Moreover, political divisions within the Kurdish movement have been linked to social class and urban versus rural backgrounds. The political establishment prior to the revolution in 1958 was largely dominated by Sunni Arabs while the government of 'Abd al-Karim Qasim was more inclusive of all ethnic and religious groups. Outside politics, women's social and cultural lives were also not solely dictated by ethnicity or religion, but social class and respective political and intellectual orientations influenced people's social circles, cultural production and consumption.

Although many women whom I interviewed pointed to the political repression, social injustices and the big gap between rich and poor as characteristics of the monarchy, a number of women (and indeed many men of that generation) remembered the days of the King with great nostalgia. I expected women from the former political elites and upper class backgrounds to reminisce with sadness about the 'good old days' of the monarchy. Maybe not surprising considering all what followed, also many women of more modest social backgrounds were contemplating the relative social and political freedoms people had under the monarchy. Several women acknowledged that they had re-thought their views and attitudes towards the monarchy in light of the severe political repression and suffering experienced over the succeeding decades. One of the most surprising accounts came from a devout Shi'i woman, today a sympathizer of the Islamist *Da'wa* Party. Zeynab B. was full of praise for the young king Faisal II, who only came of age in 1953, and the political and social conditions during the monarchy:

> The King lived on the other side of Baghdad in Karkh, close to the British embassy. He had a humble house. They called it Flower Palace. We saw him every day in the morning and every day in the afternoon. All the people really loved him. He was so cute and so nice. He would stop by the grocery store to buy something. We even saw the king walking in the street. People saw him every day in an open carriage giving salute to people or walking in al-Rashid Street. He had one servant, no one else. No guard. The palaces had no guards. You might see one or two guards, but no more. You did not see police or military on the street. We saw them only once a year, during the military parade. We had democracy. We had congressmen. We had laws. We had a parliament. We had freedom. As I remember we had equality. I recall that with me in school there was the daughter of the Prime minister. Other ministers' children were with us in public schools. You could see the ministers picking up their children.[2]

Zeynab's extremely positive account has to be understood in the context of her strong dislike, even hatred, of the Communists, who were instrumental in turning the 1958 coup d'état by a group of military officers into a full-fledged revolution. In her view, the traditions associated with the monarchy were much more in line with her family's and her own social and political attitudes than the secular ideas propagated by the Communists.

[2] Ibid., p. 61.

While Zaynab's account is extreme in terms of the praise and lack of criticism about economic exploitation and political repression during the monarchy, I came across many other positive recollections of women's everyday lives, their education and their involvement in public and political life. However, what needs to be stressed is that the oldest women I talked to came from a social background that allowed for a relatively comfortable life, encouraged education and a degree of freedom where social lives were concerned. Their fathers were lawyers, doctors, or government employees in ministries. Women of less bourgeois backgrounds had fathers who mainly worked as teachers or government clerks. The mothers of the women I interviewed were housewives, although some were working as teachers and doctors.

Members of or sympathizers with the Iraqi Communist Party generally describe the Revolution of 1958 with great enthusiasm. Soraya M. has been living in London in a nice apartment decorated with paintings and photos from the 'good old days', including a photo of 'Abd al-Karim Qasim on one of her side-boards. Soraya is full of despair and anger about the current situation inside Iraq. Yet, her facial expressions change and her eyes light up when she speaks about the days of the Revolution:

> The 14th of July 1958 is the most important day of my life. The joy we had! I had my first boy. He was seven months old. We lived in al-Mansur behind Qasr al-Malik [the King's Palace]. We were sleeping on the roof as we always used to do during the hot summer nights. My son and the baby of my brother, who was married to a German woman, had woken up early and we were preparing milk for them. All of a sudden the house was shaking. Two days before, the party [communist party] distributed a message, saying: 'There will be big events coming soon. Be prepared!' We did not know what it would be. I said: 'Barbara, the king's house has been attacked.' She did not believe me. I took my son to my mother's and I went to the street. All of Baghdad went out. People had found out what happened by word of mouth. Later there was a radio announcement. Most people did not think it was a bad thing to pull the body of the king through the streets. I did not think it was bad at the time. But now we feel differently about it. The communists were blamed for it. But people were angry. They had been exploited and had lived in poverty and they reacted badly.[3]

Memories about the shooting of members of the royal family, the hanging of political leaders and the display of executed members of the *ancien régime* evoked contrasting feelings amongst most of the women I talked to. It has been argued that given the strong anti-British sentiments at the time, the violence associated with the 1958 Revolution was relatively contained, certainly in comparison with what was to come.[4] Yet women across the political spectrum mentioned the violence that took place in the first days of the Revolution although several communist women, even of upper class background, acknowledged that they did not think about it a lot at the time. 'These things happen in revolutions'. Hana R., a communist activist told me, 'It's the mob. We could not stop it at the time'. Nadia R. who had not been involved in any political activism in the 1950s recalls: 'At 6 o'clock in the morning on the radio, we heard the news. The driver was saying in a very happy way: "They are dragging people in the streets!" I can never

[3] Ibid., p.76.
[4] M. Farouk-Sluglett and P. Sluglett, *Iraq since 1958: From Revolution to Dictatorship*, 4th ed. (London and New York: I.B. Tauris, 2003), p. 49.

116

forget my shock. But they were wise enough to put a curfew and by 1 o'clock things started to settle down'.[5]

III. The Political Spectrum

The generation of young and educated Iraqi women and men who experienced the revolution were divided across political lines, reflecting the wider political spectrum: some favouring Iraqi nationalism, and others being attracted to pan-Arab nationalism. The more radical and popular wings of both trends were represented by the Iraqi Communist Party (ICP) and the Ba'th party, the latter representing a radical wing of Arab nationalism. Other anti-monarchical yet less radical political forces were the National Democratic Party (NDP) and the Independence Party. The NDP advocated social democracy and political reform by parliamentary means, concentrating on conditions inside Iraq, including opposing the continued British military presence and influence. The Independence Party, on the other hand, although largely ineffective after the Second World War, was much more interested in the promotion of pan-Arabism and denounced British influence in the context of Arab nationalism.

The major opposition force in the 1940s and 1950s was the Iraqi Communist party, founded in 1934. Notions of social justice, egalitarianism, class struggle, anti-British Iraqi nationalism and secularism were appealing to an intellectual elite as well as impoverished workers and peasants, shanty town dwellers and students. Many of the older women I talked to had become politicized in the context of the student movement in the late 1940s. Not officially licensed by the government, members of communist-led organizations had to work underground and were regularly subjected to repression and persecution. Nevertheless they were growing in numbers. For example, the women's organization *Rābitat al-Difā' 'an Huqūq al-Mar'a* (the League for the Defence of Women's Rights) grew considerably in the 1950s and was active both in humanitarian work and political mobilization. The ICP's inclusive nationalism was particularly popular amongst Iraq's minority communities, including the Kurds and the Jews.

The leftist critique of social injustices was appealing to many Kurds in the North, who despite being unified by Kurdish nationalism and aspirations of independence, were divided in terms of 'haves and have-nots', especially in terms of landowners and tribal leaders on the one side, and the impoverished majority of the population on the other. Many Kurds joined the ICP or the distinctly urban leftist parties such as the Kurdish Communist Party or *Shoresh* (Revolution).[6] The most popular nationalist party to emerge was the Iraqi wing of the Kurdish Democratic Party (KDP), later headed by Mulla Mustafa Barzani after his return from exile in the Soviet Union. Although 'conspicuously silent on questions of social or economic reform',[7] the KDP supported the aim of anti-monarchical forces and embraced the revolution in 1958.

Many contemporary commentators argue that Arab nationalism is not appealing to the majority of the Shi'i population who feel alienated by a movement that is dominantly Sunni. Yet, during the 1950s, Shi'i leaders and general supporters were found in the pan-Arab movements, including the Ba'th party. However, prior

---

[5] Al-Ali (2007), p. 77.
[6] C. Tripp, *A History of Iraq* (Cambridge, Cambridge University Press, 2000), pp. 115–116.
[7] Ibid.

to 1958, the Ba'th party was very small and while the first Ba'th secretary general, Fu'ad al-Rikabi, was a Shi'i from Nasiriya, most of the members at the time were his friends and kin. Rather than thinking of themselves as Shi'i or Sunni, people would think of themselves as Arab or alternatively Iraqi, before anything else. With the establishment of the state of Israel, xenophobic attitudes towards minorities were most tragically in evidence with Iraq's Jewish population, but later on also targeted the Kurds and increasingly the Iraqi Shi'is. However, it was only after the Ba'th *coup d'état* in 1963 that sectarianism deepened and became institutionalized.[8] Across the political spectrum, resentment against the established political regime grew throughout the 1950s. In 1952, mass demonstrations initiated by student discontent, known as the *Intifada* (Uprising), resulted in martial law, increased repression and mass arrests of political leaders. In 1954, three of the opposition parties (NDP, ICP and the Independence Party) joined forces in a National Front. The return of Nouri al-Sa'id as Prime Minister for the twelfth time brought even worse repression, including the banning of all opposition parties and newspapers.[9] This did not stop people from expressing their discontent though. Salwa N., a retired paediatrician who left Iraq for the UK during the mid 1990s, was studying engineering at Baghdad University at the time. She recalls the period just before the revolution:

> I was not a member of any political party, but I remember that my friends and I were always demonstrating against this or that. Some of my friends were Communists and others were Arab nationalists. In the mid-50s, we were protesting against the Baghdad Pact, an alliance with Britain and the US. We demonstrated in support of Nasser, especially in '56 when he was attacked for nationalizing the Suez Canal. Sometimes we were just shouting anti-government slogans. The police were violent at times. On several occasions, people got shot at. But we would still continue. Lots of girls and women took part in these demonstrations. There was never a sense that women should not be part of these actions, on the contrary.[10]

Most women I talked to stressed that their political activism cut across ethnic and religious lines as well as the wider range of inter-communal contacts, co-education of students of different religious and ethnic backgrounds, the sharing of religious celebrations and every-day lives. More than being Sunni, Shi'i, Kurd, Christian, Mandean or Yazidi, and until the early 1950s Jewish, it was social class that would be the main marker of differences and commonalities. As Hana N., a woman of Shi'i origin who is now supporting the Shi'i Islamist Da'wa party, put it: 'We grew up with all the ethnic and religious groups. We went to school with Jews and Christians. And we celebrated all holidays together.'

Nuha, whose family had moved to Baghdad from Mosul when she was five, recalls:

> I only had one experience with sectarianism when I was young. When we were living in Karrada in the 1950s, our next door neighbour invited us for dinner. The next day we saw all the plates chucked out in the back yard. My mother called my sister and they saw all the plates and the cutlery. They thought we were dirty because we were Sunni. The next time I was 20 at university. My best friend was Shi'i. I asked her: 'When are you going to stop

---

[8] E. Davis, *Memories of State: Politics, History and Collective Memory in Modern Iraq* (Berkeley, CA: University of California Press, 2005), p. 85.
[9] Farouk-Sluglett Sluglett (2003), p. 45.
[10] Al-Ali, (2007), pp. 74–75.

beating yourself every year' She asked me: 'Do you know anything about the tenth day of Muharram?'[11] She asked me questions and I had no idea what she was talking about. She asked me: 'Do you want to learn?' So she started telling me religious stories in great details and I started weeping. My friend laughed.[12]

Despite some incidents of prejudice and sectarianism, all the women I talked to were in agreement that they lived in relatively multi-cultural and to some extent cosmopolitan environments that encouraged education, political awareness and activism, travel abroad and cultural appreciation. The increasing opportunities in education went hand in hand with considerable accumulation of wealth and development programmes that started in the early 1950s. Yet, once again, it is important to point out that the specifically urban and middle and upper class backgrounds distinguished the women I talked to from the majority of the Iraqi population at the time. Most Iraqis, especially girls and women, did not have access to education and were struggling to survive under harsh economic conditions. Social injustice and exploitation led to social unrest and later on to the revolution, but there was also an increasingly politicised class of educated young people who wanted total independence from Britain, the former colonizer, and a fairer and just social system. At the same time as there was a strong and urgent move to change the existing political order, Iraqi intellectuals and artists were also involved in creating new cultural movements and found new expressions and forms in literature and the arts.

IV. Iraqi Women and Gender Relations under the Ba'th Regime

Women's experiences of the early Ba'th period differed not only in terms of ethnic and religious affiliation, but also, and maybe more significantly, in terms of class and political orientation. Many secular and apolitical middle class Shi'i, Kurdish and Christian women concur in their perceptions of the achievements of the Ba'th with many of the middle class Sunni women I interviewed. Even many women who were imprisoned or had to flee as political refugees during the early 1970s or early 1980s acknowledge the positive impact of developmental modernist policies on women during that period. Historically, Iraq is not the only country in which a repressive dictatorship did initially open up certain social, economic and professional spaces for women.

Many Iraqi women gained in terms of socio-economic rights during the 1970s and 1980s within the general context of political repression. Living conditions improved for the majority of the population as the state relied not only on force and its power to control and co-opt, but also devised generous welfare programmes and opened up opportunities for investment and capital accumulation which were of great benefit to a large number of people within the expanding middle classes. During my interviews with middle-class women who had not directly suffered state repression during the 1970s, I started to realize that the state

---

[11] Nuha is referring to the Shi'i rituals associated with 'Ashurah, the tenth day of the Islamic month of Muharram. For Shi'i Muslims, the day commemorates the martyrdom of Husayn ibn 'Ali, the grandson of the Prophet Muhammad at the Battle of Karbala' in the year 61 AH (AD 680) and is a day for mourning. Plays re-enacting the martyrdom are often staged and many take part in mourning rituals. Some Shi'i observe 'Ashurah with a traditional flagellation ritual called zanjeer zani or zanjeer matam, involving the use of a zanjeer (a chain with a set of curved knives at the end). The practice is not universal – many Shi'i enact the ritual by beating their chests symbolically.

[12] Al-Ali (2007), p. 65.

didn't just rely on its coercive and repressive control mechanisms to rule the country. The regime also managed to silence dissent and even obtain people's approval by providing a prospering socio-economic context in which many Iraqi families flourished. Siham A., recalls how her family moved from a relatively modest and small home in Al-Kadhimiya, a pre-dominantly Shi'i area, to al-Mansur, an ethnically and religiously diverse upper- middle class neighbour-hood. Siham's father ran a family-based construction company that had expanded rapidly in the context of the economic boom and state-led development projects in the 1970s. Many small businesses, companies and small-scale industries benefited from the economic policies of the state, and experienced instant capital accumulation and wealth.[13] Siham was reminiscing about the 'good old times':

> We moved to a nice big house in al-Mansur in 1978. It had many rooms and the garden was so nice. I got my own room with my own bed. Before we moved, I had to share the bed with two of my sisters. We bought new furniture, a big new fridge and freezer and a TV. My parents had lots of parties at home. In the summer, my parents' friends and relatives would come late in the evening and sit in the garden until the early hours of the morning, chatting, eating, and sometimes singing. My mother was a fantastic cook, but we all used to help her. And then there was Bahira, our maid, who would chop all the onions as none of us children wanted to do that job. On the weekend, my parents would take us to the club where I spent most of the time swimming or playing with my friend Amina by the pool. In the summer, we sometimes travelled abroad. I went shopping to London twice, and I also visited Beirut. Life was good before the war with Iran started.[14]

Siham acknowledges that her parents and her relatives were initially very sympathetic to the new regime. Her family was just one of thousands who experienced dramatic upward social mobility through rapid wealth and became part of an expanding middle class, made up of increasingly new social groups with 'new money'. As a secular Shi'i family they were also hopeful that the Ba'th would not pursue sectarian policies and enforce the stability and calm needed for economic prosperity.

Despite the far-reaching powers of the centralized state, some women benefited more than others. For women in the countryside or women of low-income background, Saddam Hussein's speeches about women's emancipation and the passing of new more women-friendly laws and policies did not change prevailing gender norms, roles and expected behaviour. At the same time, although limited and driven by pragmatic considerations, the Ba'th regime's policies of pushing women into the public sphere, especially the education system and the labour force, started to impact positively on some of the traditional attitudes and roles between women and men. This was particularly the case within the expanding urban middle-classes. For women of the old upper and upper middle classes, education and more liberal attitudes had been part of their parents' upbringing. However, for the newer middle classes, that emerged in the context of economic boom and expansion, tensions between modernization policies leading to women's greater participation in education and the work force clashed with traditional conservative ideas about women's and men's roles and forms of conduct.

[13] Farouk-Sluglett Sluglett (2003), p. 232.
[14] Al-Ali, (2007), pp. 128–129.

What one might coin 'state feminism', the state's active promotion of women's rights and attempt to change existing gender relations, might prove to be problematic when the state lacks credibility amongst the population. By providing women with certain legal rights, social services and access to education and the labour market, the Iraqi regime tried to shift patriarchal power away from fathers, husbands, brothers, sons, and uncles. The state became the main patriarch and patron of the country. Many of the middle class men and women went along with the relatively progressive social policies of the Iraqi state as long as the economic conditions were right. Yet, amongst the more religious and conservative forces in Iraqi society, such as tribal leaders and Islamists, there was a strong resentment against the state's attempt to interfere in people's traditions and sense of propriety. As so often when reforms and changes are imposed from above, they prove fickle and can easily be reverted.

However, for those who voiced their resistance to the Ba'th, the initial period of the new regime is remembered as a series of systematic attempts to eradicate any opposition and stabilize the regime. Political repression, mass arrests, torture and executions fill the memories of those women who were politically active themselves or had family members that were involved in opposition politics.

V. Shift in State Policies and Social Attitudes

Worsening political repression, a series of wars and the militarization of society seriously affected women, families and gender relations, not only in terms of the loss of loved ones, but also in terms of a deteriorating economy, changing government policies and shifting norms and increasingly conservative values surrounding women and gender. After the end of the Iran–Iraq war (1980–1988), and under the sanctions in the 1990s and early 2000s, a radical shift took place in terms of women's diminishing participation in the labour force, restricted access to education, inadequate healthcare and other social services. Women were increasingly pushed back into their homes as unemployment rates sky-rocketed, the economy faltered and the infrastructure collapsed.

During the eight-year period of the war with Iran, there was a shift in state rhetoric and government policies *vis-à-vis* women and gender relations. Maybe more so than before, women were needed by the state to keep the country running as thousands and thousands of Iraqi men were fighting and dying in the war. Women were carrying the conflicting double burden of being the main motors of state bureaucracy and the public sector, the main breadwinners and heads of households but also the 'mothers of future soldiers'. At some point the regime's ambivalent position towards women, as educated workers and mothers of future citizens, tipped towards the latter role as both the ideological climate and pragmatic needs had changed.

Women were increasingly used to demarcate boundaries between communities and carry the heavy burden of honour in a society that became increasingly militarized. Women's patriotic duties shifted to producers of loyal Iraqi citizens and future fighters. Their bodies became progressively more the sight of nationalist policies and battles. During the Iran–Iraq war, a series of legal decrees were introduced to control women's marital and reproductive freedoms. In December 1982, the Revolutionary Command Council (RCC) issued a decree forbidding Iraqi women to marry non-Iraqis as well as another decree prohibiting

Iraqi women married to non-Iraqis to transfer money or property to their husbands as inheritance.[15] At the same time, Iraqi men were encouraged to divorce their Iranian wives while Iraqi Arab men were encouraged to marry Kurdish women as part of the regime's Arabization policies in the north. During this period, Islamist and Kurdish women were tortured and sexually abused, humiliating not only the women but 'dishonouring' their male relatives as well.

It is, however, the 13 years of the most comprehensive sanctions system ever imposed on a country (1990–2003) which had the most devastating effects on women and gender relations throughout the country and across social classes. Aside from the most obvious and devastating effects of economic sanctions, related to dramatically increased child mortality rates, widespread malnutrition, deteriorating health care and general infrastructure as well as unprecedented poverty and an economic crisis, women were particularly hit by a changing social climate. The breakdown of the welfare state had a disproportionate effect on women, who had been its main beneficiaries. State discourse and policies as well as social attitudes and gender ideologies shifted dramatically during the sanctions period.

Women were clearly pushed back into their homes and into the traditional roles of being mothers and housewives. From being the highest in the region, estimated to be above 23% prior to 1991, women's employment rate fell to only 10% in 1997, as reported by the UNDP in 2000.[16] Monthly salaries in the public sector, which, since the Iran–Iraq war, had increasingly been staffed by women, dropped dramatically and did not keep pace with high inflation rates and the cost of living. Many women reported that they simply could not afford to work anymore, since the state had to withdraw its free services, including childcare and transportation.[17]

Teenage girls and young women in their twenties and thirties frequently referred to the changes related to socializing, family ties, and relations between neighbours and friends. Often a parent or older relative was quoted as stating how things were different from the past when socializing played a much bigger role in people's lives. Zeinab, a fifteen-year-old girl from Baghdad, spoke about the lack of trust between people. On the change in dress code for women and the social restrictions she and her peers experience constantly, she said:

> People have changed now because of the increasing economic and various other difficulties of life in Iraq. They have become very afraid of each other. I think because so many people have lost their jobs and businesses, they are having loads of time to speak about other people's lives, and they often interfere in each other's affairs. I also think that because so many families are so poor now that they cannot afford buying more than the daily basic food, it becomes so difficult for them to buy nice clothes and nice things and therefore, it is better to wear *hijab*. Most people are somewhat pressured to change their lives in order to protect themselves from the gossip of other people – especially talk about family honour.[18]

[15] S. Omar, 'Honour, Shame and Dictatorship', in F. Hazelton (ed.), *Iraq since the Gulf War: Prospects for Democracy* (London and New York, Zed Books, 1994), p. 63.
[16] *1999–2000 Country Report*, Iraq Country Office, June 2000.
[17] N. Al-Ali, 'Gendering Reconstruction: Iraqi Women between Dictatorship, wars, Sanctions and Occupation', *Third World Quarterly*, 26(4/5) (2005), pp. 7–47.
[18] N. Al-Ali and Y. Hussein 'Between Dreams and Sanctions: Teenage Lives in Iraq', in Akbar Mahdi (ed.), *Teenagers in the Middle East* (Westport, CT: Greenwood Publishing Group, 2003), p. 46.

The fears related to a woman's reputation may have been aggravated by the occurrence of so-called 'honour killings' during and after the sanctions period. Saddam Hussein, in an attempt to maintain legitimacy after the Gulf War by appeasing conservative patriarchal constituencies, brought in anti-woman legislation such as a 1990 presidential decree granting immunity to men who committed honour crimes.[19] Fathers and brothers of women who are known or often merely suspected of having 'violated' the accepted codes of behaviour, especially with respect to keeping their virginity before marriage, may kill the women in order to restore the honour of the family. Despite the fact that the law was abrogated after only two months without naming specific reasons,[20] knowledge about the existence of honour killings worked as a deterrent for many Iraqi women and teenagers. Others might have been less worried about the most dramatic consequences of 'losing one's reputation'. For educated middle-class women from urban areas it was not so much honour crimes they feared, as diminished marriage prospects.

The most obvious signs of this shift towards greater social conservatism where women and gender relations are concerned were changed dress code (many girls and women started to wear *hijab*), restrictions in mobility and public spaces for socializing in mixed gender settings, and an overall shift towards more traditional gender roles. Sanctions also changed class differences in Iraqi society as it led to the impoverishment of a previously broad and educated middle class at the same time as it allowed a new class of *nouveau riche* war and sanctions profiteers to emerge.

VI. Developments Since 2003

While Iraqi men are bearing the main brunt in terms of the deteriorating security situation and escalating armed violence, women are particularly hard hit in terms of survival in harsh living conditions, poverty, malnutrition, lack of adequate health services and infrastructure, including electricity which in some areas of Iraq only works for about two hours per day. Over 70% of the more than 2 million displaced people inside Iraq are women and children. Many have found shelter with relatives who share their limited space, food and supplies. But this has created rising tensions between families over scarce resources. Many displaced women and children find themselves in unsanitary and overcrowded public buildings under constant threat of being evicted.

While aerial bombings of residential areas are responsible for a large number of civilian deaths, many Iraqis have lost their lives while being shot at by American or British troops. Whole families have been wiped out as they were approaching a check point or did not recognize areas marked as prohibited. In addition to the killing of innocent women, men and children, the occupation forces have also been engaged in other forms of violence against women. There have been numerous documented accounts about physical assaults at check-points, and during house searches. American and British forces have also arrested wives, sisters and daughters of suspected insurgents in order to pressure them to surrender. Aside from the violence related to the arrests itself, those women who were detained by

---

[19] See http://www.womenwarpeace.org/iraq/iraq.htm.
[20] A. Rohde, 'Facing Dictatorship: State Society Relations in Ba'thist Iraq', unpublished PhD dissertation, Freie Universität Berlin (April 2006), p. 236.

the troops might suffer as well from the sense of shame associated with such a detention.

Islamist militias linked to political parties in government and insurgent groups opposing the government and the occupation also pose a particular danger to Iraqi women. Many women's organizations and activists inside Iraq have documented the increasing Islamist threats to women, the pressure to conform to certain dress codes, the restrictions in movement and behaviour, incidents of acid thrown into women's faces and even targeted killings. Suad F., a former accountant and mother of four children who lives in a neighbourhood in Baghdad that used to be relatively mixed before the sectarian killings in 2005 and 2006 was telling me during a visit to Amman in 2006:

> I resisted for a long time, but last year also started wearing *hijab*, after I was threatened by several Islamist militants in front of my house. They are terrorizing the whole neighbourhood, behaving as if they were in charge. And they are actually controlling the area. No one dares to challenge them. A few months ago they distributed leaflets around the area warning people to obey them and demanding that women should stay at home.

By 2008, the threat posed by Islamist militias as well as the mushrooming Islamist extremist groups goes far beyond imposed dress codes and calls for gender segregation in universities. Despite, or even partly because of the US and UK rhetoric about liberation and women's rights, women have been pushed back even more into the background and into their homes. Women who have a public profile; either as teachers, doctors, academics, lawyers, NGO activists or politicians, are systematically threatened and have become targets for assassinations.

Criminal gangs also contribute to the lawlessness and chaos by kidnapping women for ransoms as well as sexually abusing them and increasingly trafficking young women outside of Iraq to sell them into prostitution.

One hundred and thirty-three women were killed last year in Basra alone, Iraq's second largest city, either by religious vigilantes or as a result of so-called 'honour killings', a report said on December 31, 2007. The report, released by Basra Security Committee at a conference on women's rights in the city, said 79 of the victims were deemed by extremists to be 'violating Islamic teachings', 47 others died in 'honour killings' and the remaining seven were targeted for their political affiliations.[21] 'Politically active women, those who did not follow a strict dress code, and women [who are] human rights defenders were increasingly at risk of abuses, including by armed groups and religious extremists', Amnesty said in a 2007 report.

VII. Conclusion

One of the many problems in the post-invasion era is the failure by many sections of society to acknowledge different experiences of the past, therefore alienating parts of the population who do not see themselves represented in a particular narrative. In reference to the present situation, I always feel uneasy when I hear people say: 'Iraqi women think . . .' or 'Iraqi women want . . .' generalizing from what is inevitably a wide variety of opinions, views and visions. What arguably has emerged from my research, however, is that difference is historically based on

[21] http://www.irinnews.org/report.aspx?ReportId = 76065

a complex set of variables and can not simply be reduced to ethnicity and religion as is often construed nowadays.

The period after the first Ba'th coup (1963) is generally associated with increased political violence, greater sectarianism and a reversal of progressive laws and reforms. The experiences of these periods differ most significantly in terms of class and political orientation. Many secular and apolitical middle class Shi'i, Sunni, Kurdish and Christian women concurred in their appreciation of the achievements of the early Ba'th in education, modernization of infrastructures and welfare provisions. However, the memories of those who were politically active in opposition to the regime are filled with accounts of political repression, mass arrests, torture and executions. Yet, even some of those women who had first hand experiences of the regime's repressive practices retrospectively appreciate its developmental policies.

At the same time, accounts of Iraqi women reveal that an urban middle class identity, especially the more cosmopolitan Baghdadi identity, continued to subsume ethnic and religious differences even throughout the period of the sanctions. In other words, a middle class Shi'i family in Baghdad had more in common with its Sunni Arab and Kurdish middle class neighbours in mixed neighbourhoods than the impoverished Shi'is living in Madina al-Thawra (renamed Saddam city and now called Sadr city), or the majority of Shi'is in the south. Indeed, Baghdadi families have frequently been multi-religious and multi-ethnic, and mixed marriages amongst urban Baghdadi middle classes were quite common.

Since the late 1970s, differences on the lines of secular and Islamist political positions started to assume greater significance and influence women's experiences of the regime. Members or sympathizers of the Islamist Shi'i *Da'wa* party, for example, were targeted not so much because of their religious affiliation but because of their opposition to the regime and their aim to establish an Islamic state. Without wanting to diminish the suffering and hardship that members of the Shi'i Islamist opposition parties endured, the narrative about being the main recipients of state repression not only belittles the suffering of Kurds, but also other segments of the population, including those Sunni Arabs who actively resisted the regime.

In the context of the aftermath of the invasion in 2003, the escalating violence and sectarian tensions, contestations about power and national identity, history becomes a very important and powerful tool. Contesting narratives about what happened in the past relate directly to different attitudes towards the present and visions about the future of the new Iraq. They relate to claims about rights, about resources, and about power. More crucially, the different accounts of the past lay down the parameters of what it means to be Iraqi, who is to be included and who is to be excluded. History justifies and contains both narratives of unity and narratives of divisions and sectarianism.

Despite the clearly political nature of the violence in Iraq, the media tend to portray violence against Iraqi women as an unfortunate part of Arab or Muslim 'culture'. A commonly held assumption is that gender-based violence, when committed in the Middle East, derives from Islam. Of course, pinning violence against women on Islam is politically useful: it helps to dehumanize Muslims and justify foreign intervention in their countries. It also deflects attention from the many ways that US and UK policy has ignored and enabled violence against the women of Iraq.

However, Iraqi women are not suffering because of anything specific to Islam. They are suffering because there is an incredible scale of violence on all levels, and no functioning state to provide security, services and adequate humanitarian assistance. No one is willing nor is able to guarantee and implement women's legal rights. The legal rights enshrined in the contested constitution are flawed to start out with and do not promote equal citizenship. Iraqi women are also deprived because of widespread and crippling poverty, large scale unemployment and lack of access to adequate resources.

And, yes, women are suffering because Islam is used by various political parties, factions, militias and insurgent groups to gain credibility and legitimacy. Iraqi politicians, Islamist militants as well as insurgents are pursuing gender ideologies and policies that are conservative at best and extremist in most cases. We are witnessing a radicalization of armed groups and their political leadership in which women are central to the attempt to gain control, impose rules and inscribe a new order rooted in narrow interpretations that are based on political-strategic considerations and ideological righteousness rather than a learned approach to religious texts and traditions.

The Discursive Occupation of Afghanistan

ANILA DAULATZAI

ABSTRACT   *In this paper I argue that feminist (inspired) writings have largely obfuscated the history of gender, violence, and subjectivity in Afghanistan. I contend that western and non-western feminisms – while having served important roles in keeping discussions on Afghanistan alive – fail to adequately relate to war and western imperialism, and therefore fall short of tracing the formations of subjectivity of women in contemporary Afghanistan. In building on a preliminary discussion of my ongoing ethnographic work with widows, I argue that the feminist project needs to more critically engage with notions such as agency and freedom in order to broaden a perspective that is often focusing too narrowly on (and thus perpetuating) under-studied notions of 'gender' and 'culture' in Afghanistan.*

I. Introduction: Occupation

Throughout Afghanistan, there are 86 bakeries operated by the World Food Program. These bakeries are run by widows and provide subsidized bread made from fortified flour to more than 170,000 mostly female-headed households throughout the city (WFP 2004). The bakery project and its focus on women in general, and widows in particular are exemplary for the way the international community has prioritized its interventions of aid and reconstruction in Afghanistan: While women are considered to be severely disadvantaged in all aspects of life in Afghanistan, widows are seen to be suffering even further grievances. The alleviation of women's suffering and the improvement of their roles in Afghan society, are considered to be one of the most urgent tasks at hand in rebuilding the country. This is in line with writings that assume a feminist approach and advocate a gender perspective to analyze and address the concerns of Afghanistan. While the potential benefits of such interventions are undeniable, this paper seeks to question the privileging of under-studied notions of gender as the primary axis along which the experience (and the suffering) of being a woman in Afghanistan can be understood and attended to.

I will argue that this privileging of gender is part of a two-pronged problem: firstly, there is a substantial lack in current knowledge on everyday life and subjectivity of Afghans, and secondly, this lack of knowledge is held in abeyance, while a limited set of analytical concepts occupies the respective discursive space. Coming to grips with Afghanistan by exclusively relying on this limited set of parameters ultimately results in an impossibility to acknowledge the experience and the suffering of Afghan women.

Although feminist (-inspired) writings have served an important role in keeping discussions of Afghanistan alive, they have largely obfuscated the history of war, violence, and subjectivity, particularly and paradoxically, as they relate to women in Afghanistan. While what lingers behind this paper is an assertion that feminist projects have failed to adequately engage with Afghanistan, my intention is not to render feminism, or a feminist perspective, useless or ineffective, but instead to add force to the advancement of feminism as a political and an epistemological project. I will begin by illustrating the limitations caused by the discursive over-determination of certain terms, especially gender, and then move on to discuss some possibilities for overcoming this inertia.[1]

Two articles by Leila Abu-Lughod,[2] and by Saba Mahmood and Charles Hirschkind,[3] respectively, lay bare what is at stake with regards to re-configuring Afghan women as subjects of inquiry, and allow insights into both the political, and the epistemological dimensions of the problematic. For the purposes at hand, their argument can be summarized as a critique of the following three essentializing tropes: (1) the suffering Afghan woman; (2) culture, as a deterministic explanatory device; (3) Islamic fundamentalism (in the form of the Taliban) as a scapegoat to summarily account for all forms of distress in Afghanistan. I would contend that the currently predominant mode of engaging with the suffering of Afghans, and Afghan women in particular, is through either one, or varying combinations of these three tropes. I have argued elsewhere, that this engagement is limited and has resulted in an impasse prohibiting an investigation of the forms and the extent of suffering endured by Afghans.[4] In the literature, as in politics, the tropes often collapse and a discussion of the 'suffering Afghan women' almost instantly becomes a treatment of other clichés: the Taliban, Islam/Islamic fundamentalism, or Afghan 'culture'.

In order to highlight the shortcomings of the prevailing formulaic conceptualizations of Afghan women and their predicament Abu-Lughod, Hirschkind and Mahmood refer to a radio address by Laura Bush on November 17, 2001,[5] as well as to the so-called 'Campaign to Stop Gender Violence in Afghanistan' by the Feminist Majority.[6] These two interventions were both emblematic and rather problematic in the ways in which they capitalized on the schematic idea of the suffering, veiled, and oppressed Afghan woman, as well as in the manner in which they distorted the recent history of Afghanistan for reasons of political expediency. The latter was accomplished by privileging the damage caused by the Taliban over a cumulative etiology of sufferings that would account

[1] My plea for acknowledging the suffering of Afghans derives from the importance I see (a) to study the subjectivities of contemporary Afghans, and (b) to recognize the severe impact that more than two decades of war, drought, and earthquakes have had in combination with the almost complete neglect of Afghanistan's hardships by the international community. I do not wish to imply that the only subjectivity Afghans can inhabit is one marked by suffering, and even less do I intend to suggest that Afghans are merely traumatized victims. However, the direly needed ethnographic study of contemporary Afghanistan will necessarily have to account for the impact of violence on the experiences and the social worlds of Afghans. Acknowledging their suffering therefore means nothing else than lending an ear to their pain, and thus retrieving their subjectivities from the discursive violence enabled by the existing analytical limitations.
[2] Leila Abu-Lughod, 'Do Muslim Women Really Need Saving? Anthropological Reflections on Cultural Relativism and its Others', *American Anthropologist* 104(3) (2002), pp. 783–790.
[3] Charles Hirschkind and Saba Mahmood, 'Feminism, the Taliban and Politics of Counter-Insurgency', *Anthropological Quarterly* 75(2) (2002), pp. 339–354.
[4] See Daulatzai, 'Acknowledging Afghanistan: Notes and Queries on an Occupation', *Cultural Dynamics* 18(3) (2006), 293–311.
[5] cf. http://www.whitehouse.gov/news/releases/2001/11/20011117.html
[6] cf. http://www.helpafghanwomen.com/

for the decades of crisis. While the Laura Bush address is criticized for hijacking the feminist agenda in order to justify the invasion and occupation of Afghanistan, the Feminist Majority campaign utilized feminism's reputation as a liberating ideology in order to advance an agenda of cultural imperialism. Although the Feminist Majority Campaign and the Laura Bush address are striking examples of the points made by Abu-Lughod, Hirschkind and Mahmood, I am ultimately more troubled by the writings of scholars who build their arguments – placed within cogent and critical political contexts – in apparently more nuanced ways, but following similar uncritical analyses. Attending to an example from this literature may help to expose some of the problems recurring in recent writings on Afghanistan propagating an apparently feminist agenda. I am especially concerned with the blurring and collapsing of fundamental analytical distinctions. The consequential neglect of feminism's analytic potential perhaps even more problematic than the hijacking of feminism in the two media interventions just discussed.

II. Feminism of Limit

An article titled 'Feminisms in the Aftermath of September 11' by Zillah Eisenstein begins with a critical assessment of the United States' foreign policies, including a discussion of the US role in the Gulf War, the assassination of President Allende in Chile, and the effect of the economic sanctions on Iraqi children between 1991 and 2002.[7] She continues her critical inquiry by writing about the bin-Laden family and its close investment ties with Western firms such as Microsoft and Boeing. This is closely followed by phrases like 'gender apartheid', 'sexual terrorism', and 'Muslim fundamentalist misogyny'. She uses such phrases as if they were semantically transparent, as if the associations she is making are obvious, and with great ease she locates the supposed problems she identifies in areas as diverse as Bosnia, Chechnya, Rwanda, Algeria, Nigeria, Afghanistan and Palestine. The following sentence indicates how Eisenstein effortlessly jumps from one Islamic country to another:

> After the Taliban retreat from Kabul, we were shown women's faces smiling as the air hit their skin. In all this, we need to be reminded that it has been women, since the Algerian revolution in that country, who have fought tirelessly for democratic rule.[8]

Eisenstein repeatedly collapses the distinctions between the various roles Muslim women have played in different struggles, and she reduces diverse Islamic movements to the cliché of 'misogynism'. Corresponding to what Abu-Lughod, Hirschkind and Mahmood criticized in both the Laura Bush address and the Feminist Majority campaign, i.e., a neat scapegoating of the Taliban for all that was unfortunate in Afghan society, particularly with respect to women, Eisenstein seems to assert that life before the Taliban was bountiful and uplifting for Afghan women, 'The war on "terrorism" exacerbates the misery for most Afghan women with *new* problems of starvation, homelessness, and their own terror'.[9]

While Eisenstein acknowledges the misery caused by the US led invasion of Afghanistan in 2001, she states that starvation and homelessness brought about by the war on terrorism are 'new' problems, and thus denies much of the suffering

---

[7] See Zillah Eisenstein, 'Feminisms in the Aftermath of September 11', *Social Text*, 20(3) (2002), pp. 79–98.
[8] Ibid., p. 80.
[9] Eisenstein, ibid., p. 84 (emphasis added).

Afghans endured in the decades of wars, droughts, earthquakes, and international neglect prior to the 2001 invasion and occupation.

> Pre-Taliban, Afghan women were participating in government, schools, and other civic institutions. Women accounted for 70 percent of all teachers, 50 percent of civil servants, and 40 percent of medical doctors. Pre-Taliban Afghan women were active in most parts of life, much like women in Iran and Algeria, before the takeover by misogynist fundamentalists. But now, after years of war, Kabul is home to some 70,000 war widows who live in abject poverty. Pregnant women throughout Afghanistan face the grave risk of miscarriage and other obstetric problems.[10]

Eisenstein never defines what she means by 'pre-Taliban'. While preferring to keep this time-period ambiguous her remarks posit a clear correlation between the poor health indicators and the miserable social conditions for Afghan women and the Taliban, thus establishing a causal link between the two.

The idea that health ramifications for women in Afghanistan need to be attributed to Taliban rule is not unique to Eisenstein. It was well received also among health professionals: In 1998, the Physicians for Human Rights (PHR) published an influential article on women's health in Afghanistan (Rasekh et al. 1998). It concluded that women in Afghanistan have poor overall health, especially poor mental health,[11] and that the Taliban were the main cause for these desperate conditions. The investigators deduced the following: '[t]he Taliban regime, a radical Islamic movement that took control of Kabul in September 1996, has had extraordinary health consequences for Afghan women'.[12]

The investigators did not address whether the ill health manifestations they found were entirely attributable to Taliban rule or whether they were results of the confounding factors of deaths of family members due to war, prior disease or poor health, displacement, lack of sanitation and overall poverty. The authors detailed alarming health indicators and risk factors, such as the infant mortality rate (165/1000), landmines that remain in Afghanistan (10 million), access to safe drinking water (urban access, 39%; and rural, 5%), malnutrition rates in children (35% of children younger than 5) as well as the dependence on external assistance for health care (70%). Considering the history of contemporary Afghanistan, the claim that these indicators are due to the Taliban regime is exaggerated and grossly over-simplifies the structural causes of the destruction and the suffering that the total population of Afghanistan, particularly the women and children, had endured for almost two decades prior to the study in 1998. Any study of women's health in a war-torn country needs to consider the processes that render some parts of the population more vulnerable than others while taking into full account that women are commonly the sub-population most affected by wars (Palmer and Zwi 1998). This is explicated in a report by MSF (MSF 2004):[13]

[10] Ibid., p. 95.

[11] Ninety-five percent of the 40 Afghan women interviewed for the study reported a decline in their physical health between 1996 and 1998, 77% indicated poor access to health care services in Kabul, while 20% reported no access at all; 97% of respondents met the diagnostic criteria for major depression and 86% demonstrated significant symptoms of anxiety (Rasekh et al. 1998). Zohra Rasekh et al., 'Women's Health and Human Rights in Afghanistan', *The Journal of the American Medical Association*, 280(5) (1998), pp. 449–455.

[12] Ibid., p. 449.

[13] Medecins Sans Frontiers was, apart from the International Red Cross, the only international NGO that remained in Afghanistan throughout the conflict since 1979.

The maternal mortality rate in Afghanistan is among the highest in the world, and is largely attributable to a lack of access to medical care. In rural areas, in particular, there is an acute shortage of qualified medical staff to provide care in the health centers that are functioning – symptomatic of a deteriorating health care system suffering the effects of war and lack of funding (MSF 2004).[14]

The 1998 PHR study is typical for the ways in which schematic conceptions of *religion* (in the form of the Taliban) and *gender* over-determine the discourse on contemporary Afghanistan.[15] The deterioration of women's health during the two years prior to the study may be attributed to longer-term structural causes and the cumulative effects of ill health, and not necessarily to the immediate political circumstances.[16] The study's findings, poor mental health, and poor overall health of women, would thus require research methods that allow determining etiologies with long-term social, political, and economic points of origin, rather than the accounting for health parameters and outcomes at a specific moment in time. By strictly following a gender-oriented line of analysis, as the PHR study did with its exclusive focus on women's health in Afghanistan, the underlying issue of a completely devastated health infrastructure in Afghanistan is largely disguised. The aim of my critical assessment is not to claim that women in Afghanistan did not suffer under the Taliban. In fact, my overarching concern is that as long as the parameters for studying Afghanistan remain limited as such, the ability to acknowledge the suffering of Afghans, both female and male, will remain elusive.

A direct and predictable manifestation of prolonged conflicts and unrest due to war and natural calamities in Afghanistan is a profound lack in accurate and current information on the everyday life of Afghans, since ethnographic

[14] Afghanistan has the second highest maternal mortality rate in the world, with 1700–2200 deaths per 100,000 live births (UNFPA, 2002; Abouzahr et al. 1996; Burnham and Smith 2005). The United Nations Population Fund reported in 2002 that 'most medical facilities are run down and in dire need of trained personnel'. The physician to citizen ratio in Afghanistan was 1 per 1700 in Kabul and other urban areas, and 1 per 434,000 in rural areas. The Afghan Ministry of Health estimated a national average of one doctor per 15,000 persons. In 2002, less than 12% of all Afghans had access to any health care, meaning a clinic within five miles, and two-thirds of the country had no access to reproductive health services at all. It was estimated that a woman died in childbirth every thirty minutes in Afghanistan and the life expectancy for an Afghan woman was 44 years (UNICEF 2002). Another major obstacle to extending reproductive health services to Afghans is the severe shortage of trained female doctors and midwives. 'Afghanistan inherited a health system from the eighties, which was geared to curative care and not for public health problems. This system has suffered not just from the fighting, but also from the succession of different regimes and consequently a high turnover of senior staff as well as constant changes in policy-making' says a report of the United Nations Assistance Mission in Afghanistan (UNAMA 2003).
[15] In a unique twist on the oppressive aspects of Afghan customs of veiling, the investigators of the 1998 PHR study also found that the burqa was a health hazard. One physician is quoted saying 'that the garment may cause eye problems and poor vision, poor hearing, skin rash, headaches, increased cardiac problems and asthma, itching of the scalp, alopecia (hair loss), and depression'. This particular finding of 1998 PHR study was later disputed by Lynn Amowitz, the principal investigator of the 2001 PHR study. She found that many women outside Kabul did not object to wearing the burqa and that approximately 90% of the women no longer living under Taliban control still chose to wear the burqa (Brown 2001). It is interesting to note that the 2001 PHR report (Amowitz and Iacopino 2001), which refuted many of the findings of the 1998 study (Rasekh et al. 1998) received very little attention. The 1998 PHR study was widely received, and its problematic findings were discussed in popular media, including on *Oprah* (Brown 2001).
    Janelle Brown: http://archive.salon.com/mwt/feature/2001/10/9/amowitz/index.html Accessed September 25, 2008.
    Lynn Amowitz and Vincent Iacopino, 'Women's Health and Human Rights in Afghanistan: A Population-Based Assessment', *Physicians for Human Rights Study*, December 2001.
[16] It is unfortunate that the PHR study tried to ascertain suffering purely by quantitative means in the form of a survey instrument. I acknowledge the need for methodological compromises due to cost, limited time, and security concerns for research under circumstances of war and political unrest, however, the findings based on such constrained research are not sufficient to support the claims made in the PHR study.

or sociological fieldwork could not be carried out there during most of the past three decades. Zillah Eisenstein's article discusses contemporary Afghanistan nevertheless, assuming that terms like 'Taliban' and 'fundamentalism' were sufficient as descriptors of the Afghan social and political environment. She repeatedly uses the word 'misogyny' to portray the Taliban, which seems to foreclose the necessity to further substantiate any claims made about how specific Taliban policies were implemented, and how they affected women. Apart from certain drastic, and certainly shocking, examples that repeatedly appear in the literature,[17] little to no information exists so far on how the Taliban functioned as an organization, and how their presence was felt in the everyday lives of Afghans. Eisenstein's usage of such discursively effective terms is exemplary for other authors who attempt to describe the concerns of Afghan women notwithstanding the absence of corroborating information.[18]

Valentine Moghadam,[19] on the other hand, uses the available sociological, ethnographic, and historical archives as the basis for her descriptions of Afghan women's lives. Her writings build on careful research, but the sources she consults, however, frequently date back to the period before the Soviet invasion in 1979. Her reputed accounts, which often render gender relations in Afghanistan as steeped in archaic patriarchal tribal codices, thus gloss over a gap of decades of research. This might be problematic, since the situation on the ground has changed drastically during this period, and the analytical categories employed 30 years ago might now have taken on different meanings, or simply not be applicable to contemporary circumstances. While she certainly cannot be held accountable for the lack of substantial ethnographic or sociological information on contemporary Afghanistan, it is worth noting that neither she nor those who reference her work do seem to make this lacuna evident in their analyses and conclusions. Moghadam's glossing over of this substantial lack of information is not unique, yet it is consequential, considering that Moghadam's work is influential and frequently cited.[20] Such descriptions might thus not so much account for gender relations in a traditionalistic society, rather than evoke gender in Afghan society using traditionalist ethnological terms.

[17] These examples include the RAWA footage of the public execution of a woman, and accounts of beatings of females for not being properly veiled (cf. Dupree 1998 and Azarbaijani-Moghaddam 2004 for a discussion of the effects these representations had in the West).

[18] See for example: Larry Goodson, 'Perverting Islam: Taliban Social Policy Toward Women', *Central Asian Survey*, 20(4) (2001), pp. 415–426; Ivy Schweitzer, 'Women: Canary in the Mine', *Gender and Cultural Memory* 28(1) (2002), pp. 466–468; Anne E. Brodsky, *With All Our Strength: The Revolutionary Association of the Women of Afghanistan* (New York: Routledge, 2003).

[19] Valentine M. Moghadam, 'Revolution, the State, Islam, and Women: Gender Politics in Iran and Afghanistan', *Social Text*, 22 (1989), pp. 40–61. *Modernizing Women: Gender and Social Change in the Middle East* (Boulder, CO: L. Rienner, 1993). *Gender and National Identity: Women and Politics in Muslim Societies* (London and New Jersey: Zed Books, 1994). 'Revolution, Religion, and Gender Politics: Iran and Afghanistan Compared', *Journal of Women's History,* 10(4) (1999), pp. 172–204. 'Patriarchy, the Taliban, and Politics of Public Space in Afghanistan', *Women's Studies International Forum*, 25(1) (2002), pp. 19–31. *Global Feminism and Women's Citizenship in the Muslim World: The Cases of Iran, Algeria and Afghanistan. Citizenship, Borders, and Gender: Mobility and Immobility* (New Haven, CT: Yale University, 2003).

[20] See, for example: Rosemary Skaine, *The Women of Afghanistan Under the Taliban* (Jefferson, NC: McFarland and Company, 2002). Judith Lorber, 'Heroes, warriors, and 'burqas': A Feminist Sociologist's Reflections on Sept 11', *Sociological Forum*, 17(3) (2002), pp. 377–396. Brodsky, *With All Our Strength*. Carol J. Riphenburg, 'Gender Relations and Development in a Weak State: The Rebuilding of Afghanistan', *Central Asian Survey*, 22(2/3) (2003), pp. 187–207, and 'Post-Taliban Afghanistan: Changed Outlook for Women', *Central Asian Survey*, 44(3) (2004), pp. 401–421. Elaheh Rostami Povey, 'Women in Afghanistan: Passive victims of the borga or active Social participants?' *Development in Practice*, 11(2/3) (2003), pp. 266–277. Saba Gul Khattak, 'Adversarial Discourses, Analogous Objectives: Afghan's Women's Control', *Cultural Dynamics*, 16(2/3) (2004), pp. 213–236.

Abu-Lughod, as well as Hirschkind and Mahmood locate some of the shortcomings of the recent scholarship on Afghanistan in the context of distinct problematics that arise in writings on Muslim women. They point out that the undifferentiated foci of much of this genre of work often result in the elision of history and geo-politics. Abu-Lughod explains this on the example of contemporary Afghanistan:

> ... the question is why knowing about the 'culture' of the region, and particularly its religious beliefs and treatment of women, was more urgent than exploring the history of the development of repressive regimes in the region and the U.S. role in this history. Such cultural framing [...] prevented the serious exploration of the roots and nature of human suffering in this part of the world. Instead of political and historical explanations, experts were being asked to give religio-cultural ones.[21]

Instead of being portrayed as complex individuals with varying sensibilities, affects, as well as abilities and inabilities to remake their selves and others, Afghan women are frequently reduced to the uni-dimensional figure of a passive, oppressed woman who is forced to wear a veil. I do not mean to assert that women in Afghanistan were not anguished under the Taliban, or that some of them were not deeply oppressed by the Taliban edicts that forced them to wear the *burqa*, or that prevented them from attending school or leaving their home unaccompanied. But I want to stress the point made by Abu-Lughod, as well as Hirschkind and Mahmood, that the almost exclusive attention that forced veiling (which only impacted a small percentage of Afghan women)[22] and certain Taliban edicts on women's movement and employment received has eclipsed the larger and perhaps more consequential modalities of suffering experienced by Afghan women as a result of more than two decades of armed conflict, war, and natural disasters. Abu-Lughod identified such calamities as the 'structural violence of global inequality', and 'ravages of war'.[23] Such modalities of suffering, I would like to add, could include, but are not limited to: widespread poverty, malnutrition, unremitting mourning stemming from multiple deaths of children or spouse or other family, repeated displacements, war-related disability, the effects of an ongoing catastrophic drought that began in 1998, the pain and discomfort resulting from untreated medical conditions such as prolapsed uterus, and the stresses associated with pregnancy. Not only are the various modes of suffering reduced by simply limiting the scope of concern to the restrictions put in place by the Taliban, but the duration of the suffering (regardless of its nature) is also misrepresented by being contained within the five-year Taliban rule. Hirschkind and Mahmood ask a pertinent question: 'Why are conditions of war, militarization, and starvation considered to be less injurious to women than the lack of education, employment, and most notably, in the media campaign, Western style dress?'[24]

---

[21] Abu-Lughod (2002), pp. 784.

[22] In personal communication with the author, the well-respected archaeologist and Afghanistan researcher Nancy Dupree pointed out that it was only a small percentage of western-oriented, upper-class women in Kabul who were impacted by the Taliban dress code policies. She agrees that it was unfortunate that the choice to remain unveiled was taken away from these women, but is also astounded by the attention this issue has received, considering the small number of women affected (the sensibilities of the vast majority of women in Afghanistan are in line with veiling).

[23] Abu-Lughod, pp. 783–790.

[24] Hirschkind and Mahmood (2002), p. 345.

Similar tendencies towards slippages surrounding discussions on 'gender' that quickly turn into verdicts on 'culture' have been pointed out by Kamala Visweswaran in her work on female asylum seekers from South Asia in the United States.[25] She notes that asylum cases of women from India, Pakistan, Afghanistan, Sri Lanka and Bangladesh necessarily collapse into cases of gender persecution and that frequently, essentializing and monochromatic caricatures of 'culture', rather than analyses of political and legal structures, or of policy failures and implementation practices by the state, serve as grounds upon which political asylum is granted or denied. Visweswaran argues that human rights claims, specifically involving cases from South Asia invoke feminism and human rights in strategic and particular ways ultimately portraying certain countries as being more prone to human rights abuses towards women than others,

> First, culture is gendered and violently masculinized so that particular countries or nation-states are marked by their crimes against women: to say India is to think dowry deaths, to say Pakistan is to think honour killing, to say Bangladesh is to think of acid-throwing disfigurement. [...] How is culture gendered so that particular countries or nation-states are marked by their crimes against women, so that they assume certain identities, not as democracies or dictatorships, but as bride-burners or honor-killings?[26]

I read Visweswaran's work as articulating a firm cautionary note regarding the use of gender essentialisms over thorough political, historical, and sociological or ethnographic analyses, particularly with regards to women from South Asia.

Now that I have outlined the contours of the stagnant trajectory in which a majority of feminist-inspired writings on Afghanistan have remained I would like to make a gesture away from what I see as a *feminism of limit*, and towards what I imagine to be a *feminism of possibility*. I consider feminism to be limited, when its analyses remain restricted to partial reflections on existing power constellations – e.g., in the case at hand, (a) the gender inequities in Afghanistan, (b) the role the international community, and particularly the USA, had in creating the conditions of possibilities for forces like the Taliban, or al-Qaeda to emerge, (c) the hypocritical nature of the US-led invasion and occupation, and the hijacking of feminist rhetoric for purposes of justification, (d) the media's role in conjuring up the ubiquitous image of Afghan women as veiled, oppressed victims of men, traditions, and Islam. But a *feminism of possibility* would not stop at this point, without utilizing its analytical potential for a critical reassessment of the epistemological underpinnings, of the very terms and concepts that make up the current textures of women's subjectivity and experience. I would therefore like to dwell here on the commentaries of a small number of scholars who make such compelling demands of feminist methodologies, and who are imbued with deep concerns and curiosities about what is at stake in Afghanistan. They continue to assert the importance of a feminist analytics in general, and specifically for Afghanistan, but they seem unconvinced that the exclusive privileging of a gender perspective will get to the issues of utmost concern, i.e., supporting Afghan women and alleviating the suffering of Afghans.

[25] Kamala Visweswaran, 'Gendered States: Rethinking Culture as a Site of South Asian Human Rights Work', *Human Rights Quarterly*, 26 (2004), pp. 483–511.
[26] Ibid., p. 509.

III. Feminism of Possibility

Joan Scott's corpus of work has played a seminal role in shaping the sensibilities of generations of feminists. She reminds us that thorough analyses of the operations of difference and the workings of power are central to a feminist methodology.

Gaining acuity from Scott's work, and applying it to Afghanistan, would mean to insist on non-static formulations, and on nuanced understandings, which – at minimum – require historical depth:

> At least since the 1980's, feminist scholarship has learned to make nuanced distinctions along multiple axes of difference; its theories don't assume fixed relationships between entities but treat them as the mutable effects of (temporally, culturally, historically) specific power dynamics.[27]

A feminist mode of inquiry in Afghanistan would thus require a fundamental overhaul and investigation of the terms often associated with the country: gender, culture, Islam, tribe, tradition, kinship, patriarchy, etc. What do each of these terms mean now? What is, for example, 'gender' in contemporary Afghanistan considering that women's and men's roles have shifted dramatically throughout the past thirty years of unrest and calamity? Since experience and life circumstances of both men and women have altered so drastically as a result of consecutive and ongoing wars, repeated droughts, and massive earthquakes, 'gender' might have taken on a different range of meaning, and similar things are to be said about 'Islam', 'tradition' and 'culture',[28] etc. All these concepts refer to elementary aspects of life in Afghanistan that have not been thoroughly investigated for decades. Suppositions and outdated anthropological or sociological research cannot be relied upon to describe contemporary life in Afghanistan.

In her book *Precarious Life*,[29] Judith Butler articulates what I consider crucial for examining Afghanistan, and for communicating understandings about it. Butler invokes the concept of the 'face' as explored by Emmanuel Levinas to illuminate how it is that the 'Other' makes an ethical claim or demand on a person. Butler turns to Levinas to reflect on the urgency of the contemporary context primarily because he provides tools to think through questions of representation and processes of humanization and dehumanization, and also to contemplate the links between ethics and violence. Butler quotes from Levinas' *Ethics and Infinity*: 'I have not looked at him in the face, I have not encountered his face … To be in relation with the other face to face is to be unable to kill. It is also the situation of discourse'.[30]

Butler brilliantly applies her understandings of the implications of the Levinasian face to the well-known images of unveiled Afghan women, which circulated after the US invasion of Kabul:

> According to the triumphalist photos that dominated the front page of the New York Times, these young women bared their faces as an act of liberation, an act of gratitude

---

[27] Joan Wallach Scott, 'Feminist Reverberations', *difference: A Journal of Feminist Cultural Studies*, 13(3) (2002), p. 6.

[28] 'Tradition' and 'culture' are problematic concepts under any circumstances (cf. Hobsbawm and Ranger 1983; Trouillot 2001).

[29] Judith Butler, *Precarious Life: The powers of mourning and violence* (London and New York, 2004).

[30] Quoted in Judith Butler, ibid., p. 138.

to the US military and an expression of a pleasure that had become suddenly and ecstatically permissible. The American viewer was ready, as it were, to see the face [. . .]. It became bared to us, at that moment, and we were, as it were, in possession of the face; not only did our cameras capture it, but we arranged for the face to capture our triumph, and act as the rationale for our violence, the incursion on sovereignty, the deaths of civilians. Where is the loss in that face? And where is the suffering over war? Indeed, the photographed face seemed to conceal or displace the face in the Levinasian sense, since we saw and heard through that face no vocalization of grief or agony, no sense of the precariousness of life.[31]

Instead of fixating on gendered violence, Butler contemplates the 'suffering over war' that is lost in the visual representations of 'liberated' Afghan women. The visibility of their unveiled faces momentarily humanizes the women, but the absence of their face in the Levinasian sense simultaneously dehumanizes them.

[. . .] although we might want to champion the suddenly bared faces of the young Afghan women as the celebration of the human, we have to ask in what narrative function these images are mobilized, whether the incursion into Afghanistan was really in the name of feminism, and in what form of feminism did it belatedly cloth itself. Most importantly, though, it seems we have to ask what scenes of pain and grief these images cover over and derealize.[32]

The 'we' in Butler's quotation have not looked at the face of an Afghan woman, because if 'we' had, 'we' surely would have seen and felt the affectual residue of decades of violence and hardship. Butler's hesitation to celebrate the unveiling of Afghan women as their liberation is of utmost importance for my argument, because she indicates that the subjectivities and the experience of being a woman in Afghanistan are lost if we are preoccupied with a perspective that only allows to perceive them as just that, women in Afghanistan. In other words, Butler's usage of the Levinasian face is a successful attempt at showing that gender is not the only dimension – maybe not even the most important one – of Afghan women's lives.

As I argue, the over-determination of gender in addressing the suffering of Afghans has led to an impasse, thereby creating the conditions of impossibility for acknowledging this very suffering. According to my assessment, the privileging of gender is due largely to a severe lack of rigorous and sound current research, which is caused by more than two decades of prolonged violence and instability that significantly constrained the possibilities for scholarly work in Afghanistan. To address the dearth in information in the wake of Afghanistan's reentry into spheres of general interest in the West, many anthropologists recently re-issued their work originally published in the sixties and seventies.[33] The vacuum has thus not been filled, but patched over with outdated research and modes of anthropological inquiry. Security concerns and logistical difficulties notwithstanding, without long-term, ethnographic research the current impasse will remain. I do not want to claim that only anthropologists are in a position to contribute valuable research data, but my contention is that the elemental aspects

[31] Judith Butler, ibid., p. 142.
[32] Ibid., p. 143.
[33] David Chaffetz, *A Journey through Afghanistan: A Memorial* (Chicago, IL: University of Chicago Press, 2001). David B. Edwards, *Before Taliban: Genealogies of the Afghan Jihad* (Berkeley, CA: University of California Press, 2002). M. Nazif Mohib Shahrani, *The Kirghiz and Wakhi of Afghanistan: adaptation to closed frontiers and war* (Seattle, WA: University of Washington Press, 2002).

of social life and experience in Afghanistan are largely unknown and desperately need to be studied. Any attempt to comment on problems, needs, or the struggles of Afghans in general and Afghan women in particular will thus remain elusive and subject to conjecture without sustained and engaged inquiries into the everyday lives and subjectivities of Afghans. For example, in order to offer insightful remarks on the conditions of women in Afghanistan it cannot suffice to regurgitate a limited set of clichés about misogynistic practices in Islamic, tribal societies. Instead, methodologies are required that enable the study of hopes, desires, and anxieties, of sensibilities, affects, and insecurities, and of the moral calculus of life, of the impacts of violence inflicted by forces within and without, as well as of kinship structures, social networks, and the reproduction of meaning.

IV. Ending the Occupation

In the following, I would like to offer some thoughts on how one could begin to re-engage with Afghanistan, yet I do not intend these remarks to be prescriptive by any means.[34] Instead, I want to consider them an invitation for others and for myself to re-cast the terms by which we have come to know Afghanistan. The work of physician-anthropologist Paul Farmer could serve as a potential beginning to find a conduit through the current impasse. His contention is that 'to understand suffering, one must embed individual biography in the larger matrix of culture, history, and political economy'.[35] The structuring of risk, as he argues, is not determined by the immediate conditions only, but must be traced back historically, as well as contextualized within contemporary political economies. Central to his work is the concept of *structural violence*, which was first discussed by John Galtung,[36] and describes harms caused by long-standing social, political, and economic inequalities that are perpetuated by institutions and result in differential access to resources and life choices. Farmer uses case studies from his clinical work to illustrate that structural violence thus determines the conditions for suffering, and often, survival.[37] For Afghanistan, this would mean locating the roots of suffering in more than twenty years of armed conflict, but also, and especially, recognizing geopolitical configurations which propelled the country into the last big battle of the Cold War, and for which it was no longer relevant after the Soviet Union had collapsed. In other words, while Afghans took upon themselves the responsibility to fight this war on behalf of foreign powers, these powers never assumed the responsibility to prevent the country from descending into chaos and devastation after the big battle was won. The absence of infrastructure, the political turmoil, and the brutality that mark the daily struggle for survival of many Afghans can thus be traced back to deliberations of the very same forces which now put the blame on the victims. Hence, it is not the interventions of international aid agencies, which are imbued with the affect of charity that will alleviate the suffering caused by these

---

[34] A version of Hila's story has been published in *Cultural Dynamics*. Please see Anila Daulatzai, 'Acknowledging Afghanistan: Notes and Queries on Occupation', *Cultural Dynamics*, 18(3) (2006), pp. 293–311.

[35] Paul Farmer, *Pathologies of Power: health, human rights, and the new war on the poor*, 2nd edn (Berkeley, Los Angeles, London: University of California Press, 2005), p. 41.

[36] John Galtung, 'Violence, Peace and Peace Research', *Journal of Peace Research*, 6(3) (1969), pp. 167–191. Paul Farmer, 'On Suffering and Structural Violence: A View from Below', in Arthur Kleiman, Veena Das and Margaret Lock (eds.), *Social Suffering* (London and Berkeley: University of California Press, 1997), pp. 283.

[37] Paul Farmer, 'On Suffering and Structural Violence: A View from Below' and *Pathologies of Power*.

deliberations and their aftermath, but perhaps the affect of compensation. But I am getting ahead of myself here. The purpose of locating the roots of the suffering of Afghans in these geopolitical configurations is not to reallocate blame, say, from the Taliban to the US, but I argue that what is at stake is precisely an acknowledgement of the genealogy of the suffering that Afghans have endured. The analytical framework, however, should not only be 'historically deep', as Farmer contends, but also 'geographically broad'[38] in order to account for the ways, as he tries to show with his work among the poor in Haiti, in which large-scale social forces become embodied as sickness, suffering and degradation.[39] To comment on contemporary Afghanistan one thus needs to trace the genealogies of suffering not just back in history, but also to the super powers and the international institutions that are presently 'reconstructing' Afghanistan, and to their agendas, and their rhetoric. I would like to illustrate the importance of this with an example from my ongoing ethnographic research among widows in Kabul. For this purpose, I will now return to one of the bakeries run by the World Food Program, which I mentioned at the outset of this paper.

Hila works a ten-hour shift every day, baking bread in a local bakery in Kabul. She is a twenty-five-year-old woman who has survived the deaths of her three brothers and her father. These deaths left Hila alone to care and provide for herself and her mother. She says that she lost all the men in her life. She tried to get married several times, but the prospective grooms, or their families, could not afford to provide for both her and her mother. She cannot leave her mother since there is nobody else that could care for her; her mother only had brothers, all of whom died during the wars, and her father's family who would customarily assume the responsibility, is too poor to accept another household member. Hila, therefore, imagines her future not to include marriage. The widows working in the bakery, and the community, thus presented her to the WFP as a '*zaneh beh sarparast*', a widow (literally: *woman without a head of household*), who should be given a job. Although she was never married, classificatorily, Hila is a widow.[40]

The predicament of this young woman does not only need to be traced back to the harshness of her life circumstances, but also to the parameters with which international aid institutions categorize the experiences of Afghan women: the figure of the war-destitute, dependent and subjugated widow has emerged as the paradigmatic object of intervention for the many international aid agencies that currently work in Afghanistan. This is related to the ways in which images of women as powerless victims circulate in the literature on Afghanistan (as outlined above), and which ultimately impact discourses and policies pertaining to development and state-building in Afghanistan. It is also grounded in demographic circumstances: among a total population of nearly 24 million Afghans, more than 3 million are young and middle-aged war widows, with 300,000 widows living in Kabul itself. It is estimated that one of eight households in Afghanistan is headed by a widow (UNFPA 2002). Hila's access to the bakery was thus gained through this category of widowhood as defined by the WFP, and which was, in turn, creatively engaged with and transformed by her community. Would she still articulate her predicament as that of a classificatory widow if the figure of the widow would not

---

[38] Paul Farmer, *Pathologies of Power*, p. 42.

[39] Ibid., pp. 29–50.

[40] *Sarparast* comes from the word *parastar*, which means guardian or head of the family. In colloquial Dari, therefore, *zaneh beh sarparast* refers to a woman without a *male* head of household.

epitomize the trope of the suffering, oppressed Afghan woman in the discourses of the international aid community? What role does this trope play in mitigating, or extending her suffering? Or, more generally, what are the impacts on the possibilities for social reconstruction in Afghanistan of an analysis that conceptualizes women as victims, and ultimately, men and 'culture' as perpetrators? These questions need to be addressed because the tropes of the suffering Afghan woman, of culture as a deterministic explanatory device, and of fundamentalist Islam as represented by the Taliban have not only governed representations of contemporary Afghanistan (as discussed in this paper), but have now moved from the discursive into the domain of everyday life and are thus impacting the social worlds of Afghans. I argue strongly for an epistemological shift away from understandings that are determined only by such tropes, and towards the systematic investigation of their impact on the everyday life and the subjectivities of Afghans.

Among the international aid community the World Food Program bakeries are considered a highly successful example for interventions directed at improving the lives of women in Afghanistan. The project has been operating since 1996, that is, it was put in existence as the Taliban came to power. Despite Taliban edicts against women working outside their homes, or for Western aid agencies, the WFP bakeries were allowed to run in Afghanistan. The bakery project became known in the international community as a space of resistance where what was seen as the otherwise suppressed spirit of feminism defied repressive Taliban edicts. Remarkably, the unique success the WFP had in negotiating with the unyielding Taliban on the other hand went largely unnoted. The widows working at the bakeries, as I found in my research, appreciated the project because it provided them with a job, and because it allowed them to feed their children, as well as to assist other widows in the community by making low-cost, fortified bread. The praising of the alleged resistance of the widows working at the bakeries, reminiscent of what Abu-Lughod has criticized as the 'romance of resistance (1990)', is thus at odds with the meanings that the widows themselves give to their role as community bakers. This incompatibility parallels a potential discrepancy between the priorities of Afghan women, and the ones of international/Western feminists and others in feminist disguise. For, one might have to recognize, as Abu-Lughod carefully stated addressing anthropologists, 'that even after 'liberation' from the Taliban [Afghan women] might want different things than we might want for them'.[41] The privileging of heroic and explicit forms of resistance might in fact even lend implicit support to explicitly imperialist sentiments, as Leila Ahmed remarked:

> Whole books are still being published in which the history of Arab women is told within the framework of the paradigm [...] that the measure of whether Muslim women were liberated or not lay in whether they veiled and whether the particular society had become 'progressive' and westernized or insisted on clinging to Arab and Islamic ways. In its contemporary version this essentially still-colonial (or colonial and classist) feminism is

[41] Abu-Lughod, p. 787. Similarly, I would like to raise a cautionary note about the way in which feminists have endorsed a particular form of 'indigenous' women's activism in Afghanistan. The Revolutionary Association of the Women of Afghanistan (RAWA) claims to work for democracy and secularism in the interest of Afghan women. While I have criticized the discrepancy between their commitment to secularism and the sensibilities of the great majority of women in Afghanistan elsewhere (Daulatzai 2004), others noted the disconnect between the organization's fetishization and its commitment to values which are representative of only a small elite (Puar and Rai 2002; Spivak 2004), or the legitimacy and motivations of their work more generally (Azarbaijani-Moghaddam 2004).

only slightly more subtle than the old version. It may be cast, for example, in the form of praising heroic Arab feminist women for resisting the appalling oppressions of Arab culture and Islam. Whereas this is its stated message, the unstated message when the inherited constructs of Western discourse are reproduced unexamined is often, just as in colonial days, that Arab men, Arab culture, and Islam are incurably backward and that Arab and Islamic societies indeed deserve to be dominated, undermined, or worse.[42]

In addition to pitting the widows working at the bakery against Afghan men or a misogynistic, patriarchal cultural environment, the celebration of their alleged feminist resistance implies that the most salient forces which women in Afghanistan would want to oppose are Afghan men, and traditional social structures and institutions. In maintaining such perceptions, international aid institutions are glossing over the possibility that their own presence in the lives of Afghan widows (as well as women and society at large, for that matter) could be experienced as that of a force that needs to be negotiated, and might be opposed. Obviously, the widows working at the bakery are happy that they have a job and that they can feed their children. But, what about the impact that the prioritizing of improving the conditions of women's lives has on the society as a whole (and by extension of that, on women, including widows)?

As I showed in the example above, Hila was forced, due to the deaths and the poverty in her family, to find a job that would feed herself and her mother. But even in a 'liberated' Afghanistan she could not do that freely, but had to submit herself to the conditions under which the World Food Program allowed her to work in the bakery; she had to become a widow. Her story is not unique. The priorities of the international aid community to help Afghan women have created circumstances under which it is much more difficult for men than for women to find paid work. As a consequence, many families are now provided for by women. Men are not only left unemployed, a condition that has serious psychological consequences anywhere in the world,[43] but they have to live in an environment that is controlled by foreign agents who consider Afghan men to be inherently misogynistic and anachronistic.[44] It therefore needs to be considered that the ways in which the international community determines the conditions of possibility under which Afghans, men and women alike, can or cannot make ends meet are not primarily perceived as liberating, but as very stringent, very limiting, and very arbitrary.

Furthermore, the mapping of a feminist political consciousness over the everyday concerns of widows sets up a dichotomy between the oppressed, voiceless woman on one side, and the heroic, autonomous figure of the resister on the other. The maintaining of such a dichotomy, and the exclusive celebration of only certain forms of resistance, ultimately discounts the everyday struggles of Afghan women in general and represents a misreading of the complex forms of agency they enact. I take my understanding of agency from Talal Asad, who defines it as 'a complex term whose senses emerge within semantic and institutional networks that define and make possible particular ways of relating

---

[42] Leila Ahmed, *Women and Gender in Islam: Historical Roots of a Modern Debate* New Haven and London: Yale University Press, 1992), pp. 246–247.

[43] cf. McKee-Ryan (2005).

[44] The presence of the ISAF forces and the international aid community has drastically skyrocketed the cost of living in Kabul. The dependence on a steady income has thus increased dramatically, which further exacerbates the pressure of making a livelihood in an already stressful environment.

to people, things and oneself'.[45] For Asad, to locate 'agency' is not primarily to attempt to locate moments in which individuals act to change their lives, but to examine and analyze the structures of possibilities that exist in which one is able to act. It becomes important to look at how relations are formed, situated and sustained rather than defining singular actions by individuals as agentive. Saba Mahmood has further complicated Asad's notion of agency, relating it to Islamic feminism in her work on women in the piety movement, a non-liberal movement in Cairo.[46] In addition to providing an ethnographic account of the Islamic Revival in Egypt, she applied Asad's notion of agency to open up ways of analyzing modes of women's agency that are not reduced to the language of resistance or subversion of norms. Her work challenges feminist assumptions about women's self-determination that see the voluntary limitations to which the women in the Islamic Revival movement submit themselves, as misguided or false consciousness. Mahmood thus raises questions about why women's self-determination should be understood only in terms of particular, 'enlightened' ideas about freedom or liberty, and not also in terms of the liberty to submit oneself to other, for example religious, norms and values. I find her insights useful because she calls into question feminist assumptions about what is good for women that are considered to be living under conditions where their freedoms are curtailed by religious or social norms. A feminist herself, Mahmood raises the following questions:

> Do my political visions ever run up against the responsibility that I incur for the destruction of life forms so that 'unenlightened' women may be taught to live more freely? Do I even fully comprehend the forms of life that I want so passionately to remake? Would an intimate knowledge of lifeworlds distinct from mine ever lead me to question my own certainty about what I prescribe as a superior way of life for others?[47]

Applying Paul Farmer's plea for the study of structural violence to Afghanistan would certainly include the need to attend to the complex problems that the exclusive privileging of gender entails, as well as to the genealogies of the institutions and interests that enable this privileging. Yet his work has not been attentive enough to the formations of subjectivities as they unfold within social networks and through everyday practices and experiences. The temporality of the clinical encounter, which is where his ethnography takes place, certainly enables the diagnosing of the conditions of suffering and the identification of vulnerabilities, such as race, gender, and class. However, it does not permit careful accounting for the inner workings of those vulnerabilities, and their contingencies. This ultimately results in formulaic descriptions of risks and vulnerabilities, and seems to homogenize the subjectivities of the poor with whom he works.

Direction for circumventing such homogenization of subjectivities can be found in Veena Das' work on violence and social suffering.[48] The way she achieves to detail how drastic events or circumstances are folded into the everyday relations of individuals is what I consider of great importance for understanding the predicament of contemporary Afghanistan. In the case of the Hila, this might entail not only the death of all her male relatives, but also her subjection to the

[45] Asad (2003).
[46] Saba Mahmood, *Politics of Piety: The Islamic Revival and the Feminist Subject* (Princeton and Oxford: Princeton University Press, 2005).
[47] Mahmood (2005), pp. 197–198.
[48] Das (1995a; 1995b; 1997; 2000), Kleinman et al. (1998).

ANILA DAULATZAI

narratives of vulnerability propagated by the international aid community, and her consequent assuming the status of widowhood. It is the unfolding of such intricacies against the background of Afghanistan's recent history, which make the study of subjectivities a dire necessity for a project to re-cast the terms by which we have come to know Afghanistan. Das follows Judith Butler in stating that subjectivity is not only constituted by experiences of subjugation, but also by the manner in which the subject inhabits the respective subject position. She explains that 'individual lives are defined by context, but they are also generative of new contexts'.[49] Das' idea of the ordinary not as something primarily uneventful, but as that which is recovered from the rubbles of tragic circumstances might thus be helpful in making sense of the predicament of women (but not only women) in Afghanistan today. For Hila it was not an oppressive system of gender imbalance that took away her husband before she ever had one, it was her life in a war-torn, poverty-struck, neglected environment, and the pressure to submit to scripts that others had written for her, those who had come to 'liberate' women like herself. Kinship structures and social networks had to be redrawn for her to inhabit something like the ordinary.[50]

V. Conclusion

The suggestions I make in this article are not exclusive, the examples I discuss are not conclusive, and the analyses I attempt are not complete. I am merely offering the approach which currently guides my own investigations as an invitation for others to re-imagine and further the available modes of engagement with Afghanistan.

My critical assessments of contemporary writings on and representations of Afghanistan are not motivated by desires to belittle the work of other scholars, or by an inclination to malign the approaches feminists have taken to improve the lives of Afghan women. Rather, it grows out of the realization that the conceptual tools used to understand Afghanistan and its predicaments urgently need to be reassessed. Discussions of contemporary Afghanistan have reached an impasse and consequently seem to spin in circles. Explanatory frameworks privileging mechanistic descriptions of the workings of *gender, culture,* or *religion* in Afghanistan need to be recognized as tropes, and these tropes can no longer serve as the underlying epistemological axes, along which our understandings unfold, but need to be incorporated into the analyses as objects of investigation. The tropes themselves, and not just the social forces they were supposed to describe, have become contingencies inflecting the details of everyday life in Afghanistan. My plea is simple: the lives of Afghans, men and women alike, need to be situated within the larger social, historical, political, and economic webs of significance, and not only within the narrow grid of tropes (lest understandings be gridlocked); it would not be fair to privilege certain vulnerabilities over others. But as we zoom out to incorporate these larger-scale contingencies, we simultaneously need to zoom in and carefully focus on the social worlds and the experiences of Afghans; the ways in which the decades of violence and deprivation are mapped onto the lives of Afghans need to be studied in detail, as must the subjectivities rendered

[49] Veena Das, *Violence and Subjectivity* (Berkeley, CA: University of California Press, 2000), p. 210.
[50] Hila's story, however, should not be seen as concluded – her quest for the ordinary is not over, and neither is my interaction with her.

142

dependent on international and institutional interventions. When I am thus searching for ways to acknowledge the suffering of Afghans I am not typecasting Afghans as victims, and I am also not replacing the tropes I write against with a new one. Rather, I am asking what it might mean to acknowledge suffering. Veena Das has recognized the violence that occurs when suffering is rendered as a trope: suffering then is separated from the pain of those who suffer and utilized to legitimize those who fashion such discourses (Das 1995), in her case the state after an industrial accident, in my case an indifferent international community and a well-intentioned, yet somewhat ill-informed world of scholars, feminists, and others. In advocating an epistemological shift away from their tropes I am thus asking, with Das, how we could retrieve suffering from the tropes and return it, bring it closer to the pain of those who suffer. Only when the process of retrieval has begun, can we then begin to illuminate the gendered aspects of suffering in Afghanistan.

Gender, Citizenship and Political Agency in Lebanon

LINA KHATIB

ABSTRACT *This paper examines the condition of women as political agents in Lebanon in the context of legislation and political participation. It focuses on the effect of the Civil War on women's conditions of living in Lebanon, and their lives in the post-war period. War had negative effects on women, reinforcing their patriarchal subjugation, furthering their economic deprivation, and diverting attention from issues like women's rights, which have only added to women's political and social marginalization. The war also had a positive effect on women as it opened up new avenues for them to participate in public life. This paper analyzes gender relations in Lebanon through the frameworks of social change and the rise of civil society, but also emphasizes the challenges facing women in post-war Lebanon, where they are still governed by patriarchal values that hinder their political participation and their identification as full citizens.*

I. Introduction

Women in Lebanon are often perceived as enjoying a better status than their sisters in other Arab countries, whether economically, socially or politically. While women in Saudi Arabia are not allowed to drive, women in Lebanon have no such legal restrictions. While women in Kuwait have only acquired the right to vote relatively recently, Lebanese women attained the right to vote in 1952. Women in Lebanon are allowed to own businesses, and since 1988 they have been admitted into the Lebanese army. Since 1974, married Lebanese women no longer need the permission of the husband to travel abroad or to obtain a passport.[1] And the number of Lebanese women seeking higher education matches that of men.[2] More women in Lebanon are forming part of the workforce. Females constituted 18.4% of workers in 1975; this figure jumped to 27.2% in 1995,[3] and 29% in 2007.[4] All those issues contribute to painting a rosy picture of the condition of women in Lebanon. The Lebanese media play a part in sustaining this image, with a number

Dr Khatib would like to thank Dima Dabbous-Sensenig and Rana Issa for their help with providing crucial research material for this paper.

[1] Kirsten Schulze, 'Communal Violence, Civil War and Foreign Occupation: Women in Lebanon' in Rick Wilford and Robert L Miller (eds.), *Women, Ethnicity and Nationalism: The Politics of Transition* (London: Routledge, 1998), pp. 150–169.

[2] UNICEF, *The Situation of Children and Women in Lebanon* (Beirut: UNICEF and the Government of Lebanon, 1995).

[3] Ibid.

[4] Khatoun Haidar, 'Antiquated Laws Violate Women's Civil Rights', *The Daily Star*, 27 August 2007.

of prominent female journalists like Maguy Farah, Giselle Khoury and Mai Chidyac playing an active on-screen role in televised political debate programs.

However, behind this glossy façade lies a patriarchal legislative, social and political system where women do not enjoy an equal status to men. A UNICEF report on the condition of women in Lebanon in 1995 concluded that:

> Women are usually excluded and marginalized at various levels including: a) discrimination against women in... existing laws. b) in norms, habits, traditions and social culture. c) political discrimination especially... in the real participation in political leadership and decision making positions at all levels. d) economic discrimination regarding attaining production resources, type of jobs, salaries and... participation in the economic process. e) statistical discrimination where there is a need for specific information on women.[5]

Those problems identified in 1995 continue to be relevant today. Women are still discriminated against in Lebanese law, and their political participation remains minimal. Although Lebanese law does not discriminate against women regarding political participation and voting, women's involvement in politics in Lebanon is marginalized. The first female to gain a parliamentary seat was Mirna Boustany in 1963, but she only gained that seat after the death of her father, whom she was elected to replace. Until 2005, there were no females in the Lebanese cabinet (when Leila Solh Hamadeh, Wafaa' Diqa Hamzeh and Nayla Moawad were appointed Minister of Industry, Minister of State and Minister of Social Affairs, respectively), while the subsequent cabinet, appointed in 2008, contained only one woman: Bahia Hariri as Minister of Education. The number of women in the Lebanese parliament after the 2005 parliamentary elections was the highest in Lebanon's history, but remained very low. As Ekmekji points out, '[i]n the 2005 legislative elections, only six women out of the 128 members made it to parliament (4.7 percent), thus ranking Lebanon 125th (out of 138) on the IPU list'.[6]

On the social level, Lebanese women remain governed by what Suad Joseph calls the 'kin contract', which she says hinders the positioning of women as full citizens. She argues that rather than looking at the sexual contract (between husbands and wives) as the main constraint on women's position in Lebanese society, one needs to focus on:

> ... extended kin relationships. Rather than vulnerability by marriage, I focus on vulnerability by 'birth'. Rather than the sexual contract, I focus on the 'kin contract'. It is the mobilization of patriarchal extended kinship, as a venue of social control, and the state's mobilization of religion to sanctify extended kinship that has been the most significant deterrent to citizenship equality for women in Lebanon.[7]

This paper seeks to tease out the complexities underlying Joseph's above statement in arguing that one cannot examine the position of women as citizens and political agents in Lebanon without linking it to the wider social processes within which women exist.

---

[5] UNICEF (1995), p. 85.

[6] Arda Arsenian Ekmekji, 'Implementation of a Women's Quota System'. *Al-Raida*, XXIII(111–112), 2005/6, p. 56.

[7] Suad Joseph, 'Civic Myths, Citizenship, and Gender in Lebanon', in Suad Joseph (ed.), *Gender and Citizenship in the Middle East* (Syracuse, NY: Syracuse University Press, 2000), p. 110.

II. Lebanese Women and Personal Status Laws

Charlton, Everett and Staudt[8] divide policies regarding women into three categories. Waylen explains that those categories are: (1) 'policies which are aimed particularly at women'; (2) 'policies which deal with relations between men and women'; and (3) 'general policies', which are 'supposedly gender neutral but have a different impact on men and women. These can be further subdivided into those policy areas linked to the public sphere and somehow seen as "masculine", such as state-defined politics, war, foreign policy, [and] international trade'.[9]

Women in Lebanon are subject to inequality in all three categories. But while in the last category, the inequality is indirect – because the policies themselves do not discriminate against women, but the social frameworks within which they exist do – the first two categories see direct discrimination.

Lebanon is a democratic state where the constitution grants all its citizens equal rights. Article 7 of the Lebanese constitution asserts that 'all Lebanese are equal under the law, they enjoy equality in civil and political rights and they assume duties and responsibilities without any difference between them'. It should be noted, however, that no article or clause explicitly prohibits gender 'discrimination'.[10] The paradox in Lebanese law is that gender discrimination is in fact institutionalized. 'While the civil code grants equality for all its citizens, the Personal Status Laws, which regulate gender relationships, contradict all the basic legal principles of equality and non-discrimination'.[11] This applies to two main areas: citizenship, and family status laws. The late Laure Moghaizel, one of Lebanon's most prominent campaigners for women's and human rights, summarized the first area as follows: 'In Lebanon, children only inherit their father's nationality. A mother can only pass her Lebanese nationality to her children in two cases: if the child is illegitimate and she recognizes him before the father, and if she is a foreigner and after the death of the husband, who is also a foreigner, she takes on Lebanese nationality'.[12]

Family status laws on the other hand are governed by the religious authorities, as opposed to the civil state. Lebanon is constituted of 18 recognized sects divided among three religious groups: Muslim, Christian and Druze. Laws governing issues like marriage, divorce, inheritance, and child custody are dependent on the rulings of the different sects within each religious group. So, for example, not only do Christian women enjoy different rights from Muslim women; Muslim Shi'ite and Muslim Sunni women also follow different laws. Dima Dabbous-Sensenig summarizes the situation:

[8] Sue Ellen Charlton, Jana Everett and Kathleen Staudt (eds.), *Women, State and Development* (Albany, NY: SUNY Press, 1989).

[9] Georgina Waylen, 'Gender, Feminism and the State: An Overview'. In Vicky Randall and Georgina Waylen (eds.), *Gender, Politics and the State* (London: Routledge, 1998), p. 13.

[10] Dima Dabbous-Sensenig (2005), 'Incorporating an Arab-Muslim perspective in the re-assessment of the implementation of the Beijing Platform for Action'. *Expert Consultation Paper on 'Priorities in follow-up to the ten-year review and appraisal of implementation of the Beijing Declaration and Platform for Action'*, United Nations, p. 7.

[11] Naila Nauphal, 'Women and other War-Affected Groups in Post-War Lebanon', in Focus Programme on Crisis Response and Reconstruction, Working Paper 2: Gender and Armed Conflicts: Challenges for Decent Work, Gender Equality and Peace Building Agendas and Programmes, Geneva: Recovery and Reconstruction Department, 2001, p. 58.

[12] Moghaizel, interview in Nelda La Teef, *Women of Lebanon: Interviews with Champions for Peace* (North Carolina: McFarland and Company, 1997), p. 209.

A Christian woman divorced because of adultery is not entitled to remarry. Child custody laws favor the Muslim father and the patrilineal family in general, with divorced Shi'ite mothers having custody of their children for a shorter period than Sunni mothers. In the area of inheritance, Lebanese Muslim women, unlike their Christian counterparts who get an equal share, inherit half what their brothers inherit in case one or both parents are dead. Not only is the above list of discriminatory practices in family status laws far from exhaustive, discrimination varies in intensity according to the confession of the woman.[13]

The Lebanese government ratified the Convention on the Elimination of all Forms of Discrimination Against Women (CEDAW) in 1997; however, it only did this after expressing reservations dealing with Personal Status Laws. In particular, the government expressed reservations about Articles 9 (2), 16(1) (c) (d) (f) (g) and 29 (1), dealing with nationality, marriage rights, divorce rights, child custody, parenting, and the 'same personal rights as husband and wife, including the right to choose a family name, a profession and an occupation'.[14] In this sense, the above areas of discrimination against women in Lebanese law have been maintained. As Naciri and Nusair argue, '[t]hese reservations not only render CEDAW ... ineffective, they also *de facto* preclude any future or further discussion on how to improve the various existing international human rights and women's rights conventions'.[15]

III. The Personal is the Political

Why should personal status laws matter in the context of women's political participation in Lebanon? One of the most known statements of second-wave feminism is 'the personal is the political'. Second-wave feminists argued that far from existing outside the realm of politics, issues seen as belonging to the private sphere of women's lives and bodies should form part of the public debate. As Phillips states, one of the achievements of the women's movement in general is stressing how '[t]hings that used to be dismissed as trivial can no longer be viewed as the haphazard consequence of individual choice, for they are structured by relations of power. Things once shrouded in the secrecies of private existence are and should be of public concern'.[16] However, in the case of Lebanese women, the relationship between personal status laws, citizenship and political participation is a more concrete one. Naciri and Nusair argue that Personal Status Laws 'govern what typically is seen as belonging to the private sphere – marriage, divorce, maintenance, child custody and inheritance – but has [sic] an equal effect on women's public lives, acting as a potent control mechanism over women's economic, political, social, civic and cultural activities'.[17]

First, the inability of women to pass on citizenship to their husbands and children constitutes them as markers of social and national boundaries. As Waylen puts it, citing Deniz Kandiyoti (1991), the 'identification of women as bearers of cultural identity and boundary markers will have a negative effect on their

[13] Dabbous-Sensenig (2005), p. 8.
[14] Rabéa Naciri and Isis Nusair, The Integration of Women's Rights into the Euro-Mediterranean Partnership: Women's Rights in Algeria, Egypt, Israel, Jordan, Lebanon, Morocco, Palestine, Syria and Tunisia (Copenhagen: Euro-Mediterranean Human Rights Network, 2003), p. 70.
[15] Ibid., p. 30.
[16] Anne Phillips, *Engendering Democracy* (Cambridge: Polity Press, 1991), p. 92.
[17] Naciri and Nusair, p. 5.

emergence as full-fledged citizens'.[18] How can a woman be a full citizen if she does not possess the same citizenship rights as men? Second, women's inequality within the law sits uncomfortably within a supposedly democratic system. As Philips argues, '[d]emocracy implies equality but, when it is superimposed on an unequal society, it allows some people to count for more than others'.[19] Lebanese law has sustained the social inequalities that existed before the birth of the Lebanese state. By institutionalizing them, it has relegated women to a secondary level of citizenship. Third, the way different Personal Status Laws apply to different women from different sects means that 'not only are Lebanese women discriminated against vis-à-vis Lebanese men in general, they are not even equal among themselves according to Lebanese personal status laws'.[20] This begs the question of who is a *Lebanese* woman, but also, who is a *Lebanese* citizen?

This brings us to the final point, that this discrimination against women highlights their powerlessness in the nationalist project. Wilford complicates Benedict Anderson's[21] characterization of the nation as an imagined community by posing the questions 'Who, exactly, does the imagining?' and 'What roles are assigned to women in the nationalist project?'[22] In the case of Lebanon, it is clear that the Lebanese nation is one determined by men, where women are either relegated to the margins (their needs being regarded as less important than men's as demonstrated in the Personal Status Laws), or not paid attention to (as seen in the gender-neutral language used in the Lebanese constitution). This construction of a 'non-gendered, abstract citizenship' stems from the long traditions of political theory that 'operate to center the male'.[23] Phillips critiques political theory by saying that '[w]ith the odd exception, the entire debate on democracy has proceeded for centuries as if women were not there'.[24] Political theory 'writers seemed to take women's unworthiness so much for granted that they did not even notice they were leaving them out',[25] but this male centrism remains when women are taken into consideration. The controls over women in Personal Status Laws emphasize identity as physically embodied rather than abstract. It is through this embodiment that men's and women's different experiences of power are highlighted:

> Our discussions of sexual equality have always silently privileged this male body. When men and women are treated the same, it means women are treated *as if they were men*; when men and women are treated differently, the man is the norm, against which the woman is peculiar, lacking and different.[26]

Hatem argues that Western modernization theories initially also constituted a gender divide. Therefore, when such theories were adopted in the Middle East as

[18] Georgina Waylen, *Gender in Third World Politics* (Boulder, CO: Lynne Rienner Publishers, 1996), p. 15.

[19] Anne Phillips, *Democracy and Difference* (Cambridge: Polity Press, 1993), p. 91.

[20] Dabbous-Sensenig (2005), p. 8.

[21] Benedict Anderson, *Imagined Communities: Reflections on the Origin and Spread of Nationalism* (London: Verso, 1983).

[22] Rick Wilford, 'Women, Ethnicity and Nationalism: Surveying the Ground', in Rick Wilford and Robert L. Miller (eds.), *Women, Ethnicity and Nationalism: The Politics of Transition* (London: Routledge, 1998), p. 11.

[23] Phillips (1991), p. 6.

[24] Ibid., p. 2.

[25] Ibid., p. 3.

[26] Ibid., p. 37, my emphasis.

LINA KHATIB

states formed, they accommodated 'the asymmetrical definitions of gender roles and relations within the family'.[27] The emerging modern systems in the Middle East were inherently patriarchal and,

> combined new public roles for women with the culturally specific concepts of male leadership (*Quwamma*) over women, the assumption of women's diminished mental and religious capacity (*Naqisat 'Aql wa Din*) in comparison to men (and hence their exclusion from key religious, judicial, and political positions), and finally a female familial obligation to obey (*ta'at*) men. This did not represent a form of distorted modernization... Western modernization did not begin by extending the principles of liberty and equality to women.[28]

So, in addition to sustaining traditional forms of social and religious forms of discrimination against women, what is seen in the Middle East, and Lebanon is no exception, is an uncritical adoption of Western modernization.

Having highlighted the links between the legal, social and political structures that govern women in Lebanon, the paper will now proceed to unearthing the barriers facing Lebanese women in being full citizens and political agents. Those barriers are both practical resulting from historical particularities, and conceptual.

IV. Citizenship and the Public/Private Paradox

Referring to second-wave feminists, Anne Phillips argues that the 'public and private cannot be dealt with as separate worlds, as if the one exists in a rhythm independent from the other... it is a nonsense to think of the "personal" as something outside of politics, or to conceive of politics as immune to sexuality and "private" concerns'.[29] However, in Lebanon there is a paradox in the relationship between the private and the public. On the one hand, Lebanese politics is conceived of as a public arena that is more hospitable to men. This is in line with patriarchal notions of the public sphere, where, by default, women are relegated to the 'private' arena of the home. By extension, because politics is identified with a male public sphere, democracy itself becomes associated with men.[30] This is reinforced in the historical tales about the formation of the independent Lebanese republic, which name a number of prominent men (such as Bshara al-Khoury and Riad al-Solh, the independent republic's first president and prime minister), but ignore women completely. As such, any role played by women is absent from the dominant historical discourse.

On the other hand, the women's movement in Lebanon since the Civil War has largely concerned itself with 'private' issues. A significant proportion of Lebanese women take part in running and joining women's groups, but the activities of those groups remain limited to what is seen as the private realm. Women's groups seem largely unwilling to engage in activities that go beyond their primary focus on charity and social welfare. Very few groups are engaged with women's and human rights, and there are none that specifically aim at political reform. Rana Issa, an activist for women's rights in Lebanon, expressed her frustration at attempting to

[27] Mervat Hatem, 'Toward the Development of Post-Islamist and Post-Nationalist Feminist Discourse in the Middle East', in Judith Tucker (ed.), *Arab Women: Old Boundaries, New Frontiers* (Bloomington, IN: Indiana University Press, 1993), p. 39.
[28] Ibid.
[29] Phillips (1991), p. 95.
[30] Phillips (1991).

150

raise the issue of sectarianism within a women's group she wanted to work with in Lebanon. The group, CRTDA, was formed to lobby for women's citizenship rights in Lebanon:

> I found it odd that they shied away from engaging in any political discussions. They said they only wanted to deal with gender issues and leave the politics to the politicians ... The irony is the issue they chose to work on was citizenship, a core political issue. Deciding who is a citizen in a democratic system is a crucial and most basic element in the democratic process. So, I pushed on and suggested that we deal with sectarianism because in my opinion sectarian representation in Lebanon is one of the major reasons why women cannot pass on their citizenship to their children. But sectarianism is a taboo topic to discuss, plus ... feminism is not political in their eyes: it is after all limited to abortion, wife beating, your right to work and dress the way you like, marry who you like and be like those Western women we admire so much who give their citizenships to their partners and children.[31]

T.S. Marshall famously stated that citizenship is a 'status bestowed on those who are full members of a community generally the nation state. All who possess the status are equal with respect to the rights and duties with which the status is endowed'.[32] However, '[b]ecause the nation is often constructed by elites who have the power to define the nation in ways that further their own interests, the same elites are also able to define who is central and who is marginal to the national project'.[33] The problem of the women's movement identified above is that by drawing a line between 'the private' and 'the public', the 'private sphere is ... deemed politically irrelevant',[34] which means that the groups involuntarily sustain the disregard of women as political agents. This further serves to 'secure a version of the individual [in politics] that remains resolutely male'.[35] In this sense, citizenship itself becomes male, even if it is expressed in gender-neutral terms in the Lebanese constitution.

V. Sustained Political Patriarchy

What the above context means in a practical sense is that politics in Lebanon is conceived of within a patriarchal framework. This framework has hindered women's participation as electoral candidates.[36] One result of the framework is the lack of recognition of the ability of women to be politicians. Schulze points out that the three women elected into Lebanese parliament in 1992 only managed to acquire those positions through their familial connections to men: a brother in the cases of Bahia Hariri and Maha Khoury; and an assassinated husband in the case of Nayla Moawad. As she puts it, 'all three women can be seen as an extension of the politics of a male family member'[37] rather than politicians in their own rights. Nayla Moawad herself acknowledged this: 'Carrying my husband's name has

---

[31] Rana Issa, Interview with the author, November 2, 2007.

[32] T.S. Marshall (1950), quoted in Waylen (1998), p. 12.

[33] Tamar Mayer, 'Gender Ironies of Nationalism: Setting the Stage', in Tamar Mayer (ed.), *Gender Ironies of Nationalism: Sexing the Nation* (New York: Routledge, 2000), p. 12.

[34] Judith Squires, *Gender in Political Theory* (Cambridge: Polity Press, 2004), p. 29.

[35] Phillips (1991), p. 31.

[36] The percentage of female candidates in the Lebanese parliamentary elections stands at 3%. United Nations, 'Consideration of reports submitted by States Parties under Article 18 of the Convention on the Elimination of All Forms of Discrimination against Women' – *Third Periodic Report of States Parties* (Lebanon: United Nations Publications, 2006).

[37] Schulze (1998), p. 163.

given my voice an added weight. I have not had to start from scratch to prove myself. For two years, I was the only woman in parliament'.[38]

In the parliamentary election of 2005, those women (except for Maha Khoury, who was not re-elected) were joined by Solange Gemayel, the widow of the assassinated president Bachir Gemayal, and Sitrida Geagea, the wife of the then imprisoned leader of the Lebanese Forces, Samir Geagea. Both women seemed to stand for men for whom running for the elections was impossible. Another elected woman was Gilberte Zouain, daughter of ex-minister and legislator Maurice Zouain. The only non-kin affiliated woman in the Lebanese parliament formed in 2005 was Ghinwa Jalloul, but even she was elected on the basis of her being a member of the parliamentary 'list' affiliated with former Prime Minister Rafiq Hariri and his supporters. It is questionable whether she would have been able to succeed had she run as an independent candidate. To do so would have meant overcoming a number of hurdles: 'any female [in Lebanon] seeking greater political involvement, particularly on the national level, has to overcome the obstacles of religion, family patronage and gender'.[39] Schulze's observation has been reflected in the 2006 UN report on the implementation of CEDAW in Lebanon, which states that '[t]he continuing active influence of traditional factors (family allegiance, services, client networks, family or partisan political legacy) in determining the chances of women's success is clear'.[40]

The other problem faced by any woman who might want to run for elections in Lebanon is one of attitudes. As Peterson and Runyan argue, 'negative attitudes toward women's political participation are expressed as lack of confidence in and support for female candidates and politicians',[41] in other words, the unacceptability of women as political agents. Moreover, 'the underrepresentation of women in political office is often "explained" by the stereotype of their being uninterested in power and politics'.[42] Unfortunately, the focus of Lebanese women's groups on activities detached from politics only serves to sustain this stereotype.

This stereotype is held by both men and women, who pass them on to future generations through socialization. Peterson and Runyan explain: 'socialization into appropriate "masculine" behavior makes men more likely than women to identify with political activities. Just as important, gender stereotypes... create a "climate" that encourages male participation while discouraging female participation in politics'.[43] The low number of women in parliament therefore 'not only indicates the reluctance of the patriarchal society to accept females as politically equal, but also suggests the reluctance of women to demand such equality'.[44] This is again reflected in the CEDAW UN report in its reference to the lower number of female candidates in the 2005 elections (18 candidates) than in the 2000 elections (14 candidates): 'This reduction in the number of female candidates may be attributable to the conviction among women of the futility of

[38] Quoted in Nelda LaTeef, *Women of Lebanon: Interviews with Champions for Peace* (Jefferson, NC: McFarland and Company, 1997), p. 201.
[39] Schulze (1998), p. 163.
[40] United Nations (2006).
[41] V. Spike Peterson and Anne Sisson Runyan, *Global Gender Issues* (Oxford: Westview Press, 1993), p. 62.
[42] Ibid., p. 22.
[43] Ibid., p. 60.
[44] Schulze (1998), p. 163.

standing as a candidate'.[45] It is telling that the female members of parliament in Lebanon are largely unconcerned with pushing for a change in Personal Status Laws or for implementing legislation against gender discrimination. The same applies to female Cabinet members. For example, despite several good initiatives by the Ministry of Social Affairs (headed by a woman, Nayla Moawad, from 2005 until 2008), such as reproductive health programs for women, few are aimed at women as *women* (as opposed to them as mothers). The only exception is member of parliament Ghinwa Jalloul who tried to start a public debate about women's citizenship rights and to raise this issue in parliament, but her calls fell on deaf ears.

In this sense, it is the women themselves who take part in sustaining patriarchy. This is not helped by the characterization of femininity as 'different' by a number of prominent female public figures in Lebanon,

> For example, Sitt Rabab [al-Sadr, sister of the Shiite Imam and leader Musa al-Sadr], in looking at the changing role of women in the Shi'a community, has voiced concern that women may become 'too harsh'. Her view on male-female relations reveals some of the barriers women still face: 'It may be very easy to dispute and argue with her husband, but is much braver and stronger to bear him silently'.[46]

Athias and Yuval Davis argue that while '[f]emininity may be seen as a coping mechanism', this strategy also means that 'women can be both individually and collectively active agents in their own subordination'.[47] What we have then is a situation where women have internalized 'oppressive stereotypes',[48] and are reinforcing, rather than challenging, gender inequalities.[49]

VI. The Effect of the Civil War and Subsequent Conflict

Another reason behind Ghinwa Jalloul's failure in her attempt to raise awareness about and call for a change in nationality laws is that her campaign overlapped with the 33-day war between Hizbullah and Israel in July 2006. Earlier that Spring, a number of events had taken place as part of this campaign. The Women's Rights Clubs at the American University of Beirut and the Lebanese American University had staged public debates and workshops about the issue. They also led awareness campaigns on the street, and even disseminated merchandizing (in the form of posters and handbags) displaying the phrase: 'My nationality: a right for me and my family'. But as the pace of the war quickened and the scale of destruction widened, the campaign was ground to a halt as the country was overtaken by more pressing concerns. As the air, road and sea routes leading into Lebanon were blocked, there was fear of a shortage of food and medical supplies. Maksoud's comments on the situation of women during the Civil War apply to the July 2006 war too:

> When abstract concerns such as feminism persist in the consciousness of a society at war, the level of purpose in the debate has diminished, because to have a purpose beyond survival becomes in the minds of people a factor interrupting their quest for

---

[45] United Nations (2006).
[46] Ibid., p. 162.
[47] Floya Anthias, and Nira Yuval Davis, *Radicalized Boundaries* (London: Routledge, 1993), p. 108.
[48] Peterson and Runyan (1993), p. 22.
[49] Ibid.

self-preservation. In such an atmosphere, there invariably develops a diminishing of political and social consciousness, which is what happened in Lebanon.[50]

In this way, the July 2006 war's negative impact on the nationality campaign mirrors a much larger one in the days of the Civil War that ravished Lebanon from 1975 until the early nineties. The Civil War was an economic, political and social disaster, during which the actions of women's movements geared towards women's rights were largely suspended.[51] The Civil War contributed to the channelling of the energies of the members of those groups towards providing more 'essential' needs. Over a decade and a half, this trend further reinforced the association of women with an ethics of care.

However, some scholars believe that the Civil War had a positive effect on women. Nauphal for example argues that 'the war has opened new avenues for women by redefining their role and increased their involvement in public life'.[52] This position is mainly based on the fact that the Civil War increased the number of women working outside the home. The deterioration in the economic situation during the Civil War, coupled with the absence of men who had either joined the war as militiamen or emigrated, meant that there was an increase in women's economic involvement. Nauphal explains, 'Women's survival strategies in this context included selling assets such as gold and land..., transforming their domestic skills into marketable ones, and in the worse cases, resorting to socially unacceptable jobs such as prostitution'.[53] A survey conducted by UNFPA in 1992 showed that the percentage of households headed by females stood at 20%, having risen from 9.2% before the Civil War.[54]

The increased visibility of women in the work sphere also had an impact on the way women's groups in Lebanon conceived their campaigns. The UNFPA report says that the women's movement in Lebanon is basing its campaigns on the premise that economic independence will lead to emancipation.[55] Hala Maksoud says that this is typical of feminist literature in general:

> Feminist literature on the subject adopted this paradigm and drew on later experiences of women's involvement ... to argue that women, through their struggle in wars of liberation, liberate not only themselves but also their male oppressors from their chauvinism ... Although that literature was developed with particular reference to wars of liberation, it was later applied to all wars, on the assumption that war opens up opportunities for women, which, if properly used, are bound to lead to their empowerment.[56]

But working outside the home does not bring automatic freedom. One burden is that work was not coupled with a change in perceptions of women's roles. As Peterson and Runyan[57] argue, women who work outside the home had to negotiate an added workload when they arrived home as they were still expected

---

[50] Hala Maksoud, 'The Case of Lebanon', in Suha Sabbagh, (ed.), *Arab Women: Between Defiance and Restraint* (New York: Olive Branch Press, 1996), p. 93.
[51] Suha Sabbagh, 'Lebanon's civil war through different eyes: an interview with Jean Said Makdisi' in Suha Sabbagh (ed.), *Arab Women: Between Defiance and Restraint* (New York: Olive Branch Press, 1996), pp. 100–103.
[52] Nauphal (2001), p. 58.
[53] Ibid.
[54] UNICEF (1995).
[55] Ibid.
[56] Hala Maksoud (1996), p. 91.
[57] Peterson and Runyan (1993).

to be responsible for most, if not all, household chores. Added to this is the fact that the destruction of the infrastructure during the war increased the time women spent on daily chores.[58] Another hurdle is that although women's presence outside the home was tolerated, even encouraged, they were still expected to observe the same social mores that applied to them before. The association of women with family honour for example has meant that female workers have had to be aware of this link when conducting their economic affairs, namely in their relationships with men in the workplace.

Orloff mentions another hurdle, this time a conceptual one. He argues: 'just as the independent male householder serves as the ideal-typical citizen in classical liberal democratic theory, the *male* worker serves as the ideal-typical citizen in the literature on social rights'.[59] The increased presence of women in the workplace carried some positive changes in laws governing women's rights (the right of married women to own a business for example was changed in 1994 to lift the restriction of needing the husband's permission). However, it did not carry a change in the way women were conceived as citizens, neither socially nor politically.

The Civil War also saw women engaging in conflict, but not in decision-making processes about this conflict. Julinda Abu Nassr argues:

> Women had no say over when the war started, neither in the decision making processes, nor in the efforts to achieve reconciliation. Their roles were those of the recipients of the consequences and the outcomes of the war on the one hand, and the makers and manufacturers of the laws of survival on the other hand.[60]

But Nauphal presents an alternative view, saying that '[d]espite the fact that they were absent from decision-making as military and political actors, many women performed war-related tasks and provided essential support for militiamen. Thus, their involvement was through 'active resistance'.[61] Nauphal's notion of 'active resistance' is nevertheless romantic. The number of women who joined the militias was not substantial, and amongst those that did, most had roles that were limited to those of nurture and care, such as making and delivering food to the male fighters and caring after the wounded. Moreover, women's contribution to the war was seen as momentary. Those women who had fought in the militias and taken more active roles retreated to assume traditional female roles after the war ended. None of the former militias or political groups in post-war Lebanon have any prominent female leaders. As Schulze puts it, '[s]ociety tolerated female "warriors" since they were perceived as temporary, often not being taken seriously by their male counterparts or those in politically important positions'.[62]

Ekmekji cites a 2005 United Nations study on women and elections in post-conflict societies as noting that 'since men are usually the warmongers, peace negotiations consequently further exclude women in post-war parliaments'.[63] Men seem to 'suffer a collective and convenient memory loss about the contribution

[58] Maksoud (1996).

[59] A.S. Orloff, 'Gender and the Social Rights of Citizenship: The Comparative Analysis of Gender Relations and Welfare States', *American Sociological Review*, 58 (1993), p. 308, emphasis in original.

[60] Julinda Abu Nassr, 'The Effects of War on Women in Lebanon' in Suha Sabbagh (ed.), *Arab Women: Between Defiance and Restraint* (New York: Olive Branch Press, 1996), p. 96.

[61] Nauphal (2001), p. 58.

[62] Schulze, p. 157.

[63] Ekmekji, p. 56.

made by women'.[64] As Cynthia Enloe argues, "forgetting" ... appears to be a frequent effect of reconsolidating centralized control of authority... [it] is part of the process of legitimatizing privilege, including gender privilege'.[65] The Civil War therefore, far from emancipating women, confirmed the character of the Lebanese society, state and public sphere as a 'gendered hierarchy'.[66]

At times women were able to use this gendered hierarchy to their benefit. According to Jean Said Makdissi, sometimes women were able to use the traditional respect given to them in Lebanese society to confront the militias during the war.[67] But the overall effect of the war was a marginalization of women's position as women. The Civil War resulted in the breakdown of the social order, and the reaction to what was an even stronger adherence to the family and tradition.[68] The increased adherence to the family can be understood in the context of a society lacking an official protector, but it diverted attention from campaigning for women's rights. This meant that during the war, women 'were not organized as women around an agenda. In fact, the only organized women's activities during the war were demonstrations and sit-ins against the war',[69] activities sanctioned by the traditional view of women as peace keepers.

VII. Religion and Sectarianism

What adds to the marginalization of women as political agents is the governance of political participation by codes derived from sectarian beliefs and practices. As Suad Joseph explains, '[p]olitical parties have not been so much sectarian in the sense of representing the interests of particular sects as a whole as they have been the personal followings of individual leaders (zu'ama') rooted largely within specific sects and organized around highly personalized patron−client relationships'.[70]

This creates a problem within Lebanon's system of sectional representation, that citizens are not represented by those sharing their interests as citizens, but by those who are supposed to be representing the interests of wider communities that those citizens belong to.[71] This transforms people from 'citizens' to 'bearers of interest'.[72] Kirsten Schulze explains how this status quo affects women's political roles:

> Arab society in general and Lebanese society in particular, has prided itself on male leadership though the za'im, the epitome of the 'macho man' (Accad 1994: 41). He embodies the perceived masculine values of conquest, domination, competition and war... Before the civil war, the za'im was the political and secular leader of his community. During the war he became its military leader along with a new, younger generation of militia leaders. Afterwards he resumed his traditional role, based on notions of political and social differentiation, class privilege, or class status. Thus, it can be seen

[64] Wilford, p. 3.
[65] Cynthia Enloe, *Bananas, Beaches and Bases: Making Feminist Sense of International Politics* (London: Pandora, 1989), p. 138.
[66] Waylen, p. 8.
[67] Sabbagh (1996).
[68] Maksoud (1996).
[69] Maksoud, p. 94.
[70] Joseph (2000a), p. 122.
[71] Phillips (1991).
[72] Phillips (1991), p. 69.

that he never relinquishes the control of his community, making it difficult even for women involved in combat to assume decision-making positions.[73]

It is not only women who are affected by this situation. Dima Dabbous-Sensenig, the Director of the Institute for Women's Studies in the Arab World at the Lebanese American University, explains that

> both Lebanese women and men in general lack political agency in a country where confessionalism and not party politics determine the parameters of political involvement. In other words, both genders suffer exclusion from political life in a political culture where parties with clear issue-oriented platforms basically do not exist, where clientelism and not meritocracy largely determine who has access to positions of power inside existing parties or in the larger political institutions of the country, and where one's confessional identity is the single most important factor in determining one's role in society and which 'side' (I find it difficult to use 'political party' in the Lebanese context) one belongs to.[74]

The Civil War also reinforced sectarianism 'and the division of the population along confessional lines. These phenomena have ... thwarted the evolution of social integration. They have weakened civil institutions, which became polarized'.[75] Large segments of the Lebanese population lived through the war segregated from communities from other sects. This long-term segregation resulted in the creation of negative myths about those unseen Others, and a sense of mistrust that persisted after the war ended. Lebanon today is still plagued by the traces of this sectarianism. Despite attempts during the Cedar Revolution of 2005 to foster a sense of national identity in Lebanon, the country remains a fragile one when it comes to its population's national imagination. This imagination is almost non-existent, with quasi-tribal loyalties to the kin, the clan and the sectarian community remaining stronger than those towards the nation. This divisive atmosphere has an indirect effect on women (and men); how can women (or men) conceive of themselves as citizens of a nation when the notion of citizenship itself is being continuously contested by competing loyalties?

Another problem with sectarianism is that it reinforces religious notions of selfhood which can be discriminatory towards women. For example, the problem with Islam-based gender movements is that they are influenced by the concept of fairness rather than equality— the 'fairness' of respecting 'the differences between and inherently complementary nature of men and women and their corresponding roles'—and thereby 'maintain the power structure that oppresses women'.[76]

This religious-based power structure merges with politics in Lebanon, creating a dogmatic effect on the political environment. Najla Hamadeh elaborates on this point and its wider implications:

> When laws are supported and perpetrated by religious or political powers that cannot be questioned or cannot be held accountable or by the claim that the legislator is speaking in the name of such authority, the need to be convincing becomes trivial. Indeed, in such cases the general public may sense the futility of subjecting the laws to the scrutiny of reason and may learn to either accept the authoritarian legal system without discussion or

---

[73] Schulze, p. 159.
[74] Dabbous-Sensenig, 2007.
[75] Nauphal, p. 60.
[76] Naciri and Nusair (2003), p. 7.

to ignore its shortcomings, focusing on ways to get around it. Such a public may even lose the habit of rational scrutiny altogether.

Lebanon is a democracy and as such its laws are expected to be more likely to be amenable to criticism and discussion and hence to be more rationally convincing. However, a high proportion of Lebanese laws that tackle issues related to women suffer from contradiction and weak argumentation. The Lebanese public, albeit democratic, is expected to accept irrationality and injustice in its legal system not only because some rulings purport to be backed up by the high authority of religion, but also because of certain 'special' conditions that have nothing to do with the law or justice but with factors like tradition, precarious multi-confessional coexistence or the necessity to give Palestinians no option other than 'the right of return'.[77]

VIII. Conclusion

This paper has put forward the context necessitating the establishment of a civil status law in Lebanon that is not gender-biased.[78] It has linked this with the wider political and social context in Lebanon. The chapter has argued that there is a need to examine this context in detail to unearth the inequalities hidden beneath Lebanon's seemingly benevolent image. For example, even though the percentage of female and male voters in Lebanon is similar,[79] this paper has shown that voting per se 'does not create space for transformation or change'.[80] It has argued that there is a need instead to focus on changing the systems and perceptions that trap women into 'a culture of passivity and self-denial'.[81] Dima Dabbous-Sensenig argues that in Lebanon, women suffer from what Naomi Wolf calls a 'fear of power',[82] where women are afraid to engage in politics.

One way of countering this fear has been a proposal put forward by Arda Arsenian Ekmekji, the only female member of the newly appointed Commission for a New Lebanese Electoral Law (appointed in August 2005 by the Lebanese Cabinet), to implement a quota system that guarantees between 10 and 30% of parliamentary seats for women as a temporary measure for the three rounds of elections after the 2006 round (covering a period of 12 years).[83] While acknowledging the limitations of a quota system, Ekmekji defends the quota measure in light of the limited participation of women in government in Lebanon. In the 2006 report on CEDAW implementation, the United Nations published the results of a survey on the adoption of a female quota, which stated that 46% of those surveyed were in favour of some form of female quota.[84] Adopting a quota is reliant on the Lebanese Cabinet and the Parliament approving it; however, with political instability continuing to plague Lebanon, the Lebanese government has put the proposal on the back burner.[85] Hala Maksoud argues,

---

[77] Najla Hamadeh, 'Editorial: One Way or the Other', Al-Raida (2005/6), XXIII (111–112), p. 2.

[78] Nada Khalifeh, 'Lebanon's reservations to CEDAW', Al-Raida, 111–112 (2005/6), pp. 14–18.

[79] United Nations (2006).

[80] Phillips (1991), p. 41.

[81] Ibid.

[82] Wolf (1993), p. 236, quoted in Dabbous-Sensenig (2006), p. 60.

[83] Elkmekji (2005/6).

[84] United Nations (2006).

[85] After sectarian clashes erupted in Lebanon in May 2008, a new Lebanese cabinet was formed and approved re-implementing the 1960 electoral law which does not accommodate gender-based quotas; however, lobbying for a quota is still being pursued by the Civil Campaign for Electoral Reform.

In light of the fact that most Arab countries live in a period of social transformation, with many experiencing wars and struggles for liberation, it is only natural that although realizing the necessity for social change and the importance of women's issues, the political sphere overrides their concerns, and its immediacy often deflects from other pursuits. In such situations, women's priorities cannot be the same as those of women living in peaceful, post-industrial societies.[86]

But even a quota system is not necessarily going to cause a major change in the political status quo. As Anne Phillips says, 'most supporters of women's equality cherish a belief that the changes they desire have as much a qualitative as a quantitative side. It is not just a matter of more women in politics; it is a chance of transforming the political realm'.[87] Only by changing the social and cultural constraints that dominate the political realm in Lebanon and by overcoming the shackles of sectarianism and clientelism can the political sphere in Lebanon become a truly open one, where men and women can be full political agents and citizens.

---

[86] Hala Maksoud (1996), p. 90.
[87] Phillips (1991), p. 4.

Gender and Violence in Algeria: Women's Resistance against the Islamist Femicide

ZAHIA SMAIL SALHI

ABSTRACT In 1984 the Algerian government passed into law the Family Code, which Algerian women have perceived as a major act of state violence against them because it codifies their subjugation and renders them more vulnerable in the face of growing conservatism and gender segregation in both the private and public spheres. Women found themselves stranded between a patriarchal society generally hostile to women and a set of laws that institutionalized discrimination against them.

The discriminatory provisions of the Family Code are symptomatic of the growing misogyny in Algerian society and have facilitated violence against women, legitimized discrimination in practice and made it particularly difficult for women to deal with the consequences of widespread human rights abuses brought about by Islamic terrorism, which have amounted to femicide, the most extreme form of sexist terrorism.

Throughout the 1990s Algerian women led a dual struggle: while the urgency of the situation engaged them to resist the Islamist femicide whose main aim was to preserve male supremacy under the cover of Islamic legitimacy, this did not detract the women's groups from their primary battle to have the Family Code repealed. This violent decade was a formative period for women who intensified their actions to raise awareness and build strong solidarity networks among women both nationally and internationally.

This chapter argues that Islamist violence in Algeria reached the level of femicide, as it targeted women's bodies as a battlefield and executed women with unprecedented violence not even seen during the Algerian war of independence. The terrorists' conduct displayed the depths of inherent misogyny which validates the term femicide as opposed to murder. Jane Caputi and Diana H.E. Russell argue that 'Calling misogynist killings femicide removes the obscuring veil of non gendered terms such as homicide and murder'.[1] In the case of the Middle East and North Africa (MENA), honour killings and Islamist violence against women which results in murder are the most frequent forms of femicide.[2]

---

[1] M. Lazreg, 'Gender and Politics in Algeria: Unravelling the Religious Paradigm', *Signs* 15 (4) (Summer 1990), pp. 775–780, at p. 777.

[2] Femicide is defined as the killing of women because they are women. Feminist sociologists differentiate between the intentional killing of males (homicides) and the intentional killings of females (femicides). Gupta elucidates, 'Femicide is the killing of women … because they are strong and practicing their freedom of choice, because they are entering male-dominated fields, because they are intelligent and choosing to live their lives without depending on men for survival'. Balbul Gupta, 'Femicide from a Feminist Perspective', *GW Feminist Review* 9(10) (1999), pp. 9-10.

For more definitions of femicide, see Jane Caputi and Diana E.H. Russell (eds.), *Femicide: The Politics of Woman-Killing* (New York: Twayne, 1992). Available at http://www.pinn.net/sunshire/book-sum/femicide.html (accessed 3.9.2009).

While this chapter strives to understand the causes and roots of Islamist femicide and the reasons why women are at the centre of the Algerian Islamist venture, it also looks at the ways in which organized and spontaneous resistance by women worked together for the same cause, and analyses the conditions which favoured the coming of age of the Algerian feminist movement and the new prospects for Algerian women in the post-terrorism era.

By exposing Islamist violence against women as femicide, this chapter hopes to change existing perceptions of violence against women and alter the way in which public opinion in both MENA and beyond responds to acts of femicide.

Introduction

In Algeria's modern history the 1980s was the decade which witnessed the birth of the movements for democratic liberties. Actors within civil society[3] took over the street[4] and expressed various demands which in essence were fuelled by a deep identity crisis. This crisis was mostly stimulated by an economic malaise resulting from the failure of President Boumedienne's socialist programme, embodied in the 'industrializing industries' and agrarian reforms. The falling oil revenues, especially after 1985, the expansion of a newly urbanized population, the rising unemployment figures coupled with the housing crisis were all elements that contributed to social dissatisfaction and unrest.[5]

Nevertheless, such expressions of discontent would not have been possible under the rule of President Boumedienne. With President Chadli Benjedid's accession to power in 1979, the political atmosphere became relatively relaxed and people's movements became less controlled.

On the intellectual level various factions were also growing and making diverse demands on a weakening state. What had started in the 1970s as a conflict between the Arabophones and the Francophones as they competed for power[6] was joined by

[3] In this research we adopt the London School of Economics, Centre for Civil Society's definition of civil society, 'Civil society refers to the arena of uncoerced collective action around shared interests, purposes and values. In theory, its institutional forms are distinct from those of the state, family and market, though in practice, the boundaries between state, civil society, family and market are often complex, blurred and negotiated. Civil society commonly embraces a diversity of spaces, actors and institutional forms, varying in their degree of formality, autonomy and power. Civil societies are often populated by organizations such as registered charities, development non-governmental organizations, community groups, women's organizations, faith-based organizations, professional associations, trade unions, self-help groups, social movements, business associations, coalitions and advocacy groups.' For more details see *http//:www.lse.ac.uk/collections/CCS (accessed 3.9.2009).*

[4] On 20 April 1980, Tizi-Ouzou had seen three days of rioting. The insurgents demanded the recognition of the Berber/Amazigh language and culture. From 1980 the Berbers annually celebrated the Berber Spring to commemorate the Black Spring and reiterate their demands.

On 28 October 1981, a 'Hundred Angry Women' demonstrated in the streets of Algiers expressing their anger at the government's decision to debate the Family Code in secret.

On 16 November 1981, 500 women gathered in front of the National Assembly as it met for a plenary session. Women have not stopped demonstrating against the Family Code, which was instituted in June 1984.

[5] For more details see Benjamin Stora, *Algeria 1830–2000: A Short History* (Ithaca and London: Cornell University Press, 2000).

[6] For more details on the language issue see Abdelrrezak Dourari, *Les malaises de la société algérienne: crise de langue et crise d'identité* (Alger: Casbah Editions, 2003); Zahia Smail Salhi, 'Between the Languages of Silence and the Woman's Word: Gender and Language in the Work of Assia Djebar', *International Journal of the Sociology of Language*, Special Issue on 'Language and Gender in the Mediterranean Region', 190 (2008), pp. 79–101.

other tendencies which were becoming rife and at the same time hostile to each other. These main tendencies were known as the Amazigh/Berber movement and the Islamist movement. While the first claimed Tamazight/Berber as the language and identity of at least 30 per cent of the Algerian population, the second was directly linked to the Arabophone faction in power and claimed Islam as the religion of the state and Arabic as its sole national language.

Islamism as a political current in the Algerian context goes back to the colonial period when the Association of the Muslim Ulema formed around Abdulhamid Ben Badis in the 1930s and then merged with the National Liberation Front in the 1950s. In the two decades following independence, the Muslim and Arab aspects of the new nation stood on a parallel line along that of the secular and leftist tendencies in power resulting in the nation being torn between two opposing forces: one Islamic/conservative and the other secular/modernist.

As such, the Islamists saw themselves as the main political and ideological opposition to the ruling elite and excluded all other tendencies that might contribute with a third political voice. In this case the Berber Cultural Movement (MCB) constituted the new voice. It was opposed by both the state and the Islamists, mainly because the Berbers were calling for the safeguarding of the Berber language and culture and for freedom of thought and speech, which directly opposed the Islamists' wholesale Arabization and Islamization project.

The first violent manifestations of the conflict between the MCB and the Islamists started at the Ben Aknoun University campus in Algiers, where on 2 November 1982 a Berber student, Kamal Amzal, was assassinated by the Islamists, known then as the Islamic Brotherhood (les frères musulmans), while he was putting up a poster to call for a general meeting to elect an independent and representative student committee. While Kamal and his group wanted to create a functioning democracy at the level of the university campus, the Islamists wanted to control the campus and leave no space for free expression.

The Algerian regime violently repressed the MCB in April 1980, a date that was from then on dubbed the 'Black Spring' (Le Printemps noir), and accused its proponents of being separatists and pawns in the hands of the ex-colonialists who were using them to destabilize the Algerian state.[7]

To control the MCB, the Algerian regime supported and encouraged the Islamist clergy. Lazreg explains, 'the Algerian government's flight into Islam can only be explained as an attempt to retain its power in the face of a dysfunctional economic program and mounting political opposition'.[8]

In fact, President Chadli's government used Islam as a rampart against civil society. In return, it had to compromise with the clergy on many vital issues. The question of language aside, the other vital area where the Islamists pressed for radical change was the Personal Status Law, with demands that targeted women's civil rights, condemning them to the status of minors for life. The Islamic conservatives endlessly argued that educated women were easy targets for Western imperialism and that their conduct was reminiscent of French colonialism.

[7] For more details on the MCB and the regime's oppression of the April 1980 demonstrations see Hocine Benhamza, *L'Algérie Assassinée* (Alger: Editions INES, 2008).
[8] Lazreg, 'Gender and Politics in Algeria', p. 777.

What is interesting at this juncture is how the MCB and the nascent women's movement were both accused of conspiring with the West, which in view of Algeria's colonial past signified treason against the principles of the national revolution and therefore lack of legitimacy for their movements, while on the opposite side of the spectrum stood the Islamist movement, enjoying wider legitimacy directly derived from Islam as the religion of the nation, which had helped it resist colonialism and safeguard its identity. For this reason alone, Islamists felt empowered to stand in the way of everything that opposed the way of Islam and claimed the right of using all means, including violence, to protect Algeria's Islamic identity.

The assassination of Kamal Amzal in 1982 and the various verbal and physical attacks throughout the 1970s and 1980s on women whose conduct was deemed too westernized and therefore non-Islamic are but a few examples of such violence.

It is the aim of this chapter to investigate and analyse the roots, reasons, and forms of Islamists' violence against women in the context of Algeria, and to scrutinize women's reactions to violence and the various resistance strategies they have adopted in the face of this violence.

Violence against Women

Violence is often defined as an assault on a person's physical and mental integrity. It is an underlying feature of all societies, and an undercurrent running through social interaction at many different levels. The World Health Organization defines violence as the 'intentional use of physical force or power, threatened or actual, against oneself, another person, or against a group or community, that either results in or has a high likelihood of resulting in injury, death, psychological harm, mal-development or deprivation'.[9]

Violence against women reflects culturally defined notions of masculinity and femininity which serve to reinforce women's subordinate position. It is in most cases, though not always, perpetuated by men against women and it embodies the power imbalances inherent in patriarchal societies. It may take an endless spectrum of forms, such as

> rape, including marital rape and rape as a tool of repression against particular classes or groups, domestic violence, child abuse, female foeticide and infanticide, denial of health care and nutrition for girl children, sexual and emotional harassment, genital mutilation, prostitution, pornography, population control, enforced sterilisation, war and state violence, exploitation of refugees, political violence, including that directed at the families of political targets, reduction in state services leading to increased stress and workload for women.[10]

Though not all of these manifestations of violence necessarily exist in the same way across the Middle East and North Africa, two levels at which violence may strike women's lives across the region can be identified as follows: private (personal) violence and public violence. The forms that these two types of violence may take

[9] World Health Organization, *World Report on Violence and Health* (Geneva: 2002), p. 38.
[10] Judy El-Bushra and Eugenia Piza Lopez, 'Gender-related Violence: Its Scope and Relevance', *Gender & Development* 1(2) (1993), pp. 1–9. Online publication 1.6.1993, http://www.informaworld.com/smpp (accessed 7.6.2009).

164

also differ from one region to another according to cultural norms and religious beliefs. To these two main factors one can add economic and political factors which may exacerbate (or alleviate) the intensity and degree of violence.

Private Violence

Private violence occurs in the private sphere and may be physical and/or mental. It takes various forms including marital rape, wife-battering, female genital mutilation, honour killing, perpetration of violence by female adult victims towards children such as in the case of battered mothers, forced marriages, discrimination against girls in terms of access to health and education, segregation between males and females in food and clothing, and exclusion of female household members from participation in decision-making.

The materialization of these types of discrimination in the private sphere cultivates an environment in which physical and mental abuse of women is seen as an acceptable practice. Female children are not only brought up into an acceptance of gender violence and segregation but also conditioned to accept their lot as part of being female. They are taught from a young age that their behaviour and dress code may provoke violence from men and that they should follow certain social norms. Male children on their part are taught from a very early age that they should be in charge of women (not only their sisters, female cousins, and in some cases neighbours but also their elder female relatives) and that they should correct their conduct if they transgress the prevailing social norm. In Muslim societies this tendency is accentuated by the religious command that a good Muslim should change what they see as wrongdoing, and it so happens that this is mostly applied in the case of women.

Consequently, while such codes boost male self-esteem and self-confidence from an early age, they totally undermine women's self-esteem and condition them to a state of subordination and total dependence on male relatives in terms of decision-making. It is often found that women are unable to take charge of their lives and have to depend constantly on male relatives. This is especially the case for widows and divorcees who in Muslim societies are compelled to return to their family homes or have a male tutor (usually a father or brother) to take care of them and act as tutor to their children.

In the case of Algeria, as is also the case across the Middle East and North Africa, private violence is not considered a major concern despite its increasing levels and direct links with public violence. State institutions across the region do not take such violence seriously, and legislation to protect victims of violence is almost non-existent. This general state of indifference to such violence arises from both religious and cultural beliefs. Wife battering, for example, is justified as a corrective measure towards disobedient wives, as prescribed in the Qur'an (IV, 34). Furthermore, speaking about wife battering is silenced by the whole society, including the victim, her family, the police, the health professionals, and so on, as a matter of family honour.[11] Dalila Djerbal-Iamarene argues that violence rests upon its toleration within

---

[11] For more details on domestic violence see M.M. Haj Yahia, 'Wife-abuse and Battering in the Socio-cultural Context of Arab Society', *Family Process* 39(2) (2000), pp. 237–255.

the family, where until recently it has been seen as a trivial topic which no one has thought to raise as a true problem.[12] Indeed, while domestic violence is largely discussed in the West and adequate policies are formulated to deal with it, in the Middle East and North Africa this type of violence is not yet considered a key concern despite its increasing occurrences and its grave consequences.[13]

Public Violence

As opposed to private violence, public violence occurs outside the home, in the public sphere. It may take place in the street or at work in the form of sexual harassment, verbal abuse, and in some cases physical abuse.

Public violence can also take the form of discrimination in employment opportunities, and the absence of adequate legislation to protect women from abuse and discrimination and guarantee equal opportunities for both men and women. In this area, the role of government bodies is crucial to ensure citizens' safety and well-being. At the same time, local culture may prevent women from reporting violence and encourage the perpetrators to wield more pressure on their victims. El-Bushra and Piza Lopez demonstrate that,

> Every government or authority structure has the power to introduce and uphold measures which guarantee women's rights in a wide range of areas, including rights to land and other property, inheritance, employment and access to services, family law, and so on. Such measures are not only positive in themselves but also foster positive public perceptions of women's rights and dignity.[14]

In most Middle Eastern and North African countries, which are known to be largely patriarchal, women often find themselves underrepresented in the public sphere which is mostly designated as the male space where male members of society aim to preserve their supremacy. In this domain women have to keep a low profile and only make timid appearances. From personal observations, I have found that a common aspect of such societies is male domination of the street and intense harassment of women, who become subjects of insult and verbal abuse in the public sphere. Another common feature, however, is women's passive reaction to such abuse: on the one hand they refrain from engaging in losing battles and on the other they fear violent reprisals which will ultimately tarnish personal reputation and family honour.

I contend that private violence against women has direct implications for public violence in that such patterns of violence are cultivated in the private sphere and are directly transposed into the public sphere. Furthermore, consciously or not the goal of violence against women is to preserve male supremacy in both spheres, and the tolerance of violence in the private sphere is ultimately reflected in the tolerance of violence in the public sphere. This is symptomatic of a misogynistic culture which

---

[12] Dalila Djerbal-Iamarene, 'Violence familiale, violence sociale, violence politique', in Hourriya/Liberté (ed.) *Droits de l'homme et violences au Maghreb et en Europe* (Paris: Hourriya, 2005), available from 1997 at http://www.maghreb-ddh.sgdg.org/liberte (accessed 25.8.2009).
[13] S. Douki, et al., 'Violence against Women in Arab and Islamic Countries', *Archives of Women's Mental Health* 6 (2003), pp. 165–171. Published online 17.4.2003 at http://www.springerlink.com/content (accessed 20.8.2009).
[14] El-Bushra and Piza Lopez, 'Gender-related Violence'.

in some societies motivates extreme violence amounting to femicide. Such extreme violence includes mutilation murder, rape murder, battery that escalates into murder, the immolation of witches in Western Europe and of brides and widows in India, and crimes of honour in some Latin and Middle Eastern countries, where women believed to have lost their virginity are killed by their male relatives.[15]

Jane Caputi and Diana H.E. Russell argue, 'Calling misogynist killings femicide removes the obscuring veil of non gendered terms such as homicide and murder',[16] and in the case of the Middle East and North Africa, honour killings and Islamist violence against women are the most frequent forms of femicide.

Violence against Women in Algeria

In Algeria, women are stranded between a patriarchal society hostile to women's presence in the public sphere and a set of laws in the form of the 1984 'Family Code' which institutionalizes discrimination against women and therefore constitutes a form of public violence against them. The discriminatory provisions of the Family Code have facilitated violence against women, legitimized discrimination in practice, and made it particularly difficult for women to deal with the consequences of widespread human rights abuses.[17]

In a briefing to the UN Committee on the Elimination of Discrimination Against Women (CEDAW), Amnesty International stated that Algerian women 'have little prospect of obtaining justice and redress for abuses they have suffered and that current laws and practice continue to discriminate against women and facilitate violence against them',[18] both in the private and the public spheres.

It has always been the case in Algerian society that male and female spaces are strictly designated in the public sphere; women are not welcome in male souks, cafes, beaches, and leisure places in general. Those who enter such places expose themselves to open harassment and are classified as having low morals.

With the rise of Islamism in Algerian society, harassment in the public sphere often amounted to extreme physical violence. Such violence is often justified by the Islamists' 're-Islamization from below' project, which justifies as religious duty all actions they take to correct whatever they see as wrongdoing (*layajouz*).

As early as the late 1970s women became a clear target for the Islamic fundamentalists, whose aim was to bully them out of the public sphere through intense harassment, verbal abuse, and segregation in the work place. This quickly escalated into physical attacks in the street against women who were dressed 'indecently', throwing acid on their bodies and attacking them with knives.

In the face of these brutal attacks, which often disfigured the victims, the government offered no rejoinder. It is often reported that when women complained

---

[15] For more details see Caputi and Russell, *Femicide*.

[16] Ibid.

[17] 'Algeria: Women Left Unprotected from Violence and Discrimination', Amnesty International Press release, 10 January 2005. Available at http://news.amnesty.org/mavp/news.nsf/print (accessed 21.12.2005).

[18] Ibid.

to the police about their assailants they were told that they had brought it upon themselves by their immoral conduct. It was in fact this silence and sometimes the complicity of the neo-conservative state that encouraged the fundamentalists' attacks on women. The way a given society chooses to control the violence inherent in it reflects the value it places on mutual respect and tolerance of difference, and on human rights, democracy, and good governance.

The institution of the 1984 Family Code is in itself symptomatic of the Algerian government's lack of respect for women and its arbitrary neglect of women's basic human rights. This move is also symptomatic of the government's lack of regard for individual liberties as it paid no heed to the numerous demonstrations led by women in 1981 and 1982 to demand the elimination of the project of the family code. The Algerian government co-opted the 'conservatives, and later, Muslim fundamentalists, to safeguard their interests and stay in power. Various governments have many times made compromises and sacrificed women's rights and safety to keep peace with the fundamentalists'.[19] While the Berber demonstrations of 20 April1980 were crushed by the military, the women's movement was crushed with institutional violence in the form of the Family Code.

The Main Provisions of the 1984 Family Code[20]

The 1984 Family Code reproduced provisions of Islamic Shari'a law that embodied the aspirations of the neo-conservative faction in society, which from the early years of independence had stood against all government initiatives to emancipate women and saw women's primary role as homemakers and men's role as breadwinners.[21]

Under this code women have no right to marry but can only be given in marriage by a matrimonial guardian (article 11). Women cannot divorce their husbands and can only obtain divorce by submitting to the *Khol'a* practice, which stipulates that they should give up their legal rights or claims to alimony. It has to be highlighted that in the case of Algeria, women are asked to pay their husbands or give up their financial share in any goods the couple owned in order to obtain a divorce. Divorce is unilateral with no duty to pay maintenance or provide housing (article 54), and men are permitted to take up to four wives (article 8).

The primary role of women, according to the Family Code is that of procreators, making it their legal duty to breastfeed their children and care for them until adulthood (article 48).

It is prescribed that women must obey their husbands, respect them, and consult them in every matter concerning them. They should ask for permission to go out and can only take employment if their husband grants them authorization. Women must also respect and look after as well as obey their in-laws (article 39).

[19] L. Ait Hammou, 'Women's Struggle against Muslim Fundamentalism in Algeria: Strategies or a Lesson for Survival?', in Ayesha Imam et al. (eds.) *Warning Signs of Fundamentalisms* (London: WLUML, 2004), pp. 117–124, at p. 118.
[20] République Algérienne Démocratique et Populaire, Ministère de la Justice, *Le Code de la famille*, (Alger: OPU, 1993). For online version see
http://www.20ansbarakat.free.fr/codedelafamille.html (accessed 8.12.2004).
[21] For more details on the institution of the Family Code and Algerian women's reaction to it see Zahia Smail Salhi, 'Algerian Women, Citizenship, and the "Family Code"', *Gender & Development* 11(3) (November 2003), pp. 27–35.

168

Women are given custody of their children; boys till the age of 10 and girls till marriage. In case a divorcee does not have a male guardian to look after her, the ex-husband will only support her if his means allow it. Furthermore, a divorcee is not permitted to take her children abroad or allow them to be involved in certain school activities without the father's signature of consent (article 52).

The 1984 Family Code codifies women's status as minors under the law, strips them of their citizenship rights, and makes them more vulnerable in a society that already favours its male members. From childhood girls are treated differently from boys and are exposed to various forms of segregation, as explained above.

In fact, the Family Code is only an expression of what is well embedded in Algerian society, despite the promises of the newly independent state under the late President Houari Boumedienne that women should be part of the development project of the state and that they should be rewarded for their active participation in the liberation process of their country from French occupation. As such, the institution of the Family Code is a clear betrayal of women and the principles of the Algerian revolution which rallied to its ranks both men and women to liberate the nation.

While the institution of the Family Code seemed to have satisfied the clergy and the neo-conservative members of Chadli's government, the Muslim Brothers were less than satisfied; in their view the code was not Islamic enough and they called for a total implementation of the Shari'a, and the institution of an Islamic State in Algeria.

The October 1988 Events and their Impact on Women

The social strife that had marked the 1980s culminated in the October 1988 riots. Many regions in the country joined the demonstrations and in some regions the movement was seen as a continuation of the Berber uprising of 1980, which is now seen as not only a cultural movement but also a civil society uprising against social injustice and government corruption.

Generally viewed as a result of a deepening economic crisis exacerbated by the severe drop in oil revenues, which resulted in rising unemployment rates together with shortages of water and housing, and soaring prices of basic consumer goods, this movement is in essence an uprising of civil society demanding social justice in the face of growing corruption.

On the 5 October 1988 the waves of discontent expressed initially through a series of strikes and peaceful marches quickly degenerated into wide scale riots. Alarmed by the intensity of the destruction caused by youths who attacked government buildings, the military resorted to violent repression, causing the death and injury of several demonstrators and the arrest and torture of many others, which ultimately led to more anger and resentment.

The Muslim Brothers capitalized on this popular anger and exploited it politically through a populist discourse which swiftly recruited many angry youths. At the same time, many other groups joined the protest and took the opportunity to voice their concerns and call for radical change and the toppling of Chadli's government.

Algerian journalists, who for many years have suffered from state censorship and absence of freedom of expression, published a declaration in which they denounced the ban on reporting and condemned the restrictions that were imposed on freedom of speech. They also denounced the violence, torture, and arbitrary arrests used by the state to try to curb the uprising.

The women's groups, who throughout the 1980s had incessantly expressed their anger at the institution of the Family Code, also joined the demonstrations and voiced their full support for the youth movement and called for the recognition of democratic liberties.

In short, the whole society joined together and more than ever before the political system came under sustained attack.

In order to save his government President Chadli Bendjedid gave promises of economic reform and political liberalization. These political reforms brought an end to the one party rule and brought to the fore a new model of societal/political organization based on citizenship rights in lieu of an abstract notion of development. It seemed that the establishment of political pluralism served as an alternative to addressing social and economic needs. It is true that since independence Algerian people had yearned for both economic development and political openness, while the ruling FLN preferred to suppress all forms of difference and repressed any kind of political opposition. Lazreg explains, 'The "discovery" of citizenship is a powerful tool of protest in the hands of political opposition groups and social groups such as women, traditionally excluded from the full enjoyment of their political rights. It opens up a new era of inquiry into the many dimensions of citizenship and their culturally specific expressions as well.'[22]

The situation of women in this new political climate is indeed most intriguing as while they remain minors under the dictates of the Family Code, which denies them their civil rights, they can now enjoy political citizenship and form their own associations through which they can make claims for equality before the law.

The institution of the Family Code in 1984 was a strong wake-up call for Algerian women and a re-launch of the Algerian feminist movement which started in the 1940s as the Algerian Women's Union (UFA: Union des Femmes Algériennes). The Union which was mainly affiliated to the Nationalist political parties joined the National Liberation Front (FLN) and the armed struggle (ALN) from 1954 to 1962. In the post-independence period it was made into a state-controlled organization, namely the UNFA (Union Nationale des Femmes Algériennes: National Union of Algerian Women). The UNFA was stripped of its militant platform and turned into a conformist organization which was ultimately deserted by feminist women.[23]

Women war veterans and a new generation of women who opposed the UNFA in their struggle to stop and eventually repeal the Family Code merged together and solidified their ranks in a new feminist movement whose political platform is the abolishing of the Family Code.

Immediately after the launch of the political reforms which followed the 1988 riots, three women's associations were created and were granted permission to operate

---

[22] Marnia Lazreg, 'Citizenship and Gender in Algeria', in Suad Joseph (ed.), *Gender and Citizenship in the Middle East* (Syracuse, NY: Syracuse University Press, 2000), pp. 58–69, at p. 58.
[23] For a more detailed study of the Algerian feminist movement see Zahia Smail Salhi, 'The Algerian Feminist Movement between Nationalism, Patriarchy and Islamism', *Women's Studies International Forum* 32(6) (2009). Online publication complete: 28-NOV-2009 DOI information: 10.1016/j.wsif.2009.11.001

as of summer 1989. These are the Association for the Emancipation of Women, the Association for Equality before the Law between Women and Men, and the Association for the Defence and Promotion of Women's Rights.

Nevertheless, despite the genuine will and determination of the women's groups to exercise full political citizenship, the disjuncture between political and civil citizenship has hampered Algerian women from enjoying full participation in public life and from achieving autonomy in the conduct of their private lives. What exacerbated this condition was the rise of the Islamic Brotherhood as a political party, namely the Islamic Salvation Front (FIS: Front Islamique du Salut). Political analysts described this move as 'the government's last-ditch effort to shield itself from the political opposition it has allowed to surface'.[24]

Women's associations and liberal political opposition parties (such as the FFS and RCD)[25] were alarmed and very worried by the Islamists' non-democratic agenda on the one hand and their populist discourse on the other; while the Islamist leaders never supported democracy, but repeatedly asserted that once in power they would fully implement Shari'a law, their populist rhetoric recruited masses of frustrated youths to whom they sold packs of dreams, and through the expression of their outright hatred of the regime they have quickly managed to pose themselves as the strongest alternative to the FLN. The danger of the domination of the public sphere by the FIS proponents is the intimidation if not silencing of other political voices, resulting in the democratic process being compromised. Michael Edwards explains,

> In its role as the 'public sphere', civil society becomes the arena for argument and deliberation as well as for association and institutional collaboration, and the extent to which such spaces thrive is crucial to democracy, since if only certain truths are represented, if alternative viewpoints are silenced by exclusion or suppression, or if one set of voices are heard more loudly than those of others, the 'public' interest inevitably suffers.[26]

Substituting the voice of the FLN with that of the FIS would indeed jeopardize the democratic process and kill the nascent democracy in its infancy. The undemocratic claims of the FIS leaders and the attitude of the FIS supporters towards other civil society members confirm this point.

Islamist Violence against Women in Algeria

This new political climate positioned women's organizations and the members of the FIS as clear opponents in a game in which the first group fought for their civil rights while the second fought to suppress them.

The members of the FIS, who used the religious space of the mosque for propagating their fundamentalist views, especially vis-à-vis women, whom they put at the centre of their populist propaganda, rallied to their cause huge numbers of unemployed youths whom they convinced that women should return to their homes to fulfil their God-given roles as homemakers and leave their jobs to the unemployed

[24] Lazreg, 'Gender and Politics in Algeria', p. 779.
[25] RCD: Rassemblement pour la Culture et la Democracie, FFS: Front des Forces Socialistes.
[26] M. Edwards, 'Civil Society', *The Encyclopedia of Informal Education* (2005). Available at www.infed.org/association/civil_society.htm (accessed 5.8.2009).

males who needed them most. Over and over again Ali Benhadj, the second leader of the FIS, portrayed women as needing male protection and reiterated that the safest place for them was the home and that their prime duty was 'to produce lions to fight for the cause of Islam'.

This discourse resulted in making the public sphere even more hostile than it already was to women, who are now designated as one of the wrongs of Algerian society and who, if Islamic salvation is to prevail, should be 'righted' as a matter of urgency. Islamist discourse repeated *ad infinitum* that society should be cleansed of moral corruption, which is mostly personified in women, who are branded as '"the avant-garde of colonialism and cultural aggression" and, because they opposed the family code which legalised polygamy, they were dubbed, "the women who wanted to marry four husbands"'.[27]

Alarmed by the Islamists' populist discourse (such as in the above quotes), and the danger they represented to the nascent democratic movement and to women's organizations, the Association for the Equality before the Law between Men and Women called for a massive gathering to celebrate International Women's Day on 8 March 1989. The members of the association emphasized their determination to continue their struggle against gender segregation as exemplified in the Family Code, which they described as an obstacle to justice, equality, and democracy, which they highlighted as the main components of the full development of the Algerian woman and of Algerian society as a whole.[28] Women's status as minors under the law prohibits the society as a whole from progressing into a democratic society, and makes them extremely vulnerable in face of the campaign of intimidation directed by the FIS members against them.

As a response to this statement the leader of the FIS Abbassi Madani told *Agence France Presse*, in an interview in 1989, that the recent anti-fundamentalist demonstrations by women were 'one of the greatest dangers threatening the destiny of Algeria'. This was because the women participants were 'defying the conscience of the people and repudiating national values'.[29] In no time at all the Islamists dominated the public sphere, and because of the religious aspect of their party and discourse, people did not have the audacity to stand against their intimidating moves, not only against women, whom they openly ordered to adopt the Islamic veil, but against society as a whole. Among their fundamentalist moves they removed satellite dishes from people's roofs and installed loud speakers which were connected to audiotapes emanating from the mosques and through which they preached their new way of life. Their discourse was loaded with threats and hatred directed at those who did not follow their way. The loud speakers, which dominated cities such as the capital, were backed up in Islamists' shops with cassettes which played the Qur'an instead of the usual music played in stores.

A whole new atmosphere dominated the public sphere, which was fully occupied by bearded men wearing *qamis* and *sirwāl* (such as worn in Pakistan), while women

---

[27] Karima Bennoune, 'S.O.S. Algeria: Women's Human Rights under Siege', in Mahnaz Afkhami (ed.), *Faith and Freedom: Women's Human Rights in the Muslim World* (London and New York: I.B. Tauris, 2000), pp. 184–208, at p. 197.

[28] Feminist declaration on 8 March 1989 in Algiers, *WAF Articles* 1 (1989), p. 15.

[29] Quoted in Bennoune, 'S.O.S. Algeria', pp. 197–198.

wore a plethora of new Islamic veils (*hijāb, niqāb, jilbāb, chador...*) which were all alien to Algerian society.

The level of intimidation against those who did not follow their dress code reached its peak at the point where they were feeling threatened in the streets, which were 'decorated' with graffiti, often in red, and subjected to shouted threats such as, 'O you woman who wears the *jilbāb* may you be blessed by God, O you woman who wears the *hijāb* [long robe and headscarf] may God put you on the right path. O you woman who expose yourself, the gun is for you.'[30]

Such intimidation resulted in many women wearing the veil out of fear and many others carrying a headscarf in their handbags which they would wear in the street and take off when reaching their destination. Bennoune quotes one such woman who testified, 'None of us want to wear the veil. But fear is stronger than our convictions or our will to be free. Fear is all around us. Our parents, our brothers, are unanimous: Wear the veil and stay alive.'[31]

In some municipalities the fundamentalists forced segregation between boys and girls in schools, and deprived girls of physical education. They intimidated people on beaches and at swimming pools and interfered with cultural life in general, prohibiting wedding ceremonies and all forms of celebrations that used music. They issued death threats against singers and performers, and cancelled all festivals. They closed all cinemas and theatres and transformed them into party headquarters. In 1990–91 they imposed a six o'clock curfew on female university students living in halls of residence. Saadi reports that anyone opposing this was 'corrected' with the aid of a whip or bicycle chain.[32]

In brief, all manifestations of social life were banned and instead a deep feeling of fear roamed the streets of the cities where the Islamists were dominant.

What started as verbal attacks, threats, and intimidations soon became transformed into outbursts of extreme violence in 1992, soon after the government annulled the December 1991 Parliamentary elections, in which the Islamists made major electoral gains, and banned the FIS as a political party.

In February 1992 a state of emergency was declared and in March of the same year the two main leaders of the FIS, Abassi Madani and Ali Benhadj, were arrested. These moves by the government resulted in the Islamic Salvation Front as a political party turning into several armed terrorist organizations, the most notorious of which were the GIA (Groupe Islamique Armé: Armed Islamic Group), the AIS (Armée Islamique du Salut: Army of Islamic Salvation), and the MIA (Mouvement Islamique Armé: Armed Islamic Movement). It has to be highlighted here that not all Islamist parties were dissolved: other religious parties 'were not banned by the various Algerian regimes that succeeded after the departure of President Chadli Benjedid and the onset of terrorism. On the contrary they were assimilated into the political process, and provision was made for the expression of dissident views', assert Roy and Sfeir.[33]

---

[30] Ibid.

[31] Ibid., p. 187.

[32] Noureddine Saadi, *La femme et la loi en Algérie* (Alger: Eds Bouchêne, 1991), p. 117.

[33] Oliver Roy and Antoine Sfeir, *The Columbia World Dictionary of Islamism*, trans. John King (New York: University of Columbia Press, 2007), p. 32.

The fear of civilians was intensified by the random killings of policemen, journalists, intellectuals, and women. The armed groups issued death threats against the intelligentsia, government security workers, and feminist activists. It became very obvious to all that the terrorists harboured a worrying misogyny.

One of the first women to be gunned down was 21-year-old Karima Belhadj, who worked as a clerk in the youth and sports department of the general office of national security. She was shot in the head and abdomen on 7 April 1993. On 23 January 1994 Mrs Mimouna Derouche, a 28-year-old mother of five children, was decapitated in front of her family. On 25 February 1994, two sisters aged 12 and 15 were kidnapped and gang raped. On 3 March 1994 Samia Hadjou, an old woman aged 69, had her throat cut. On 7 November 1994 two sisters named Saida and Zoulikha were gang raped, tortured (their fingernails and toenails were pulled out), and their throats cut. Their bodies were found on a roadside. Saida and Zoulikha received this punishment because they refused to consent to temporary marriage with the terrorists.[34] Unveiled women were now being shot down in the streets; in March 1994 three unveiled high school students were shot down,[35] one of whom had been warned but refused to wear the veil.

Feminist activists were openly targeted. Their names were listed and pinned on mosque doors and shouted over the loudspeakers. Khalida Messaoudi, whom the fundamentalists sentenced to death in 1993, testifies, 'Over the loudspeakers, whose monotonous echoes penetrate into the very centre of the surrounding houses, imams would hurl curses at me, describe me as "a woman of delinquent morals" and a "danger to the morality of women," and warn those women who might be tempted to follow my example.'[36] From this date onwards she lived in hiding, moving from one place to another and disguising herself as she moved between places.

If Khalida survived the fundamentalists' threats other feminists didn't; on 15 February 1995 Nabila Djahnine, the president of the Berber women's group, Thighri N' tmettouth (The Cry of Women), was gunned down in Tizi-Ouzou. In Sfizef (south of Mascara) eleven women teachers were slaughtered in front of their pupils by an armed group outside the Ain Adden school.[37]

It soon became evident that women were at the top of the terrorists' agenda and that their bodies were primarily targeted as symbols; the terrorists' lists of women to be killed were extensive and included women from all walks of life: women who worked in government offices; women who owned shops such as hairdressers, beauty salons, and Turkish baths; women teachers and university lecturers; women related to government officers or security workers; feminist activists, women artists and singers, schoolgirls, women who lived on their own,[38] even husbands of important women such as the husband of the government Minister Leïla Aslaoui[39] were targeted.

[34] Bennoune, 'S.O.S. Algeria', p. 186.

[35] Salim Ghazi, 'Deux Lycéenes assassinées', *El Watan*, 31.3.1994, p. 1.

[36] Khalida Messaoudi and Elisabeth Schemla, *Unbowed: An Algerian Woman confronts Islamic Fundamentalism*, trans. Anne C. Vila (Philadelphia: University of Pennsylvania Press, 1998), p. 87.

[37] Amnesty International, 'Algeria: Civilian Population caught in a Spiral of Violence', Report MDE 28/23/97 (London, 1997) p. 18.

[38] In the southern Algerian town of Ouargla, a group of fundamentalists set fire to the house of Saliha Dekkiche, a divorced woman living alone with her children, resulting in her 3-year-old child burning to death.

[39] In her book, *Les Années rouges* (Alger: Casbah Editions, 2000), Leïla Aslaoui testifies about the assassination of her husband and the atrocities of Islamic terrorism in general.

After targeting individuals the terrorists soon moved to mass murders, bombings of buses and public places, and the massacre and ransacking of remote villages.

When they attacked villages,[40] whole populations were massacred. Daily newspapers reported the kidnapping of young girls who were gang raped and turned into sex slaves, those who disobeyed them or attempted to escape had their bodies mutilated and abused, with their genitals often amputated. The hideous machine of sexual torture reached unimaginable dimensions. It was reported in daily newspapers that the terrorists used a technique they called *Tafrī'* to split women's bodies into two halves by attaching them to two vehicles which drove in opposite directions.

Ait Hamou describes the horror in the following terms, 'Women were attacked in their homes, brutally beaten, abducted, raped, taken as temporary wives of the "emirs", or as slaves. They were shot dead, torn apart when they were pregnant and their foetuses smashed on the walls.'[41] Abduction of women and rape became common practice among armed groups. In 1998, Human Rights Watch reported that more than 2,000 women were raped in five years of conflict,[42] many of them were held by armed Islamist militia, to be violated, beaten, and forced to perform domestic tasks for the men.

When some of these women managed to escape, they were unable to secure any support and were 'therefore damaged by the initial rape, but also by the shame and stigma which separates them from their families'.[43]

Such practices turned the terrorists' war against women into a genuine femicide. Women were truly petrified not of death but of torture and dishonour. Bennoune reports that one woman told her, 'I thought of buying poison so I can kill myself if taken by them alive, so all they get is a corpse. I am losing my hair from nerves.'[44]

Practices which resembled madness and rage against women were reported on a daily basis. Pondering on the Islamists' femicide Khalida Messaoudi observes,

> At the heart of their way of life, their mindset, their imprecations, and their savagery, I perceived a constant obsession, of the kind that is symptomatic of madness: an obsession with women. The truth is; no other theme looms as large as this one does in the ideology of the FIS ... According to the fundamentalists, women are the root of all evil.[45]

Targeting women's bodies and using them as battlefields makes it obvious that gender is at the core of the issue of Islamic terrorism, and inflicting violence on their bodies is a means of controlling women and terrorizing their community. As Aisha Lemsine remarks, 'The treatment of women raises serious questions about the level of faith and Islamic behaviour on the part of the protagonists in the civil war in Algeria.' She adds, 'As in Bosnia, Algerian women are the first victims of the civil war in their

---

[40] In a single night in August 1997 the terrorists massacred 100–300 women, children, and men in Hay Rais, and in September of the same year they slaughtered 64 women in Beni Messous and 100–200 in Bentalha. For more details see Anissa Barrak, 'Les Faits à travers la presse algérienne', *Confluences Méditerranée* 25 (1998), pp. 11–20.

[41] Ait Hammou, 'Women's Struggle against Muslim Fundamentalism', p. 120.

[42] Human Rights Watch, 'Algeria: Country Reports' (Washington DC, 1998), p. 4.

[43] Amnesty International and Fédération Internationale des Ligues des Droits de l'Homme and Human Rights Watch, *Algérie: Le livre noir* (Paris: La Découverte, 1997), pp. 20–21.

[44] Bennoune, 'S.O.S. Algeria', p. 185.

[45] Messaoudi and Schemla, *Unbowed*, p. 100.

country. In the Balkans, rape and forced pregnancy were tactics of "ethnic cleansing"; in Algeria, the persecution of women is a key element of "religious cleansing".[46]

Even Islamist leaders like Sudan's Hassan Al-Turabi have disavowed the war against Algerian women, and the Tunisian Islamist Rachid Ghennouchi openly declared, 'As Islamists ourselves, we are ashamed at what Algerian Islamists are doing to women!'[47]

It has to be highlighted, however, that in their attempt to suppress women and confine them to the private sphere, Islamists' violence has made women more visible and more central to the fight and resistance against their barbaric acts.

Women's Resistance Strategies

Speaking of women's resistance strategies might suggest an organized and collaborative action taken by women against terrorism, which is not the case. Their reactions and strategies were dictated by the circumstances they lived in and experienced, and to say that these women were not afraid of terrorism would be too pretentious.

Algerian women, like the rest of the population, were traumatized and deeply scared for their lives and those of their loved ones. The whole society lived through a general psychosis which they experienced day and night. No place in Algeria was safe or spared from fear and danger. To 'resist' as opposed to 'succumb' was not even an option. Women had to stand up to Islamism as a terrorist movement that opposed progress and democracy.

Trapped between the dictates of an infamous Family Code and the barbarism of the Islamic fundamentalists, women were not prepared to submit to the threats of the terrorists or to give up their struggle to repeal the Family Code. At every opportunity, women activists voiced their determination to have the code repealed and their belief that Algeria, with its principles of liberation drawn from its revolutionary not-too distant past, would eventually triumph over the retrograde forces of terrorism. Women's new struggle took a dual course of action: one was social and spontaneous and the other was political and structured, mainly led by the feminist groups.

On the social level women's motto was 'life as opposed to death'. As such their strategy was to resist and oppose the destructive powers of Islamic terrorism by simply continuing to lead 'normal' lives despite the atmosphere of war.

Women continued to go to work and do their daily errands. They continued to send their children to school despite the fact that schools were targeted by the terrorists who had burned down and ransacked many educational establishments. Both children and teachers were also targeted. Sixteen pupils were assassinated while at school on 5 October 1997,[48] and female teachers who were not sure of returning to their homes

---

[46] Aicha Lemsine, *Middle East Times* (Cairo), 16.3.2001. Available at http://www.islamfortoday.com/Algeria/htm (accessed 20.6.2009).

[47] Ibid.

[48] In September 1994 the GIA called for a boycott of schools and threatened reprisals in the form of school burnings and murders of pupils and teachers if anyone defied the order. Quoted in Meredeth Turshen, 'Militarism and Islamism in Algeria', *Journal of Asian and African Studies* 39(1–2) (2004), pp. 119–132, at p. 125.

in the evening (twelve teachers, some of whom were veiled, were assassinated in front of their pupils in September 1997 and several others had already met the same destiny) continued to attend to their duties; every time a female teacher was assassinated another filled her post.[49]

Women continued to go to hairdressers and beauty salons despite the Islamists' threats and they continued to find ways to celebrate births, weddings, and their children's birthdays and school achievements in the ways they always had done.

Despite the fear and difficulty of gathering, they continued to celebrate International Women's Day, during which they staged mock tribunals against terrorism, and showed films and staged plays that highlighted the dangers of fundamentalism and glorified women's courage, women's contribution to society, and more importantly raised the morale of women. They highlighted the importance of women's solidarity networks and the active participatory roles which they had yet to play.

In short, Algerian women celebrated life and the continuance of life while the terrorists spread death every day (more than eighty people were killed daily) and transformed the country into a huge graveyard. In the face of grief, women consoled each other and helped each other by hosting orphans and widows and aiding the needy at times of despair. The feminist groups launched many charitable organizations to help survivors of rape who were disowned by their families because of the shame they had allegedly brought on them. These organizations, such as 'SOS Femmes en Détresse', took care of the children of the women and girls who were forcibly impregnated by the terrorists and pressed the government to permit abortion in such circumstances. They recruited doctors, midwives, psychologists, and lawyers as volunteers to help in the rehabilitation process of the female survivors of violence.

In the absence of men, women stepped into new fields and positions traditionally designated as male domains. In some areas they led funerals, and in the work place they took positions in sectors such as construction and civic engineering. Women took charge of small enterprises and ran new businesses. In short, at a time when women were forcibly excluded from the public sphere they became even more visible by adopting new roles and moving into new economic domains.

On the political level, women have never given up their demands to have the Family Code repealed and have worked tirelessly to widen the spread of awareness among high school and university students about the Family Code and its perils, and most importantly about women's human rights, which were denied to them by society at large, in order to mobilize support for its abolition.

What is important to highlight here is that women's organizations refused to have their rights and claims for the abolition of the Family Code take second place, as was the case after the independence of the country when they were constantly told that economic development took priority over the issue of women's rights. It was now believed that no progress could take place and no democracy could be achieved if half the population was excluded from the equation and denied its human rights.

Despite their status as victims of terrorist violence and minors under the law, throughout the 1990s women engaged in consolidating their roles as agents of change

---

[49] Aslaoui, *Les Années rouges*, p. 9.

and resistance to Islamist terrorism. On the 2 January 1992 women were the first to
stage a massive demonstration against the FIS and their electoral victory of December
1991. Having participated in this demonstration, I was surprised to see how what
started with a group of about a hundred demonstrators gathered in the centre of
Algiers recruited followers along the march, becoming a massive crowd. Alarmed
by the urgency of the moment, women and men joined spontaneously as the march
processed by their homes or shops.

The crowd called for the cancellation of the electoral process in which many
women's voices were taken by the FIS through the proxy vote, and warned of the
danger of Algeria becoming an Islamic state.

With the choice between an Islamist regime which is known for imposing religious
law to the detriment of civil law, and a military regime that would limit democratic
freedoms in the name of national security, women chose to support the military. In
her book on the terrorist decade Leïla Aslaoui asserts, 'On the night of the third to
the fourth of June 1992, the army came out to save the republic.'[50] She explains that
without the army, which unlike the government was strong and unified, the country
would have become an Islamic republic. These same claims were shouted by the
women demonstrators whose banners carried slogans reading, 'The Army, the People
and Democracy', 'No Iran, No Kabul, Algeria is Algerian', 'Algeria: Free and
Democratic', 'Let's Save the Principles of the Republic'.[51]

The numbers of women participating in the demonstrations amounted to thousands;
their aim was to reclaim the public sphere which the Islamists were trying to dominate,
but more importantly to manifest their rejection of a fundamentalist rule which they
saw as a threat not only against women but also against society as a whole and, most
importantly, against the nascent democracy. Such demonstrations became almost
routine occurrences to affirm that Algeria would not submit to terrorist violence.[52]

On the women's demonstrations the independent newspaper *Al-Watan* wrote, 'Tens
of thousands of women were out to give an authoritative lesson on bravery and spirit
to men paralysed by fear, reduced to silence … the so-called weaker sex refused to
be intimidated by the threats advanced by "the sect of assassins".'[53]

It has to be highlighted here that since the celebrations of national independence
in 1962, women had been almost absent as civil society members and had not taken
part in demonstrations. The institution of the Family Code and the rise of
fundamentalism in Algeria were the two main wake-up calls which roused them
from their passivity to become active agents and claim their space in the political
arena. Several feminist groups started organizing themselves and working together

[50] Aslaoui, *Les Années rouges*, p. 144.

[51] Such slogans were repeatedly shouted at subsequent demonstrations such as that on 25 October 1993. Such
slogans demonstrate women's awareness of the replications of Islamic fundamentalism at the international level.
They also demonstrate a will to link the women's movement in Algeria to other women's movements internationally
but most specifically with Women Living under Muslim Laws. See http://www.newint.org/issue270/270edge.html
(accessed 21.12. 2005).

[52] For more details see *Shadow Report on Algeria to CEDAW*, submitted by International Women's Human Rights
Law Clinic and Women Living under Muslim Laws (1999). Available at http://www.nodo50.org/mujeresred/argelia-
shadwreport.html (accessed 30.6.2004).

[53] Valentine M. Moghadam, 'Organizing Women: The New Women's Movement in Algeria', *Cultural Dynamics* 13
(2001), pp. 131–154, at p. 140. Available at http://cdy.sagepub.com/cgi/content/refs/13/2/131 (accessed 17.6.2009).

to change the awareness of women's issues in Algerian society and provide women with the knowledge that would enable them to counteract fundamentalism and produce a counter-discourse on both the national and international levels.

To do so, they maintained their stand as staunch opponents of fundamentalism and terrorism, by voicing their views and making their suffering known to all. The women survivors of rape testified on national television and in daily newspapers about their ordeals, telling the whole nation and those who remained in doubt about what the terrorists were doing to women and how their savage acts contradicted the essence of Islam.

This act was a very powerful move in Algerian history and in the history of Algerian women in particular; what had been an unspoken taboo during the war of independence and in the years which followed was now spoken of openly and widely mediatized.

Rape as a repressive measure was widely used by the colonists during the Algerian war of independence. The stories of such ordeals were never told as there was general consensus that these horrors which were directly targeting the honour of the victims and their families were to be buried for ever. It is astonishing to remark that no one ever talks about this subject whether in public or in private.

In her article 'From Taboo to Transnational Political Issue: Violence against Women in Algeria'[54] Catherine Lloyd demonstrates how in the 1990s, women transformed the issue of Islamist violence in terms of rape from taboo into a campaigning issue that has taken on transnational dimensions.

The front pages of the Algerian daily newspapers carried pictures and stories of the lived horrors while the feminist organization Rassemblement Algérien des Femmes Démocratiques (RAFD) carried out the documenting of human rights violations and the collecting of women's testimonies. It is indeed interesting to remark how these survivors of rape relate their stories in minute detail to magnify the human tragedy they experienced. Their testimonies have even made the women of the war of independence break their silence after many decades and relate, as well as compare, their experiences. In summer 2000 Louisette Ighilahriz, a war veteran, came forward and testified about 'the torture of rape' she underwent at the hands of French soldiers in 1957, which she published as a book both in France and Algeria.[55]

This fusion of colonial and post-colonial stories of torture and resistance by women is also displayed in political activism and the joining of forces between the war veterans and the new feminists in the fight against the Family Code.

Algerian Women and Transnational Networking

Having strengthened their ranks on the national level as a resistance group against terrorism and fundamentalism, the Algerian feminists reached out into the international arena by forging solidarity networks with other women globally but particularly with those living under Muslim laws.

---

[54] Catherine Lloyd, 'From Taboo to Transnational Political Issue: Violence against Women in Algeria', *Women's Studies International Forum* 29(5) (September–October 2006), pp. 453–462. Available at http://www.sciencedirect.com/science (accessed 20.8.2009).

[55] Louisette Ighilahriz, *Algérienne*, récit recueilli par Anne Nivat (Alger: Casbah Editions, 2006).

In 1995 they joined the Maghreb Egalité Network together with Moroccan and Tunisian women's groups to represent Maghrebi women at the Beijing Conference in 1995, where they made violence against women a priority and cooperated in this with organizations such as Women against Fundamentalisms and Women Living under Muslim Laws. By joining such groups and international networks Algerian women also sought to secure resources for female survivors of violence and to widely publicize their cause.

According to Lloyd, in order to establish resources for women who had experienced violence, the women activists began to liaise with international funding agencies, building their capacity for effective action.[56] This work has generated solidarity and funding, most recently for equipment and premises, such as shelters for women. Algerian women's regular contacts in the diaspora provide useful resources: for example many Algerian women's organizations continue to use France as a base for activities such as confiding their funds to bank accounts in France managed by trusted colleagues who regularly send them small sums of money. Algerian women in the diaspora raised funds and bought medicines which they regularly shipped to Algeria during the years of the civil war.[57]

Along with raising funds these women were keen to secure the support of many Western countries whose media often portrayed the Islamists as victims of the undemocratic Algerian state who had crushed their victory by cancelling the electoral process in 1992. Their main aim was to create a counter-discourse to that of the FIS and demonstrate to world opinion that the FIS had used democratic means to eradicate the nascent democracy in Algeria. Feminists publicized FIS leaders' statements against democracy[58] and presented themselves as an alternative voice to that of the state, which had lost its credibility on the international scale. The women of the RAFD filed a civil action suit in Washington DC against the FIS and its US representative, Anwar Haddam. The founder of the RAFD, Zazi Sadou, was given an award for her work for Algerian women's human rights from the US-based network Women, Law and Development International.[59]

Zazi Sadou, Salima Ghozali, Khalida Messaoudi, and other feminist leaders became tireless ambassadors in various countries across the world telling Western audiences about the realities at stake in Algeria. At the height of the Islamic terror in November 1994, Saida Ben Habylas, the official Algerian representative to a UN-sponsored regional meeting that took place in Amman, gave an impassioned speech denouncing the violence against women.[60]

---

[56] Lloyd, 'From Taboo to Transnational Political Issue'.

[57] The same actions were also conducted by the fundamentalists whose supporters in the diaspora were actively gathering funds and generating financial support for their fighters in Algeria. Such groups were seen in many places, especially after Friday prayers, calling loudly for support for the 'Algerian bothers'. It is interesting to notice how women and the Islamists were the two most visible contenders in the 1990s, both nationally and internationally.

[58] As an example, this is what the two main Algerian fundamentalist leaders/co-founders of the FIS party had to say, even long before the December 1991 elections were cancelled in Algeria, about their programme and democracy: 'I do not respect either the laws or the political parties which do not have the Qur'an. I throw them under my feet and I trample them. These parties must leave the country. They must be suppressed,' Ali Benhadj, *Alger Républicain*, 5.4.1991; 'Beware of those who pretend that the concept of democracy exists in Islam. Democracy is Kofr', Ali Benhadj, *Le Matin*, 29.10.1989. Quoted in Mariemme Hélie-Lucas, 'What is your Tribe? Women's Struggle and the Construction of Muslimness', *WLULM* 26 (October 2004), p. 26.

[59] Moghadem, 'Organizing Women', p. 142.

[60] Ibid., p. 143.

The reality which the Algerian feminists aimed to explain to the world was that Islamic terrorism was not a home-grown phenomenon and a result of socialist mismanagement, as claimed by Mark Paris, the acting assistant secretary for Near Eastern Affairs, in a statement before the Subcommittee on Africa of the Foreign Affairs Committee in March 1994,[61] but the result of the US and other Western governments' actions in promoting Islamism and training Arab fundamentalist armed men in Pakistan and Afghanistan during the 1980s.

In *The Jordan Times*, Miriam Shahin wrote, 'The West indirectly supports the FIS with its IMF and World Bank demands on Algeria. It is weakening the middle class and making the poor poorer and the rich richer.'[62]

Bennoune reports that a visiting US delegation told a former Algerian Prime Minister that the continued existence of a public sector in Algeria was a far greater problem than terrorist violence.[63]

In brief, while world opinion in the 1990s supported the view that Algerian authorities should have given the FIS the opportunity to rule after winning the 1991 elections, Algerian public opinion thought the opposite; members of the FIS were terrorizing society well before they won the elections. Letting them rule the country would have resulted in the Talibanization of Algeria. The rise of the FIS in the 1990s coincided with the return of some 3,000 Algerians who had fought and trained in Afghanistan. General Belkheir declared in an interview that what the army did in Algeria was to prevent it from becoming another Afghanistan. The task was made very difficult by the moral embargo imposed by the West on Algeria, which prevented it from supplying its units and men with adequate weapons such as reconnaissance and night-vision equipment.

By the end of the 1990s the Algerian army had succeeded in neutralizing the threat that Islamism represented for the state. Yet, the international community still had not recognized the legitimacy of the war against Islamic terrorism and continued to hold Algerian authorities responsible for human rights abuses, while the terrorists' acts which resulted in a death toll of 200,000, the dislocation of thousands of people, and the destruction of both state and private infrastructure remained underestimated.

The 11 September 2001 attacks on the World Trade Centre in New York resulted in a radical change in world opinion towards Islamic terrorism and a reassessment of the violence in Algeria. At this stage charges of human rights violations by the Algerian security forces were dropped and the legitimacy of the war against terrorism in Algeria was recognized. President Bouteflika wrote in his letter of condolence to President Bush, 'Algeria understands better than others the pain of the families of the September 11 victims. For these reasons, Algeria supports the initiative of launching an international action against terrorism.'[64]

---

[61] Bennoune, 'S.O.S Algeria', pp. 200–201.

[62] Miriam Shahin, 'Algerian Women fight Terror', *The Jordan Times*, 13.11.1994, p. 1.

[63] Bennoune, 'S.O.S. Algeria', p. 201.

[64] Luis Martinez, 'Why the Violence in Algeria?', *Journal of North African Studies* 9(2) (Summer 2004), pp. 14–27, at p. 21.

Conclusion

With the end of the most terrible violence in Algeria and as the Islamist threat subsides, Algerian women are emerging from a difficult yet formative period. The legalization of their associations in 1989 has allowed them to organize themselves as pressure groups and become active actors in the public sphere. Their continuous demands for their legal rights, while combating and resisting Islamic terrorism, has made them real political actors and maintained them at the centre of political manoeuvres.

This trajectory, I would argue, is only the continuation of the political struggle they started in the 1940s which led them to become active agents in the fight against French colonial domination in the 1950s. Moving back to the centre of political action in the 1980s gave the women's movement more legitimacy and made their struggle for gender equality a concrete possibility, though fraught with difficulties in terms of changing prevailing mentalities.

In the post-terrorist period, women are once again represented in government; eleven women won seats in the national assembly in 1997 and in 2003 Khalida Messaoudi (now known as Khalida Toumi) became the government spokesperson.[65]

On the subject of gender and violence, the Algerian government has come under continued pressure from both regional and national women organizations as well as from international bodies to take serious action to address the problem of violence against women. Violence is now debated as a social phenomenon and is treated as a health problem which society has to fight. Various media have been used to encourage women to bring violence into the open and report it to the authorities, whose attitude towards domestic violence has also changed.

In October 2000 the organization SOS Femmes en Détresse[66] convened a conference in Algiers on violence against women and children and set up a network which has published its own report on the violence. Lloyd contends, 'These actions were significant in that they acknowledged the problem and recognised a role for specific legislation to protect women from violence. This would be backed up by data from bodies such as the police, social services, the courts and other state bodies that serve as points of contact for victims of family violence.'[67]

The work of NGOs resulted in lifting the veil of shame from all forms of violence, be they domestic, sexual, or institutional and the website of SOS Femmes en Détresse regularly publishes testimonies of victims of domestic violence, rape, incest, and child abuse, subjects which Algerian society refused to acknowledge in the past. They have also set up a legal and psychological aid hotline for women and children to report all forms of violence.

Women's groups asserted that the government campaign against domestic violence could not be successful as long as the Family Code remained unchanged. They insisted that women ought to be protected by laws which would punish perpetrators

---

[65] Turshen, 'Militarism and Islamism in Algeria', p. 130.

[66] The objectives of SOS Femmes en Détresse are the abolition of the Family Code, the defence of women's rights, spreading awareness about women's legal rights, eliminations of all forms of violence against women, providing shelter for distressed women (victims of all forms of violence, divorcees, single mothers, etc.) and their children, the rehabilitation of women, providing professional advice for women to create small businesses, providing legal and health advice to women and so on.

[67] Lloyd, 'From Taboo to Transnational Political Issue', p.460..

of violence. Women's NGOs pressed for government action to repeal the Code. By 2004 the group '20 ans Barakat' (20 years are enough) had become very active and was pressing hard for repeal of the Code. Although this has not been achieved, in 2005 some changes to the Code were introduced after heated debates and long protests by conservative political parties who opposed its modification.

Although the draft is believed to stop far short of eliminating all discriminatory provisions of the Family Code, most women activists and organizations in Algeria recognize these amendments to the Code as a significant improvement to the present law, and what is most important is the shifting of the sacred aspect of the Code which was viewed as an almost God-given document.

Bibliography

Abou Zahr, Carla, Wardlaw, Tessa, Stanton, Cynthia, and Hill, Ken (1996) 'Maternal Mortality', *World Health Statistics Quarterly* 49, pp. 77–87.

Abu Nasr, Julinda (1996) 'The Effects of War on Women in Lebanon', in Suha Sabbagh (ed.) *Arab Women: Between Defiance and Restraint* (New York: Olive Branch Press), pp. 95–99.

Abu-Lughod, Leila (1990) 'The Romance of Resistance: Tracing Transformations of Power Through Bedouin Women', *American Ethnologist* 17(1), pp. 41–55.

Abu-Lughod, Leila (2002) 'Do Muslim Women Really Need Saving? Anthropological Reflections on Cultural Relativism and its Others', *American Anthropologist* 104(3), pp. 783–790.

Acar, F. (2000) 'Country Papers: Turkey' in Marilou McPhedran et. al. (eds.) *The First CEDAW Impact Study, Final Report* (Toronto: The Centre for Feminist Research, York University and the International Women's Rights Project).

Ait Hammou, Louiza (2004) 'Women's Struggle against Muslim Fundamentalism in Algeria: Strategies or a Lesson for Survival?', in Ayesha Imam et al. (eds.) *Warning Signs of Fundamentalisms* (London: WLUML), pp. 117–124.

AKP Head Office Women's Auxiliaries Activity Report (2005).

Akşit, E.E. (2005) *Kızların Sessizliği: Kız Enstitülerinin Uzun Tarihi* (İstanbul: İletişim).

Al-Ali, Nadje (2005) 'Gendering Reconstruction: Iraqi Women between Dictatorship, Wars, Sanctions and Occupation', *Third World Quarterly* 26(4–5), pp. 739–758.

Al-Ali, Nadje (2007) *Iraqi Women: Untold Stories from 1948 to the Present* (London and New York: Zed Books).

Al-Ali, Nadje and Hussein, Yasmin (2003) 'Between Dreams and Sanctions: Teenage Lives in Iraq', in Akbar Mahdi (ed.) *Teenagers in the Middle East* (Westport, CT: Greenwood).

Al-Fassi, Allal (1966) *Al-Naqd Al-Dhati* (Auto-Criticism) (Beirut: Dar Al-Kashshaf).

Al-Haj, Majid (1989) 'Social Research on Family Lifestyles among Arabs in Israel', *Journal of Comparative Family Studies* 20, pp.175–195.

Al-Haj, Majid and Rosenfeld, Henry (1990) *Arab Local Government in Israel* (Boulder, CO: Westview).

Amnesty International (1997) 'Algeria: Civilian Population caught in a Spiral of Violence'. Report MDE 28/23/97 (London: Amnesty International).

Amnesty International (2007) 'Amnesty International Report: Iraq'. Available at http://thereport.amnesty.org/eng/regions/middle-east-and-north-africa/iraq

Amnesty International and Fédération Internationale des Ligues des Droits de l'Homme and Human Rights Watch (1997) *Algérie: Le livre noir* (Paris: La Découverte).

Amowitz, Lynn and Iacopino, Vincent (2001) *Women's Health and Human Rights in Afghanistan: A Population-based Assessment* (Boston: Physicians for Human Rights).

Anderson, Benedict (1983) *Imagined Communities: Reflections on the Origin and Spread of Nationalism* (London: Verso).

Anthias, Floya and Yuval Davis, Nira (1993) *Radicalized Boundaries* (London: Routledge).

Arat, Y. (1999) *Political Islam in Turkey and Women's Organizations* (Istanbul: TESEV).

Arat, Y. (2001) 'Group-Differentiated Rights and the Liberal Democratic State: Rethinking the Headscarf Controversy in Turkey', *New Perspectives on Turkey* 25, pp. 31–46.

Asad, Talal (2003) *Formations of the Secular: Christianity, Islam, Modernity* (Stanford, CA.: Stanford University Press).

Aslaoui, Leïla (2000) *Les Années rouges* (Alger: Casbah Editions).

Ayata, S. (2004) 'Changes in Domestic Politics and the Foreign Policy Orientation of the AKP Party', in L. Martin and D. Keridis (eds.) *The Future of Turkish Foreign Policy* (Cambridge, MA: MIT Press).

Azarbaijani-Moghaddam, Sippi (2004) 'Afghan Women on the Margins of the Twenty-First Century', in A. Donini, K. Wermeister, and N. Niland (eds.) *Nation-building Unravelled: Aid, Peace and Justice in Afghanistan* (Bloomfield, CT: Kumarian Press).

Badran, Margot, Sadiqi, Fatima, and Rashidi, Linda (eds.) (2002) 'Language and Gender in the Arab World', *Language and Linguistics* 9.

Barkallil, Nadira (1990) 'La Naissance et le Développement du Prolétariat Féminin Urbain', unpublished Doctoral Dissertation. University of Rabat, Morocco.

Barrak, Anissa (1998) 'Les Faits a travers la presse algérienne', *Confluences Méditerranée* 25, pp. 11–20.

Bartlett, Linda, Whitehead, Sara, Crouse, Chadd, and Bowens, Sonya (2002) Maternal *Mortality in Afghanistan: Magnitude, Causes, Risk Factors and Preventability: Summary Findings* (Afghan Ministry of Health, Centers for Disease Control, UNICEF).

Belarbi, A. (1987) 'La Représentation de la femme à travers les livres scolaires', in M. Al Alahyane et al., *Portraits de Femmes* (Casablanca: Le Fennec), pp. 47–68.

Belarbi, Aicha (1997) 'Réflexions Préliminaires sur une Approche Féministe de la Dichotomie Espace Public/ Espace Privé', in R. Bourquia (ed.) *Etudes Féminines* (Rabat: Faculty of Letters), pp. 73–82.

Benard, Cheryl and Schlaffer, Edit (2002) *Veiled Courage: Inside the Afghan Women's Resistance* (New York: Broadway Books).

Benhadj, Ali (1989) *Le Matin*, 29 October.

Benhadj, Ali (1991) *Alger Républicain*, 5 April.

Benhamza, Hocine (2008) *L'Algérie Assassinée* (Alger: Editions INES).

Bennoune, Karima (2000) 'S.O.S. Algeria: Women's Human Rights under Siege', in Mahnaz Afkhami (ed.) *Faith and Freedom: Women's Human Rights in the Muslim World* (London and New York: I.B. Tauris), pp. 184–208.

Berger, Maurice, Wallis, Brian and Watson, Simon (eds.) (1995) *Constructing Masculinity* (New York and London: Routledge).

Bilici, Mücahit (2000) "Islam and the Public Sphere: The Case of Turkey's Caprice Hotel" (İslam'ın Bronzlaşan Yüzü: Caprice Hotel Örnek Olayi), *in New Public Faces of Islam (İslamin Yeni Kamusal Yüzleri)* Nilüfer Gole, ed. Istanbul: Metis Publishers. [in Turkish with English abstract].

Bourquia, Rahma (ed.) (1997) *Etudes Féminines* (Rabat: Faculty of Letters).

Brodsky, Anne E. (2003) *With All Our Strength: The Revolutionary Association of the Women of Afghanistan* (New York: Routledge).

Brown, Janelle (2001) 'Optional Burqas and Mandatory Malnutrition', in Afghanistan- salon.com.

Burnham, Gilbert and Smith, Jeffrey (2005) 'Conceiving and Dying in Afghanistan', *Lancet* 365(9476), pp. 827–828.

Butler, Judith (1990) *Gender Trouble: Feminism and the Subversion of Identity* (New York and London: Routledge).

Butler, Judith (2004) *Precarious Life: The Powers of Mourning and Violence* (London and New York: Verso).

Çak1r, S. (1994) *Osmanl1 Kad1n Hareketi* (İstanbul: Metis).

Caputi, Jane and Russell, Diana H.E. (1992) *Femicide: The Politics of Woman Killing* (New York: Twayne).

Chadli, El-Mostafa (2001) *La société Civile ou la Quête de l'Association Citoyenne* (Rabat: Publications Faculté des Lettres et des Sciences Humaines).

Chaffetz, David (2001) *A Journey through Afghanistan: A Memorial* (Chicago: University of Chicago Press).

Charlton, Sue Ellen, Everett, Jana and Staudt, Kathleen (eds.) (1989) *Women, State and Development* (Albany, NY: SUNY Press).

Cindoğlu, D. and Toktaş, Ş. (2002) 'Empowerment and Resistance Strategies of Working Women in Turkey: The Case of 1960–1970 Graduates of the Girls' Institutes', *European Journal of Women's Studies* 9(1), pp. 31–48.

Cohen, S. and Jaidi, L. (2006) *Morocco: Globalization and its Consequences* (New York: Routledge).

Comaroff, Jean and Comaroff, John (2006) 'Criminal Accounting: Quantifacts and the Production of the Unreal', talk presented at the University of Haifa, May.

Connell, Robert W. (2000) 'Arms and the Man: Using the New Research on Masculinity to Understand Violence and Promote Peace in the Contemporary World', in Ingeborg Breines, Robert Connel, and Ingrid Eide (eds.) *Male Roles, Masculinities and Violence: A Culture of Peace Perspective* (Paris: UNESCO).

Cornwall, Andrea and Lindisfarne, Nancy (eds.) (1994) *Dislocating Masculinity: Comparative Ethnographies* (London: Routledge).

Co•ar, S. and Özman, A. (2004) 'Centre-right Politics in Turkey after the November 2002 General Election: Neo-liberalism with a Muslim Face', *Contemporary Politics* 10(1), pp. 57–74.

Dabbous-Sensenig, D. (2005) 'Incorporating an Arab-Muslim Perspective in the Re-assessment of the Implementation of the Beijing Platform for Action', in *Expert Consultation Paper on Priorities in Follow-up to the Ten-year Review and Appraisal of Implementation of the Beijing Declaration and Platform for Action* (United Nations). Available at http://www.un.org/womenwatch/daw/meetings/consult/10-review/EP9.pdf

Dabbous-Sensenig, D. (2006) 'Empowerment of Women in Politics and Media. Text of Presentation at the Role of Higher Education in the Empowerment and Achievements of Arab Women Forum', *Al-Raida* 23–24(114–115), pp. 58–61.

Daoud, Zakia (1993) *Féminisme et Politique au Maghreb* (Casablanca: Eddif).

Das, Veena (1995) *Critical Events: An Anthropological Perspective on Contemporary India* (Dehli and New York: Oxford University Press).

Das, Veena (1995) 'Voice as Birth of Culture', *Ethnos* 60(3–4), pp. 195–181.

Das, Veena (1998) 'Wittgenstein and Anthropology', *Annual Review of Anthropology* 27, pp.171–195.

Das, Veena, Kleinman, Arthur, Ramphele, Mamphela, and Reynolds, Pamela (eds.) (2000) *Violence and Subjectivity* (Berkeley: University of California Press).

Daulatzai, Anila (2004) 'A Leap of Faith: Thoughts on Secularistic Practices and Progressive Politics', *International Social Science Journal* 56(182), pp. 565–576.

Davis, Eric (2005) *Memories of State: Politics, History, and Collective Memory in Modern Iraq* (Berkeley: University of California Press).

Djerbal-Iamarene, Dalila (1997) 'Violence familiale, violence sociale, violence politique', in Hourriya/Liberté (ed.), *Droits de l'homme et violences au Maghreb et en Europe*. Available at http://www.maghreb-ddh.sgdg.org/liberte

Donini, Antonio, Wermester, Karin, and Niland, Norah (2004) *Nation-building Unravelled: Aid, Peace and Justice in Afghanistan* (Bloomfield, CT: Kumarian Press).

Douki, S., Nacef, F., Belhadj, A. Bouasker, A., and Ghachem, R. (2003) 'Violence against Women in Arab and Islamic Countries', *Archives of Women's Mental Health* 6, pp. 165–171. Available at http://*vaw.sagepub.com/cgi/content/refs/14/1/53*

Dourari Abdelrrezak (2003) *Les malaises de la societé algérienne: crise de langue et crise d'identité* (Alger: Casbah Editions).

Dupree, Nancy (1998) 'Afghan Women under the Taliban', in W. Maley (ed.) *Fundamentalism Reborn? Afghanistan and the Taliban* (New York: New York University Press), pp. 145–159.

Edwards, David B. (2002) *Before Taliban: Genealogies of the Afghan Jihad* (Berkeley: University of California Press).

Edwards, M. (2005) 'Civil Society', *The Encyclopaedia of Informal Education*. Available at http://www.infed.org/association/civil_society.htm

Eisenstein, Zillah (2002) 'Feminisms in the Aftermath of September 11', *Social Text* 20(3), pp. 79–99.

Ekmekji, Arda Arsenian (2005/6) 'Implementation of a Women's Quota System', *Al-Raida* 23(111–112), pp. 56–59.

El-Bushra, Judy and Piza Lopez, Eugenia (1993) 'Gender-related Violence: Its Scope and Relevance', *Gender & Development* 1(2), pp. 1–9.

Elran, Meir (2005) *Israel's National Resilience: The Influence of the Second Intifada on Israeli Society* (Tel Aviv: Jaffee Center for Strategic Studies, Tel Aviv University).

Enloe, Cynthia (1989) *Bananas, Beaches and Bases: Making Feminist Sense of International Politics* (London: Pandora).

Ennaji, M. (1999) 'The Arab World (Maghreb and Near East)', in J. Fishman (ed.) *Handbook of Language and Ethnic Identity* (Oxford: Oxford University Press), pp. 382–395.

Ennaji, M. (2004) *Civil Society, Gender, and Development* (Fès: Fès-Saiss Publications).

Ennaji, Moha (2005) *Multilingualism, Cultural Identity and Education in Morocco* (New York: Springer).

Ennaji, Moha (2005) *Social Policy in Morocco* (Geneva: UNRISD Publications).

Ennaji, M. (2006) 'Social Policy in Morocco: History, Politics, and Social Development', in M. Karshenas and V. Moghadam (eds.), *Social Policy in the Middle East* (New York: Palgrave Macmillan & UNRISD), pp. 116–127.

Ennaji, M. and Sadiqi, F. (2008) *Migration and Gender in Morocco* (Trenton, NJ: Red Sea Press).

Espanioly, Nabila (1997) 'Violence against Women: A Palestinian Woman's Perspective; Personal is Political', *Women's Studies International Forum* 20, pp. 587–592.

Farmer, Paul (1998) 'On Suffering and Structural Violence', in Arthur Kleinman, Veena Das, and Margaret Lock (eds.) *Social Suffering* (Delhi: Oxford University Press).

Farmer, Paul (2004) 'An Anthropology of Structural Violence', *Current Anthropology* 45, pp. 305–325.

Farmer, Paul (2005) *Pathologies of Power: Health, Human Rights, and the New War on the Poor* (Berkeley: University of California Press).

Farouk-Sluglett, Marion and Sluglett, Peter (2003) *Iraq since 1958: From Revolution to Dictatorship*, 4th edn (London and New York: I.B. Tauris).

Feminist declaration on 8 March 1989 in Algiers (1989) *WAF Articles* 1, p. 15.

Galtung, John (1969) 'Violence, Peace and Peace Research', *Journal of Peace Research* 6(3), pp. 167–191.

Gamson, William A. and Herzog, Hanna (1999) 'Living with Contradictions: The Taken-for-Granted in Israeli Political Discourse', *Political Psychology* 20(2), pp. 247–266.

Ghanem, As'ad (1998) 'State and Minority in Israel: The Case of Ethnic State and the Predicament of its Minority', *Ethnic and Racial Studies* 21, pp. 428–448.

Ghazi, Salim (1994) 'Deux Lycéenes assassinées', *El Watan*, 31 March, p. 1.

Glazer, Ilza and Abu-Ras, Wahiba (1994) 'On Aggression, Human Rights, and Hegemonic Discourse: The Case of a Murder for Family Honor in Israel', *Sex Roles* 30, pp. 269–282.

Göle, N. (1997) 'Secularism and Islamism in Turkey: The Making of Elites and Counter-Elites', *Middle East Journal* 51(1), pp. 46–58.

187

Goodson, Larry (2001) 'Perverting Islam: Taliban Social Policy toward Women', *Central Asian Survey* 20(4), pp. 415–426.

Gupta, Balbul (1999) 'Femicide from a Feminist Perspective', *GW Feminist Review* 9(10) pp. 9-10.

Haidar, Khatoun (2007) 'Antiquated Laws Violate Women's Civil Rights', *The Daily Star*, 27 August. Available at http://www.zawya.com/story.cfm/sidDS270807_dsart36

Haj Yahia, M.M. (2000) 'Wife-abuse and Battering in the Socio-cultural Context of Arab Society', *Family Process* 39(2), pp. 237–255.

Haj-Yahia, Muhammad M. (2003) 'Beliefs About Wife Beating among Arab Men from Israel: The Influence of their Patriarchal Ideology', *Journal of Family Violence* 18, pp. 193–206.

Hale, W. (2005) 'Christian Democracy and the AKP: Parallels and Contrasts', *Turkish Studies* 6(2), pp. 293–310.

Hamadeh, Najla (2005/6) 'Editorial: One Way or the Other', *Al-Raida*, 23(111–112), pp. 2–5.

Hasan, Manar (2002) 'The Politics of Honor: Patriarchy, the State, and the Murder of Women in the Name of Family Honor', *Journal of Israeli History* 21, pp. 1–37.

Hatem, Mervat (1992) 'Economic and Political Liberalization in Egypt and the Demise of State Feminism', *International Journal of Middle East Studies* 24(2), pp. 231–251.

Hatem, Mervat (1993) 'Toward the Development of Post-Islamist and Post-Nationalist Feminist Discourse in the Middle East', in Judith Tucker (ed.) Arab Women: Old Boundaries, New Frontiers (Bloomington: Indiana University Press), pp. 29–48.

Hazelton, F. (ed.) (1994) *Iraq since the Gulf War: Prospects for Democracy* (London: Zed Books).

Hélie-Lucas, Mariemme (October 2004) 'What is your Tribe? Women's Struggle and the Construction of Muslimness', *WLUML* 26, pp. 25–36.

Heper, M. (2005) 'The Justice and Development Party Government and the Military', *Turkish Studies*, 6(2), pp. 215–231.

Heper, M. (2004) 'Turkey "Between East and West"', Institute of European Studies, University of California, Berkeley, Paper no. 40516.

Hirschkind, Charles and Mahmood, Saba (2002) 'Feminism, the Taliban and Politics of Counter-Insurgency', *Anthropological Quarterly* 75(2), pp. 339–354.

Human Rights Watch (1998) 'Algeria: Country Reports', 30 June. Available at http://www.wri-irg.org

Ighilahriz, Louisette (2006) *Algérienne*, récit recueilli par Anne Nivat (Alger: Casbah Editions).

International Women's Human Rights, Law Clinic and Women Living under Muslim Laws (1999) *Shadow Report on Algeria to CEDAW*. Available at http://www.nodo50.org/mujeresred/argelia-shadwreport.html

IRIN (2008) 'IRAQ: Islamic Extremists Target Women in Basra', http://www.irinnews.org/report.aspx?ReportId=76065

Israel Central Bureau of Statistics (2002) *Ha-Ochlusiya Ha'arvit: The Arab Population in Israel* (Jerusalem: Central Bureau of Statistics).

Jenkins, G. (2003) 'Muslim Democrats in Turkey?', *Survival* 45(1), pp. 45–66.

Johnson, Penny and Kuttab, Eileen (2001) 'Where Have all the Women (and Men) Gone?', *Feminist Review* 69, pp. 21–23.

Joseph, Suad (2000) 'Civic Myths, Citizenship, and Gender in Lebanon', in Suad Joseph (ed.) Gender and Citizenship in the Middle East (Syracuse, NY: Syracuse University Press), pp. 107–136.

Joseph, Suad (ed.) (2000) *Gender and Citizenship in the Middle East* (Syracuse, NY: Syracuse University Press).

Joseph, Suad and Slymovics, Susan (eds.) (2001) *Women and Power in the Middle East* (Philadelphia: University of Pennsylvania Press).

Kanaaneh, Rhoda Ann (2005) 'Boys or Men? Duped or "Made"? Palestinian Soldiers in the Israeli Military', *American Ethnologist* 32(2), pp. 260–275.

Kandiyoti, Deniz (1991) 'Identity and its Discontents: Women and the Nation', Millennium: Journal of International Studies 20(3), pp. 429–443.

Kandiyoti, Deniz (ed.) (1991) *Women, Islam and the State: Women in the Political Economy* (Philadelphia, PA: Temple University Press).

Kardam, N. (2005) *Turkey's Engagement with Global Women's Human Rights* (Aldershot: Ashgate).

Kashua, Sayed (2004) *Let it Be Morning* (Tel Aviv: Keter) (in Hebrew).

Katz, Sheila H. (1996) 'Adam and Adama, Ird and 'Ard: En-gendering Political Conflict and Identity in Early Jewish and Palestinian Nationalisms', in Deniz Kandiyoti (ed.) *Gendering the Middle East; Alternative Perspectives* (London: I.B. Tauris), pp. 85–105.

Keyder, Ç. (2004) 'The Turkish Bell Jar', *New Left Review* 28, pp. 65–84.

Khalifeh, Nada (2005/6) 'Lebanon's Reservations to CEDAW', Al-Raida 23(111–112), pp. 14–18.

Khamaisi, Rasem (2005) 'Urbanization and Urbanism in the Arab Settlements in Israel', *Ofakim Be-Geographia* 64–65, pp. 293–310 (in Hebrew).

Khatibi, A. (1993) *Penser le Maghreb* (Rabat: SMER).

Khattak, Saba Gul (2004) 'Adversarial Discourses, Analogous Objectives: Afghan Women's Control', *Cultural Dynamics* 16(2/3), pp. 213–236.

Kleinman, Arthur (2000) 'The Violence of Everyday Life: The Multiple Forms and Dynamics of Social Violence', in Maurice Berger, Brian Wallis, and Simon Watson (eds.) *Constructing Masculinity* (New York and London: Routledge), pp. 226–241.

Kleinman, Arthur, Das, Veena, and Lock, Margaret M. (1997) *Social Suffering* (Berkeley: University of California Press).

Kogacioglu, D. (2004) 'Progress, Unity, and Democracy: Dissolving Political Parties in Turkey', *Law and Society Review* 38(3), pp. 433–462.

Kurtoğlu, A. (2002) *Günlük Hayatımızda Görgü ve Nezaket* (İstanbul:Timaş).

Laroui, A. (1987) *Islam et Modernité* (Paris: Editions La Découverte).

LaTeef, Nelda (1997) *Women of Lebanon: Interviews with Champions for Peace* (Jefferson, NC: McFarland).

Lazreg, Marnia (1990) 'Gender and Politics in Algeria: Unravelling the Religious Paradigm', *Signs* 15(4), pp. 755–780.

Lazreg, Marnia (2000) 'Citizenship and Gender in Algeria', in Suad Joseph (ed.) *Gender and Citizenship in the Middle East* (Syracuse, NY: Syracuse University Press), pp. 58–69.

Lemsine, Aicha (2001) 'Women in Islam', *Middle East Times*, 16 March. Available at *http://www.islamfortoday.com/ muslimstoday.htm*

Lévinas, Emmanuel (1985) *Ethics and Infinity* (Pittsburgh, PA: Duquesne University Press).

Lewin, Alisa, Stier, Haya, and Caspi-Dror, Dafna (2006) 'The Place of Opportunity: Structural and Individual Determinants of Poverty among Jews and Arabs in Israel', *Research in Social Stratification and Mobility* 24, pp. 177–191.

Lloyd, Catherine (2006) 'From Taboo to Transnational Political Issue: Violence Against Women in Algeria', *Women's Studies International Forum* 29(5), pp. 453–462.

Lomsky-Feder, Edna and Rapoport, Tamar (2003) 'Juggling Models of Masculinity: Russian-Jewish Immigrants in the Israeli Army', *Sociological Inquiry* 73(1), pp. 114–137.

Lorber, Judith (2002) 'Heroes, Warriors, and "Burqas": A Feminist Sociologist's Reflections on Sept 11', *Sociological Forum* 17(3), pp. 377–396.

Lovenduski, J. (1993) 'Dynamics of Gender and Party', in J. Lovenduski and P. Norris (eds.) *Gender and Party Politics* (London: Sage).

Lustick, Ian (1980) *Arabs in the Jewish State: Israel's Control of a National Minority* (Austin: University of Texas Press).

Mahmood, Saba (2005) *Politics of Piety: The Islamic Revival and the Feminist Subject* (Princeton: Princeton University Press).

Maksound, Hala (1996) 'The Case of Lebanon', in Suha Sabbagh (ed.) *Arab Women: Between Defiance and Restraint* (New York: Olive Branch Press), pp. 89–94.

Mammeri, Mouloud (1991) *Culture Savante, Culture Vécue* (Alger: Editions Tala).

Marshall, G. (2005) 'Ideology, Progress and Dialogue: A Comparison of Feminist and Islamist Women's Approaches to the Issues of Head-covering and Work in Turkey', *Gender and Society* 19(1), pp. 104–120.

Martinez, Luis (2004) 'Why the Violence in Algeria?', *Journal of North African Studies* 9(2), pp.14–27.

Massad, Joseph (1995) 'Conceiving the Masculine: Gender and Palestinian Nationalism', *Middle East Journal* 49(3), pp. 467–482.

Mayer, Tamar (2000) 'Gender Ironies of Nationalism: Setting the Stage', in Tamar Mayer (ed.) *Gender Ironies of Nationalism: Sexing the Nation* (New York: Routledge), pp. 1–24.

McKee-Ryan, Frances M. (2005) 'Psychological and Physical Well-Being during Unemployment: A Meta-Analytic Study', *Journal of Applied Psychology* 90(1), pp. 53–76.

Mejjati Alami, R. (2000) 'Femmes et Vulnérabilité sur le Marché du Travail', in F. Sadiqi (ed.) *Mouvements Féministes* (Fès: Faculty of Letters Publications), pp. 15–28.

Mernissi, Fatima (1975) *Beyond the Veil: Male–Female Dynamics in a Modern Muslim Society* (New York: Schenkman).

Mernissi, Fatima (1994) *Dreams of Trespass: Tales of a Harem Girlhood* (New York: Addison Wesley).

Mernissi, Fatima (2007) 'Le Tapis Amazigh et les Tisseuses Artistes', in Moha Ennaji (ed.), *La Culture Amazighe et le Développement Humain* (Fès: Publications of Fès-Saiss), pp. 15–20.

Messaoudi, Khalida and Schemla, Elizabeth (1998) *Unbowed: An Algerian Woman confronts Islamic Fundamentalism*, trans. Anne C. Vila (Philadelphia: University of Pennsylvania Press).

Moghadam, Valentine M. (1989) 'Revolution, the State, Islam, and Women: Gender Politics in Iran and Afghanistan', *Social Text* 22, pp. 40–61.

Moghadam, Valentine M. (1994) *Gender and National Identity: Women and Politics in Muslim Societies* (London: Zed Books).

Moghadam, Valentine M. (1995) *Modernizing Women: Gender and Social Change in the Middle East* (Boulder, CO: Lynne Rienner).

189

Moghadam, Valentine M. (1999) 'Revolution, Religion, and Gender Politics: Iran and Afghanistan Compared', *Journal of Women's History* 10(4), pp. 172–204.

Moghadam, Valentine M. (2001) 'Organizing Women: The New Women's Movement in Algeria', *Cultural Dynamics* 13, pp. 131–154. Available at http://cdy.sagepub.com/cgi/content/refs/13/2/131

Moghadam, Valentine M. (2002) 'Patriarchy, the Taliban, and Politics of Public Space in Afghanistan', *Women's Studies International Forum* 25(1), pp. 19–31.

Moghadam, Valentine M. (2003) 'Global Feminism and Women's Citizenship in the Muslim World: The Cases of Iran, Algeria and Afghanistan', Conference on Citizenship, Borders, and Gender: Mobility and Immobility, Yale University, 8–10 May.

Monterescu, Daniel (2001) 'A City of "Strangers": The Socio-cultural Construction of Manhood in Jaffa', *Journal of Mediterranean Studies* 1(1), pp. 159–188.

Naciri, Rabéa and Nusair, Isis (2003) *The Integration of Women's Rights into the Euro-Mediterranean Partnership: Women's Rights in Algeria, Egypt, Israel, Jordan, Lebanon, Morocco, Palestine, Syria and Tunisia* (Copenhagen: Euro-Mediterranean Human Rights Network).

Nashif, Esmail (2004/2005) 'Attempts at Liberation: Body Materialization and Community Building among Palestinian Political Captives', *Arab Studies* 12(2)/13(1), pp. 46–79.

Nauphal, Naila (2001) 'Women and Other War-affected Groups in Post-war Lebanon: In Focus Programme on Crisis Response and Reconstruction', *Working Paper 2: Gender and Armed Conflicts: Challenges for Decent Work, Gender Equality and Peace Building Agendas and Programmes* (Geneva: Recovery and Reconstruction Department), pp. 57–61.

Omar, Suha (1994) 'Honour, Shame and Dictatorship', in F. Hazelton (ed.) *Iraq since the Gulf War: Prospects for Democracy* (London: Zed Books).

Orloff, A.S. (1993) 'Gender and the Social Rights of Citizenship: The Comparative Analysis of Gender Relations and Welfare States', *American Sociological Review* 58, pp. 303–328.

Palmer, Celia and Zwi, Anthony (1998) 'Women, Health and Humanitarian Aid in Conflict', *Disasters* 22(3), pp. 236–249.

Pateman, C. (1988) 'The Fraternal Social Contract', in J. Keane (ed.) *Civil Society and the State* (London: Verso).

Peteet, Julie M. (1994) 'Male Gender and Rituals of Resistance in the Palestinian Intifada: A Cultural Politics of Violence', *American Ethnologist* 21, pp. 31–49.

Peterson, V. Spike and Runyan, Anne Sisson (1993), *Global Gender Issues* (Oxford: Westview).

Phillips, Anne (1991) *Engendering Democracy* (Cambridge: Polity Press).

Phillips, Anne (1993) *Democracy and Difference* (Cambridge: Polity Press).

Povey, Elaheh Rostami (2003) 'Women in Afghanistan: Passive Victims of the Borga or Active Social Participants?', *Development in Practice* 11(2–3), pp. 266–277.

Puar, Jasbir and Rai, Amit (2002) 'Monster, Terrorist, Fag: The War on Terrorism and the Production of Docile Patriots', *Social Text* 72, 20(3), pp. 117–148.

Rafea, Aliaa (2000) 'The Meanings of Hijab', in Fatima Sadiqi (ed.) *Feminist Movements: Origins and Orientations* (Fès: University of Fès Publications).

Randal, V. (1998) 'Gender and Power: Women Engage the State', in V. Randal and G. Waylen (eds.) *Gender, Politics and the State* (London: Routledge).

Rasekh, Zohra, Bauer, Heidi, Manos, Michele, and Iacopino, Vincent (1998) 'Women's Health and Human Rights in Afghanistan', *Journal of the American Medical Association* 280, pp. 449–455.

République Algérienne Démocratique et Populaire, Ministère de la Justice (1993) *Le Code de la famille (The Family Code)* (Alger: OPU).

Riphenburg, Carol J. (2003) 'Gender Relations and Development in a Weak State: The Rebuilding of Afghanistan', *Central Asian Survey* 22(2–3), pp. 187–207.

Riphenburg, Carol J. (2004) 'Post-Taliban Afghanistan: Changed Outlook for Women', *Asian Survey* 44(3), pp. 410–421.

Rohde, A. (2006) 'Facing Dictatorship: State Society Relations in Ba'thist Iraq', unpublished PhD dissertation, Berlin: Freie Universität.

Rosenfeld, Henry (1978) 'The Class Situation of the Arab National Minority in Israel', *Comparative Studies in Society and History* 20, pp. 374–407.

Rosenfeld, Henry and Al-Haj, Majid (1990) *Arab Local Government in Israel* (Boulder, CO: Westview).

Roy, Oliver and Sfeir, Antoine (2007) *The Columbia World Dictionary of Islamism*, trans. John King (New York: University of Columbia Press).

Saadawi, Nawal (1980) *The Hidden Face of Eve: Women in the Arab World* (London: Zed Press).

Saadi, Noureddine (1991) *La femme et la loi en Algérie* (Alger: Eds Bouchêne).

Sabbagh, Suha (1996) 'Lebanon's Civil War through Different Eyes: An Interview with Jean Said Makdisi', in Suha Sabbagh (ed.) *Arab Women: Between Defiance and Restraint* (New York: Olive Branch Press), pp. 100–103.

Sa'di, Ahmad and Lewin-Epstein, Noah (2001) 'Minority Labour Force Participation in the Post-Fordist Era: The Case of the Arabs in Israel?', *Work, Employment and Society* 15(4), pp. 781–802.

Sadiqi, Fatima (ed.) (1999) *Mouvements Féministes: Origines et Orientations* (Fès: Publications du CERF).

Sadiqi, F. (ed.) (2000) *Feminist Movements: Origins and Orientations* (Fès: Dhar El Mehraz).

Sadiqi, Fatima (2003) *Women, Gender and Language in Morocco* (Leiden and Boston: Brill Academic).

Sadiqi, F. and Ennaji, M. (2006) 'The Feminization of Public Space: Women's Activism, the Family Law, and Social Change in Morocco', *Journal of Middle East Women's Studies (JMEWS)* 2(2), pp. 86–114.

Sadiqi, Fatima, Nowaira, Amira, El-Khouly, Azza, and Ennaji, Moha (eds.) (2009) *Women Writing Africa: The Northern Region* (New York: The Feminist Press).

Salhi, Zahia Smail (2003) 'Algerian Women, Citizenship, and the "Family Code"', *Gender & Development* 11(3), pp. 27–35.

Salhi, Zahia Smail (2004) 'Maghribi Women and the Challenge of Modernity: Breaking the Women's Silence', in Naomi Sakr (ed.) *Women and the Media in the Middle East: Power through Self-Expression* (London: I.B. Tauris).

Salhi, Zahia Smail (2008) 'Between the Languages of Silence and the Woman's Word: Gender and Language in the Work of Assia Djebar', *International Journal of the Sociology of Language*, Special Issue on *Language and Gender in the Mediterranean Region* 190, pp. 79–101.

Salhi, Zahia Smail (2009) 'The Algerian Feminist Movement between Nationalism, Patriarchy and Islamism', *Women's Studies International Forum* Online publication complete: 28-NOV-2009 DOI information: 10.1016/j.wsif.2009.11.001. will also be published in hard copy (forthcoming).

Salim, Z. (1999) 'La femme, un potentiel d'entrepreneur et une réalité de salaire', in *Actes du Colloque sur Histoire des Femmes au Maghreb* (Kénitra: Publication de la Faculté des Lettres), pp. 123–134.

Sar1 kaya, E. and Özcan, Z.Y. (2005) *Aile Sağl1k Rehberi* (Ankara: Çankaya Belediyesi).

Sayigh, Rosemary (1993) 'Palestinian Women and Politics in Lebanon', in Judith Tucker (ed.) *Arab Women: Old Boundaries, New Frontiers* (Bloomington: Indiana University Press), pp. 175–194.

Schaefer-Davis, S. (2004) 'Women Weavers Online: Rural Moroccan Women on the Internet', *Gender Technology and Development* 8(1), pp. 53–74.

Schaefer-Davis, Susan (1979) *Patience and Power* (Rochester, VT: Schenkman).

Schneider, K. (1999) 'Les mécanismes de l'exclusion des domestiques au Maroc et leurs réponses', in *Actes du Colloque sur Histoire des Femmes au Maghreb* (Kénitra: Publication de la Faculté des Lettres), pp. 179–196.

Schulze, Kirsten (1998) 'Communal Violence, Civil War and Foreign Occupation: Women in Lebanon', in Rick Wilford and Robert L. Miller (eds.) *Women, Ethnicity and Nationalism: The Politics of Transition* (London: Routledge), pp. 150–169.

Schweitzer, Ivy (2002) 'Women: Canary in the Mine', *Gender and Cultural Memory* 28(1), pp. 466–468.

Scott, Joan Wallach (2002) 'Feminist Reverberations', *Differences: A Journal of Feminist Cultural Studies* 13(3), pp. 1–21.

Shafir, Gershon and Peled, Yoav (2002) *Being Israeli: The Dynamics of Multiple Citizenship* (Cambridge: Cambridge University Press).

Shahin, Miriam (1994) 'Algerian Women fight Terror', *The Jordan Times*, 13 November, p. 1.

Shahrani, M. Nazif Mohib (2002) *The Kirghiz and Wakhi of Afghanistan: Adaptation to Closed Frontiers and War* (Seattle: University of Washington Press).

Shahrani, M. Nazif Mohib (2002) *The Women of Afghanistan Under the Taliban* (Jefferson, NC: McFarland).

Shalhoub-Kevorkian, Nadera (1999) 'Law, Politics, and Violence against Women: A Case Study of Palestinians in Israel', *Law & Society* 21(2), pp. 189–221.

Şimşek, S. (2004) 'New Social Movements in Turkey since 1980', *Turkish Studies* 5(2), pp. 111–139.

Slackmam, Michael (2007) 'Algeria's Quiet Revolution: Gains by Women'. *International Herald Tribune*, 26 May. Available at http://www.iht.com/aeticles/2007/05/26/africa/algeria.1-62108

Smooha, Sammy (2002) 'The Model of Ethnic Democracy: Israel as a Jewish and Democratic State', *Nations and Nationalism* 8(4), pp. 475–503.

Sofer, Jehoeda (1992) 'Testimonies from the Holy Land: Israeli and Palestinian Men Talk about their Sexual Encounters', in Arno Schmitt and Jehoeda Sofer (eds.) *Sexuality and Eroticism among Males in Moslem Societies* (Binghamton, NY: Harrington Park Press), pp. 105–112.

Spivak, Gayatri Chakravorty (2004) 'Globalicities: Terror and its Consequences', *New Centennial Review* 4(1), pp. 73–94.

Squires, Judith (2004) *Gender in Political Theory* (Cambridge: Polity Press).

Stack, Carol B. and Burton, Linda M. (1993) 'Kinscripts', *Journal of Comparative Family Studies* 24(2), pp. 157–170.

Stora, Benjamin (2000) *Algeria 1830–2000: A Short History* (Ithaca and London: Cornell University Press).

Taoufik, Ahmed (1993) *Mudawwanatu Al-Ahwāl al-Shakhsiyyah ma'a Ākhiri al-ta'dīlāt* (The Code of the Personal Status Law and the Latest Amendments) (Casablanca: Dār Al-Thaqāfa).

Taussig, Michael (1995) 'Schopenhauer's Beard', in Maurice Berger, Brian Wallis, and Simon Watson (eds.) *Constructing Masculinity* (New York and London: Routledge), pp. 107–114.

Taylor, P.K. (2008) 'I Just Want to be Me', in Jennifer Heath (ed.) *The Veil: Women Writers on its History, Lore and Politics* (Berkeley: University of California Press), pp. 119–138.

Thompson, P.J. (1994) 'Beyond Gender', in L. Stone (ed.) *The Education Feminist Reader* (New York and London: Routledge).

Tripp, Charles (2000) *A History of Iraq* (Cambridge: Cambridge University Press).

Trouillot, Michel-Rolph (2003) *Global Transformations: Anthropology and the Modern World* (New York: Palgrave Macmillan).

Tuğal, C. (2002) 'Islamism in Turkey: Beyond Instrument and Meaning', *Economy and Society* 31(1), pp. 85–111.

Turshen, Meredeth (2004) 'Militarism and Islamism in Algeria', *Journal of Asian and African Studies* 39(1–2), pp. 119–132.

UNAMA (United Nations Assistance Mission in Afghanistan) (2003) 'Fact Sheet: Health and Nutrition'.

UNFPA (2002) 'Kabul Maternity Hospitals Lack Equipment and Supplies', United Nations Report, 19 February.

UNICEF (1995) *The Situation of Children and Women in Lebanon* (Beirut: UNICEF and the Government of Lebanon).

UNICEF (1997) *State of the World's Children Report* (New York: UNICEF).

United Nations (2006) *Consideration of Reports submitted by States Parties under Article 18 of the Convention on the Elimination of All Forms of Discrimination against Women—Third Periodic Report of States Parties: Lebanon* (United Nations Publications).

Visweswaran, Kamala (2004) 'Gendered States: Rethinking Culture as a Site of South Asian Rights Work', *Human Rights Quarterly* 26, pp. 483–511.

Wagner. D.A. (1993) *Literacy, Culture, and Development: Becoming Literate in Morocco* (Cambridge: Cambridge University Press).

Wali, Sima, Gould, Elizabeth, and Fitzgerald, Paul (1999) 'The Impact of Political Conflict on Women: The Case of Afghanistan', *American Journal of Public Health* 89(10), pp. 1474–1476.

Walters, Keith (1999) 'Opening the Door of Paradise a Cubit: Educated Tunisian Women, Embodied Linguistic Practice, and Theories of Language and Gender', in Mary Bucholtz et al. (eds.) *Reinventing Identities: The Gendered Self in Discourse* (New York: Oxford University Press).

Waylen, Georgina (1996) *Gender in Third World Politics* (Boulder, CO: Lynne Rienner).

Waylen, Georgina (1998) 'Gender, Feminism and the State: An Overview', in Vicky Randall and Georgina Waylen (eds.) *Gender, Politics and the State* (London: Routledge), pp. 1–17.

WFP (2004) *A Report from the Office of Evaluation* (Rome: World Food Program).

White, J.B. (2002) *Islamist Mobilization in Turkey: A Study in Vernacular Politics* (Seattle and London: University of Washington Press).

White, J.B. (2003) 'State Feminism, Modernization, and the Turkish Republican Woman', *National Women's Studies Association Journal* 5(3), pp. 145–159.

Wilford, Rick (1998) 'Women, Ethnicity and Nationalism: Surveying the Ground', in Rick Wilford and Robert L. Miller (eds.) *Women, Ethnicity and Nationalism: The Politics of Transition* (London: Routledge), pp. 1–22.

Woodhull, Winifred (1993) *Transfiguration of the Maghreb* (Minneapolis and London: University of Minnesota Press).

World Health Organization (2002) *World Report on Violence and Health* (Geneva: WHO).

Yahia-Younis, Taghreed (2005) 'Behind the Scenes: Women in Local Politics among the Palestinian-Arab Minority in Israel', in Eli Rekhess and Sara Osatzki-Lazar (eds.) *Municipal Elections and Local Government in the Arab and Druze Communities: Clanship, Ethnicity, and Parties* (Tel Aviv: Dayan Center), pp. 42–64 (in Hebrew).

Yahia-Younis, Taghreed, and Herzog, Hanna (2005) 'Gender and Clan Discourse of Governmentality: Primary Elections in Clans for Candidates for Local Authorities in the Arab-Palestinian Communities in Israel', *State and Society* 5(1), pp. 1104–1077 (in Hebrew).

Yavuz, M.H. (2000) 'Cleansing Islam from the Public Sphere', *Journal of International Affairs* 54(1), pp. 21–42.

Zahid, F. (2000) 'Femmes rurales', paper given at Women Space: International Conference, Faculty of Letters, Rabat, 15–17 February.

Zihnioğlu, Y. (1993) *Kadinsiz İnkilap: Nezihe Muhiddin, Kadinlar Halk Firkasi, Kadin Birliği* (İstanbul: Metis).

Index

For Product Safety Concerns and Information please contact our EU
representative GPSR@taylorandfrancis.com
Taylor & Francis Verlag GmbH, Kaufingerstraße 24, 80331 München, Germany

www.ingramcontent.com/pod-product-compliance
Lightning Source LLC
Chambersburg PA
CBHW080238270326
41926CB00020B/4284